STASSEN AGAIN

Harold Stassen, 1939

STASSEN AGAIN

STEVE WERLE

MINNESOTA
HISTORICAL
SOCIETY PRESS

www.mnhspress.org
The Minnesota Historical Society Press is a member of the
Association of American University Presses.
Manufactured in the United States of America
10 9 8 7 6 5 4 3 2 1
∞ The paper used in this publication meets the minimum
requirements of the American National Standard for Information Sciences—
Permanence for Printed Library Materials, ANSI Z39.48–1984.

International Standard Book Number
ISBN: 978-0-87351-962-5 (paper)
ISBN: 978-0-87351-967-0 (e-book)

Library of Congress Cataloging-in-Publication Data

Werle, Steven, 1972–
Stassen again / Steve Werle.
pages cm
Includes bibliographical references and index.
ISBN 978-0-87351-962-5 (pbk. : alk. paper) — ISBN 978-0-87351-967-0 (ebook)
1. Stassen, Harold E. (Harold Edward), 1907–2001. 2. Presidential candidates—
United States—Biography. 3. United States—Politics and government—1945–1989.
4. Republican Party (U.S. : 1854–)—History—20th century. 5. Conservatism—
United States—History—20th century. 6. Governors—Minnesota—Biography.
7. Minnesota—Politics and government—20th century. I. Title.
E748.S784W47 2015
977.6´053092—dc23
[B]
2014043567

This book is dedicated with
heartfelt admiration and appreciation
to
AL WERLE, RICH DECKER, *and* FRED SIPPEL—
three old-school sons of the middle way,
and to
JACOB, JOSHUA, *and* SIMON—
three young lads who are, God willing, well on their way.

You can't stop a politician, even by defeating him.

—WILL ROGERS

There is a better road than the extreme right or the extreme left.
There is the broad middle way.

—DWIGHT D. EISENHOWER

Contents

STASSEN AGAIN

When You Meet Him
Take a Good Look

By early February of 1988, the presidential primary season was already heating up, but you would have been hard-pressed to feel it while standing in the middle of another interminable Minnesota winter. With nearly a foot of snow on the ground and temperatures hovering below zero, few reputable journalists even considered traveling to Mondale and Humphrey country that year in search of a hot campaign story. The honorable and former vice presidents, along with their political party it seemed, were yesterday's news. New Hampshire's primary election was only two weeks away, and that is where smart money had either current Vice President George H. W. Bush or Senator Robert Dole of Kansas pulling away from the pack in pursuit of the Republican nomination. Unless Democrats could come up with an electrifying candidate of their own, George Bush or Bob Dole appeared destined to become the next president of the United States.

It must have been nostalgia or curiosity or a vindictive editor that drove *Chicago Tribune* reporter Rogers Worthington to Minnesota on this bitter winter's day. Now, as he sat in a cozy St. Paul hotel lobby sizing up the elderly gentleman he had come to interview, Worthington noted the unexpected contrasts: "He is a tall, robust man still sharp of eye and booming of voice." Eighty years old and well past his prime, the man had grown accustomed to being the source of controversy and the butt of jokes. This was, after all, his ninth attempt to win the GOP nomination for president. But at least he had a sense of humor about it. Four years earlier he remarked that he was running in the primaries to make Ronald Reagan appear younger. Today it looked like he was the one trying to look more youthful. Worthington observed that "he wore the candidate's de rigueur blue pinstripe suit and red tie, plus a brown toupee with the follicle-per-centimeter density of a nineteen-year-old." It had become, for better or for worse, Harold Stassen's signature style.[1]

That was only part of the story though, and Rogers Worthington knew it. Stassen's career in politics had already spanned six decades, coinciding with some of the most influential policy makers of the twentieth century, conservatives and liberals alike. Though long removed from elective office, the three-time governor, naval officer, and presidential advisor spoke passionately about the future of the Republican Party and the prospects for world peace, neither of which were new issues for him. By now Stassen had made a name for himself several times over as a determined if unconventional candidate who refused to take no for an answer. And along the way he had burned too many bridges to count with his fellow Republicans.

Twenty years before Worthington's visit, during the turbulent and tragic spring of 1968, a young high school student in Wisconsin met Harold Stassen for the first and only time. Fourteen-year-old Charles Reid already possessed a keen interest in politics, but the impression Mr. Stassen made upon him that day remains vivid nearly a half century later precisely because of the issues they discussed. According to Reid, the importance of Wisconsin's relatively early primary in 1968 only increased his fascination with the political process. One March day he decided to venture downtown from his

During a Stassen reelection campaign for Minnesota governor, probably in 1942, "Stassen Again" was a claim on the future.

home in Milwaukee to learn what he could about the Republican candidates who were seeking the support of primary voters. He first stopped at the Nixon headquarters, where, he recalls, "No one paid the slightest attention to me. I was a fourteen-year-old curiosity seeker who had come wandering off the street and I was treated as such."[2]

Reid continued on down Wisconsin Avenue and happened upon Stassen's campaign offices. To his astonishment, the candidate was actually present and welcomed the opportunity to talk personally with all visitors, including a teenager who was not even old enough to vote. Stassen and Reid spoke for almost twenty minutes. They discussed the deteriorating conditions in Vietnam, and Reid was surprised to hear Stassen challenging conventional wisdom regarding the war. There was no talk of falling dominoes or containing communism. No trumpeting the purity of American motives in Southeast Asia. No cheap slogans like "peace with honor," which amounted to little more than vague campaign rhetoric when what the country really needed was a concrete strategy to end the war. Stassen was candid and clear. "He wanted to deescalate the conflict," Reid remembers, "and to work toward establishing peace as soon as possible. He thought a robust United Nations involvement would be helpful and wanted the governments of both South and North Vietnam brought into the UN. His position arose out of his own religious convictions. We should be peacemakers. And the peaceful cooperation of nations, he thought, was the goal we should all strive for." Charles Reid left the encounter with a new appreciation for Harold Stassen and a large, multicolored campaign pin that read "Students for Stassen for Peace." He wore it with pride until the end of the month, by which time Harold Stassen had notched yet another electoral loss on his long, labored, and seemingly self-imposed march toward political oblivion.[3]

The newspaper headlines had been entirely different two decades earlier. Harold Stassen won the Wisconsin primary decisively in the spring of 1948, and some of the nation's leading pollsters began calculating, prematurely as it turned out, his odds for victory over Harry Truman in November. But that image scarcely squares with the impression most Americans have of Harold Stassen today—if they have heard of him at all, that is, for few of Stassen's contemporaries remain with us to recall what it was like when he was *the* rising star of the Republican Party. The traditional view of Stassen is that of an overly ambitious, midwestern politician whose quadrennial runs at the White House qualify him for little more than permanent association with America's notorious ne'er-do-well presidential candidates including Aaron Burr, William Jennings Bryan, Ross Perot, and Ralph Nader. The only notable difference, it would seem, was the toupee, which Marjorie Williams of the *Washington Post* once observed "topping his great head like a sullen possum that had been dipped in bronze." That's hardly a legacy worth hanging one's hat upon. Then again, perhaps it is entirely the wrong legacy.[4]

~

One summer day in 2008, I was visiting the Minnesota State Capitol in St. Paul and admiring its architectural splendor. Walking up the marbled staircases and along the grand, decorative halls, I noticed in the east wing that all of the former governors save one had brief descriptions of their respective careers permanently displayed adjacent to their official portraits. The exception is Harold Stassen. I asked a volunteer stationed around the corner what or who determined when a chief executive received an explanatory placard, and he kindly explained that the honor was reserved for those governors who were deceased. When I pointed out that Harold Stassen died in 2001 but his portrait contained no such distinction, the gentlemen responded, "Has it been that long?" Nearly a year later, in the spring of 2009, a group of students from my school visited the capitol with their government teacher. During a question-and-answer period in the Governor's Reception Room, a curious young girl asked (at my urging) one of Governor Pawlenty's staffers why Stassen didn't have anything written about him next to his painting. An uncomfortable smile formed on the staffer's face, and then he answered flippantly, "I guess he didn't do anything that important."

Both incidents underscore a fundamental dearth of pertinent information about Harold Stassen and his extraordinary influence upon the twentieth century. To understand the man is to appreciate the enduring value of moderation and tolerance in a democracy. Stassen loved freedom, not because it made for good campaign copy but because it is the divine right of all human beings. He was inspired by the wondrous achievements brought about in societies that value the free exchange of ideas between individuals—young and old, rich and poor, black and white, Republican and Democrat. His faith in free men and women became the cornerstone of his moral and political philosophies, and, indeed, when he did on occasion drift from that central belief, it became the source of his political undoing. Stassen was far from perfect. But his career provides a valuable object lesson for modern politicians. His accomplishments serve to remind us that seeking to understand the experiences and motives of others is a political necessity, not a sign

Cartoon by Steve Sack, *Minneapolis Star Tribune*, September 18, 1983

of weakness. Harold Stassen sought the middle way when others spurned
compromise under the petty guises of partisanship and popularity.

There is a particular portion of Carl Sandburg's *The People, Yes* (1936) that
could have been written about Harold Stassen. It captures the essential
spirit that embodied both his motives and his achievements:

> The free man willing to pay and struggle and die
> for the freedom for himself and others
> Knowing how far to subject himself to discipline
> and obedience for the sake of an ordered
> society free from tyrants, exploiters and
> legalized frauds—
> This free man is a rare bird and when you meet
> him take a good look at him and try
> to figure him out because
> Some day when the United States of the Earth
> gets going and runs smooth and pretty there
> will be more of him than we have now.[5]

At some point in our lives, all of us are called to account. We are driven
by our consciences and, in Jefferson's words, "by a decent respect to the
opinions of mankind" to publicly declare what we believe and then endeavor
to further those sacred causes. Stassen's core values resonate like a refrain
of our nation's most prized institutions—freedom, equality, justice for all,
and government of the people, by the people, and for the people. A commitment to seeing those lofty principles translated into tangible results for
citizens of the world was the key to understanding Harold Stassen's unique
political persona, and it provides the underlying theme of this study.

To accomplish this task I have spent a great deal of time reading about
Minnesota, the United States, and the world as a whole at the turn of the
twentieth century. I firmly believe that the only way to even approximate
an understanding of Stassen's political significance is to fully appreciate the
era in which he first lived, to begin knowing the collective values, priorities,
biases, superstitions, and assumptions through which young Harold Stassen
perceived his ever-broadening horizons.

One source that has proven particularly valuable in terms of getting a
feel for the times is Hamlin Garland's *A Son of the Middle Border* (1917). In
a review for the *New York Times*, literary legend William Dean Howells

characterized the importance of Garland's newly published memoir in this way: "As you read the story of his life you realize it the memorial of a generation, of a whole order of American experience; as you review it you perceive it an epic of such mood and make as has not been imagined before." That is, in a nutshell, how I have envisioned recounting Stassen's life from the beginning. It all sounds ridiculously presumptuous, but then again, after you have discovered what I have discovered about Harold Stassen, it may be nothing more than form following function. Years ago I heard someone describing how Thornton Wilder chose the subjects for his books and plays. To paraphrase, Wilder evidently said he imagined a book he'd like to read, looked around to see if it had ever been written, and if it hadn't, he wrote it himself.[6]

Here is the book I imagined but could not find at any public library or bookstore or even on Amazon.com.

1 Tyrants, Exploiters, and Legalized Frauds

In Minnesota, winter rarely gives way to spring without a fight. Temperatures rise unpredictably—sometimes making steady progress and then suddenly in fits and furies—first taking snow with them and now bringing it back with a vengeance. Farmers keep busy tinkering with their machines or mending worn-out fences, all the while waiting for the inevitable signs of spring—budding trees, puddle-filled fields, and hurried harbingers of change. Critters scurry about in search of food for themselves and their dependents, and birds travel far and wide to find building materials for new homes. There is a tremendous continuity to it all. Creatures large and small, two- and four-legged alike, emerge from yet another season of death determined to start anew the business of getting ahead.

It was unseasonably cold, even for Minnesota, when Elsbeth Stassen gave birth to her third son on April 13, 1907. The temperature outside the farmhouse dipped well below freezing several times that month, and two weeks after her new child's arrival, a late-season storm dumped thirteen inches of snow in two days. The only thing for mother, baby, and the rest of the household to do was hunker down and ride it out as best they could, a strategy doubtless sufficient to meet the many and varied challenges posed by life on the northern plains. Elsbeth and her husband William named their newborn son Harold Edward and likely offered a prayer of thanksgiving. Devout as they were, the proud parents perhaps beseeched God to render young Harold a long and fruitful life in service to his fellow man. And then their thoughts probably turned to keeping warm and making preparations to plant again.

~

Like tens of thousands of other Germans, Elsbeth ("Elsie") Mueller and her family immigrated to America in the 1880s. They first took up residence near Dayton's Bluff on the east side of St. Paul but eventually moved across the Mississippi River to the new town of West St. Paul (so named because it is west of the Mississippi River). Elsie was just six years old when she set sail for the United States, but somewhere among the necessities and keepsakes packed tightly in the Muellers' steamer trunk there must have been a few cherished values that she was expected to hold sacred for the balance of her life. Family, hard work, honesty, and faithful adherence to a moderate brand of Christianity practiced by German Baptists became the cornerstones of Elsie's existence. Years later, when she had a family of her own, it didn't take long for her children to learn that the same was expected of them.

In 1873, a decade before Elsie and the rest of the Muellers arrived in Minnesota, William A. Stassen was born into another St. Paul neighborhood on the west side of the river. His parents were of German, Czech, and Norwegian ancestry and had made their way to Minnesota after the Civil War via Wisconsin. The Stassen family moved a few miles south, where good land could be had at reasonable prices. Somewhere along the line William made Elsie's acquaintance, probably at the Riverview Baptist Church, which was just a mile down the road from the Mueller house. Nature took its course and the couple married in 1899. They acquired forty acres of land a few miles farther south in West St. Paul, and William began raising produce to sell at the St. Paul City Farmer's Market. Truck farming became the Stassens' primary source of income, however modest, but it did afford William the opportunity to dabble in local politics and spend time with their two sons who arrived in quick succession at the turn of the century.

The Stassen and Mueller families had taken part in one of the largest mass migrations in human history. They arrived about a generation after whites, through a series of forced and broken treaties followed by a bloody war, had forced the indigenous Dakota people from the land. Demographic and ecological changes came swiftly. An estimated 6,000 people—most of whom were Native Americans—lived in Minnesota Territory when the federal census was taken in 1850. By decade's end the total number of inhabitants exceeded 172,000. The earliest white settlers tended to come from New England, New York, Pennsylvania, and Ohio, but they were soon joined by European immigrants making their way to Minnesota by ship and by rail. Scandinavians and Germans composed the two largest groups, lured almost exclusively by the prospect of cheap, fertile land and establishing communities with names like Newburg, Peterson, New Richland, Christiana, and New Germany. Wisconsin-born author Hamlin Garland (1860–1940) also moved westward through Minnesota with his family after the Civil War. He later reminisced of a popular marching song from his youth that became, in his words, "a directing force in the lives of at least three generations of my pioneering race." One memorable verse went like this:

When we've wood and prairie land,
Won by our toil,
We'll reign like kings in fairy land,
Lords of the soil![1]

Immigrants kept coming, often encouraged by early settlers and entrepreneurs who had a vested interest in seeing the region's population expand. One such visionary wrote an open letter addressed to "German emigrants and especially to the cultivators of the soil . . . I wish to call your attention to that portion of the United States called Minnesota as I think it offers great inducements to emigrants from northern Germany, Denmark, and Norway." Year after year they arrived, cleared more land, built up permanent towns, and set about proving that Minnesota was destined to be, as the state's first newspaper put it patronizingly, "populated by a more useful class." That meant schools, churches, businesses, railroads, post offices, and local governments. The city of St. Paul, favorably located just east of where the Minnesota and Mississippi Rivers converged, quickly became the center of political and commercial developments, but that was not all it was known for. After visiting St. Paul in 1882, Mark Twain declared it "a land of libraries and schools." The city already contained a publicly subsidized land-grant university and several private academies and colleges. By the turn of the century, Minnesota boasted a population of nearly two million. The North Star State finally shed the frontier image typically consigned it by easterners. Minnesota had at long last come of age, and its leading citizens were soon shaping national policy instead of just reflecting it. With the arrival of each new generation came the promise of ever increasing responsibilities and rewards for those who were hearty enough to call this land their home.[2]

In this part of the country, the Mississippi River serves as a continuous reminder that from small things big things come. Within the span of a few hundred miles, history and geography have conspired to transform the river from a tiny, inconspicuous stream that children can easily traverse to an unremitting force of nature more than two miles wide and sixty feet deep. Being downstream causes one to ponder what it must be like upstream and vice versa. It tends to work that way with time, too. As a young lad, Harold Stassen was naturally unaware of the myriad figures and factors that had come before him and shaped his local surroundings. While knowledge of that sort would play a crucial role in his chosen vocation down the road, it was understandably out of reach for the first several years of Harold Stassen's life. But hindsight removes all such barriers for those of us perched high atop the twenty-first century. Or to put it another way, a wide expanse awaits us when we seek earnestly to profit from our collective past.

The political, economic, and social fissures of the late nineteenth century set the stage for this unfolding drama in which Harold Stassen plays the starring role. His story is, to a large extent, our story as well. He was born at the end of an age that defined progress primarily by quantitative measures. Laws and attitudes tended to reflect the notion that what was good for the nation was good for the individual, no matter the price paid or the burdens borne by those folks less favored by fate or circumstance. The change began haltingly at first, with efforts to organize the nation's farmers, regulate railroads, and unionize mine workers from Coeur d'Alene to the Iron Range. But as Harold Stassen grew, so too did the widespread impulse to reform America. Progressive ideas took root, became commonplace, and redefined what it meant to be a Republican in a nation about to be run by Democrats and in a world soon to be fundamentally reorganized by Americans. And his particular journey through life coincided with many of the watershed events by which we have come to mark the passage of time and temperament in the twentieth century. Understanding Stassen's career contextually requires an acknowledgment that the world into which he was born differed drastically from the world he helped to create.

~

If there was a politician in Minnesota during the late nineteenth century who most resembles the statesman Harold Stassen would become nearly a half century later, it is Cushman Kellogg Davis. Born in upstate New York in 1838, Davis migrated to Wisconsin with his family several years before the Civil War, studied law at the University of Michigan, and in 1861 put his legal career on hold to serve the Union's cause. After the war, Davis moved to St. Paul to take up law once again and quickly won office in the Minnesota State Legislature. Other victories followed in fast succession. At the age of thirty-eight, Cushman Davis could rightly claim—as Stassen would one day do—the honorable titles of attorney, war veteran, and *former* Republican governor of Minnesota. By the 1890s Davis had parlayed his considerable legal and political experience into a U.S. Senate seat that he held for almost fourteen years. And Davis's Middle Western background didn't seem to hinder his influence upon national affairs. As America's interests began to extend beyond the continental United States, Davis assumed tremendous sway as chairman of the Senate Committee on Foreign Relations. He was surely propelled in part by the jingoistic spirit of the day. That *might makes right* attitude proved decisive on matters of war and peace at the end of the nineteenth century. Emboldened by a sense of self-righteousness and confident in the superiority of their institutions, Americans with few notable exceptions embraced the "splendid little war" with Spain as a necessary if troublesome affair. Even Minnesotans, isolated as they were from the rest of the world, were quick to rally around the Stars and Stripes when it appeared destined to fly above foreign shores.

Senator Davis was headed back to St. Paul from Washington, DC, in July of 1898 when news of an American victory over Spanish forces in Cuba reached the United States. Upon his arrival by train in Minnesota, Davis boldly proclaimed his vision for world affairs in the coming century, which if fulfilled would mark a drastic change in America's standing among nations. He said:

> This Nation in the near future is to become the leading factor in international politics. We cannot retreat to our former policy of isolation . . . I believe we shall be equal to this responsibility. We can take care of all the possessions we may acquire, and comfortably shoulder all the tremendous duties we may assume. We shall find the necessary resources of statesmanship, the qualities of diplomacy, the strength of rulership that is our heritage. The future broadens before us in wonderful ways we could not have foreseen. We may go to meet its destinies calm, confident, secure in the might of the Nation and the justness of its purposes.[3]

A generous dose of chauvinism notwithstanding, Davis's impromptu speech would in time prove remarkably accurate, at least on the face of it. He envisioned the United States as a world power. And like the generation before him that viewed continental expansion as providential, Davis saw little reason to question America's motives or "the justness of its purposes."

Much of the coming twentieth century would find the purity of American ideals under attack at home and abroad, disputes in which Harold Stassen frequently played an important part. That the nation has since assumed a starring role in world affairs is beyond dispute.

In 1901 Cushman Davis published a lengthy tract he titled *A Treatise on International Law Including American Diplomacy.* In a gesture that would be virtually repeated by Stassen almost forty years later, Davis made a plea for unity in the realm of foreign policy by writing: "Whatever may be the distractions of party and the vicissitudes of political ascendency in our internal affairs, it is a maxim of this government that, whatever party may be in government, the continuity of our foreign intercourse and policy should never be broken."

Cushman Davis anticipated another significant trend in American politics that foreshadowed Stassen's career. In the half century following the Civil War, Minnesotans frequently found themselves on the front line of a struggle threatening to tear the nation apart—this time as much by class as by section. Rapid industrial growth in the late 1800s brought profound consequences for all Americans. Traditional economic and social patterns were changing drastically, and the nation's citizens grappled to reconcile the ideals of the past with the realities of the present. Writer Sherwood Anderson captured the spirit of the times in this way: "The coming of industrialism, attended by the roar and rattle of affairs, the shrill cries of millions of new voices that have come among us from overseas, the going and coming of trains, the growth of cities, the building of the inter-urban car lines that weave in and out of towns and past farmhouses, and now in these later days the coming of the automobiles has worked a tremendous change in the lives and in the habits of thought of our people of Mid-America."[4]

∼

As it turned out, Cushman Davis's profound influence upon the nation was not limited to foreign affairs. He was in the vanguard of progressive, Republican reformers for whom the prospect of change in government did not portend the end of the world. On the contrary, the perpetuation of the Republic depended upon it. By 1895 Davis was blunt in his characterization of the era, proclaiming, "The new wine is bursting the old bottles . . . If I were asked to define the controlling political and social elements and questions of this age, I would unhesitatingly say that they are the urgent and ever-increasing necessity of regulating the internal concerns of the state by government."[5]

At a time when "few men of great power had the sympathy and the vision necessary to perceive the menace contained in the growth of corporations," Senator Davis of Minnesota championed the need for government action to curb the excesses of capitalism. Though he first delivered his most famous speech—"Modern Feudalism"—while campaigning for governor in 1873, its central theme resonated with listeners for the next three decades. One passage in particular caught the attention of an up-and-coming politician from New York who would soon find himself the very agent of change Davis envisioned. His name was Theodore Roosevelt, and he agreed wholeheartedly with Davis's suggestion that

> The liberty of the individual has been annihilated by the logical process constructed to maintain it. We have come to a political deification of Mammon. *Laissez-faire* is not utterly blameworthy. It begat modern democracy, and made the modern republic possible. There can be no doubt of that. But there it reached its limit of political benefaction, and began to incline toward the point where extremes meet . . . To every assertion that the people in their collective capacity of a government ought to exert their indefeasible right to self-defense, it is said you touch the sacred rights of property.[6]

That President Roosevelt sought common cause in Cushman Davis's campaign to balance individual liberty with property rights proved enormously consequential. It set the stage for several dramatic showdowns between what Roosevelt called "great industrial combinations" and "the general welfare" of America. Roosevelt effectively threw down the gauntlet early in his presidency when he began enforcing the Sherman Anti-Trust Law. The message was clear: Big Business could expect anything but business as usual from his administration if it continued to flout the law and jeopardize the public's interest. A series of highly publicized federal lawsuits brought against the Northern Securities Company, American Tobacco, and Standard Oil firmly established Roosevelt's reputation as a trust-buster and endeared him to the masses. But by 1907, as he neared the end of his second term, Roosevelt's references to corporate America became increasingly vitriolic. Speaking at Indianapolis in late May, the president referred to the "predatory man of wealth" as the gravest threat to private property in the United States. And three months later, in August of 1907, Roosevelt renewed his pledge "to punish certain malefactors of great wealth" who seemed determined to "enjoy the fruits of their own evil doing."[7]

The tide of public opinion had finally turned in favor of progressive reform, and Theodore Roosevelt—as was his nature—exploited it for all it was
worth. He had the right temperament at the right time to transform the
meaning of government in this country, a feat for which he earned himself
a rightful place in the pantheon of American politics. It was Cushman Davis's
peculiar fate, however, to be among those who inspired the change but did
not live to see it through to fruition. At the time of his death in 1900, the
term "progressive" had not yet gained wide acceptance as a political watchword, much less a movement unto itself. But the seeds had been planted
and conditions were ripe for change as the wheel of time clicked forward to
mark the passing of one extraordinary age and the birth of another—just in
time for Harold Stassen's arrival.

~

Progress in the late nineteenth century didn't come cheaply or easily, but
that it had arrived with promises of even greater rewards in the future was
taken as an article of faith. The optimism of that era was contagious, and
it gave rise to many grandiose predictions. Newspapers from one end of the
country to the other greeted the new century with the greatest of expectations. "[The nineteenth] has been a century of such astounding achievement that it is perhaps natural to believe that there will be no other equal
to it," wrote the editors of the *Los Angeles Times* on January 1, 1901. "Past
history, however, shows no limits to the capacities for development of the
human race, and the historian of the 20th century may have full as wonderful a tale to tell." On the same morning, residents of Boise, Idaho, opened
their *Daily Statesman* to read, "The child of today, living to ordinary age, will
find himself as a citizen of the mightiest nation ever known—greater in
power and resources than all Europe and dominating the entire world." Two
weeks later a Mr. John Talman of St. Paul, Minnesota, included his two cents'
worth in a letter to the editor of the *New York Times Saturday Review:* "The
century upon which we have just entered is one of Hope most luminant."[8]
Such was the tone of most forecasters, several of whom turned out to be
remarkably prescient. But few managed to qualify that pervading sense of
idealism as well as the *Evening News* of Kenosha, Wisconsin. Its prophecy
struck a more pragmatic note: "All things considered, this old world, wicked
as it is, is a vastly better place to live in at the close of the 19th century than
it was as its beginning . . . If righteousness and justice and brotherly love
shall go hand in hand with the advance of science, with the dissemination
of knowledge and the development of nature's resources, then indeed it

[the twentieth] will be a glorious century." *If* appears to have been the operative term.[9]

If, as Victor Hugo suggested, nothing is as powerful as an idea whose time has come, then the child born in America during 1907 could look forward to a life utterly transformed by many powerful ideas—technological, social, economic, political, military, and so on. In the panorama of human history, the first few years of the twentieth century rest on what might be described as a kind of tectonic fault in time—a precarious juncture that proved for better *and* for worse strikingly oriented toward change. Age-old traditions, inert by nature and by habit, heaved under the strain of dynamic forces that showed little sign of letting up or shifting course. And the beneficiaries of said traditions pushed back with ever-increasing determination.

The tumult had already begun to take its toll by the time Harold Stassen entered the world, and ample evidence existed for those who were willing to look closely enough. It could be found in the spring of 1907 along the railroad tracks located a bit east of William Stassen's farm and among efforts to unionize workers on the Mesabi Iron Range one hundred eighty miles due north. It would within a few short months be written on the faces of panicked depositors lining up outside Wall Street's biggest banks and investment houses. And that summer at The Hague in the Netherlands, it was most certainly on the minds of negotiators from around the globe, including the young John Foster Dulles, fresh from Princeton and eager to make his mark on the world. One day in the distant future Dulles and Harold Stassen would indeed join forces to help remake that world, but for now neither was ready to influence or even comprehend the profound changes that were in store for humankind.

~

The frustration associated with changing economic circumstances that was becoming apparent to easterners like Teddy Roosevelt in 1907 was downright palpable in the Midwest. It had been for quite some time. The growing disparity between urban and rural America in the Industrial Age was hardly news to the nation's farmers. They had been fighting an uphill battle against merchants, bankers, middlemen, commission agents, wholesalers, creditors, and speculators since colonial times and had only recently begun to organize themselves into something approaching a national brotherhood. A Minnesota farmer, in fact, provided the inspiration for what became the Order of Patrons of Husbandry, better known as the National Grange. Founded in 1867 by Oliver H. Kelley and several associates, the Grange was designed as a social organization "to break down the isolation of the farmer, introduce color and interest to his life, bring about an interchange of views, and build up a solidarity of interest." Kelley was greatly influenced by his experiences working for the Department of Agriculture and touring the rural South after the Civil War. He became convinced that cooperative farm associations provided the best defense against increasing transportation costs and falling prices, the two greatest man-made threats to farmers during the Gilded Age.[10]

Kelley and his fellow Grangers insisted that their organization was not a political party, but inevitably, by virtue of its expanding membership (Minnesota had 538 local granges in 1874), the Grange began to impact state and local politics. Members of the Grange were elected to state legislatures and county boards throughout the Midwest. The most notable result of this growing influence came in the form of state regulatory agencies and statutes aimed at limiting railroad, elevator, and warehouse rates, which farmers viewed as unfair and discriminatory. In 1871 for instance, Minnesota's Republican governor declared that "freight and elevator charges as 'practiced by some of our roads are unjustifiable, extortionate and oppressive to the last degree.'" Lawmakers agreed. Referred to collectively as "Granger laws," populist legislation in Middle Western states (primarily Illinois, Iowa, Wisconsin, and Minnesota) "established the principle that railroads and other corporations 'clothed with public interest' are properly subject to public regulation."[11]

Railroad and business executives viewed things differently. To them it was not so much an issue of fairness as it was an unwarranted attack upon their freedom. They denounced the Granger laws "as legislative encroachments upon the sanctity of private property and illegitimate public meddling with the right of private businesses to be managed by their owners as they saw fit." Convinced that the state laws violated the federal constitution, business leaders retained the best attorneys money could buy to make their case to the U.S. Supreme Court. They had faith in capitalism and in due process and in an American system of jurisprudence that consistently came down on the side of property rights. If the states had gone astray because of disaffected farmers and weak-minded legislators, then it was up to the federal judiciary to bring them back to their senses. These were the railroads, after all. The nation depended upon them. Surely the justices on the Supreme Court would understand the important precedent that was at stake.[12]

Apparently they did. Unfortunately for the railroads and related interests, the court's opinion did not match their own. In a series of crucial decisions handed down in 1877, the U.S. Supreme Court validated the doctrine that private businesses affected with the public interest can and ought to be regulated in order to protect the general welfare of a community. It was a huge setback for the railroad industry, which viewed the combined rulings as nothing short of apocalyptic. One prominent lawyer went so far as to warn that the high court had essentially "opened a new gateway of attack upon private industry" and had "pushed aside the obstructions which stood in the way of communism, or, at least, of the communistic spirit." In another era, hysteria might have gotten the best of him.[13]

For the folks who benefitted most from regulated fares and freight rates—farmers, small-town merchants, train passengers, states' rights advocates, and local government officials—the celebration was short lived. While they may have won an important battle against corporate business interests, the war between private industry and the general public continued to be fought in the nation's courtrooms. And it's little wonder who had the resources and wherewithal to stubbornly press ahead with argument after argument until they received the answer they were looking for. Time and money were with the railroads.

Law is a tricky thing. The more frequently a statute is revisited by parties armed with reasonable arguments for and against, the more murky and open to interpretation the law tends to become. That sounds somewhat counterintuitive for people who believe that to know something is to command it and to know it really well is to master it. Such is the logical way of viewing knowledge in general and legal precedents in particular. But as the American jurist Oliver Wendell Holmes, Jr., declared in 1881, "The life of the law has not been logic; it has been experience." It is an astute observation and one upon which Holmes built his entire judicial reputation. He understood that members of free, democratic societies experiment all the time by trying to solve their problems through the legislative process. Sometimes it works. Sometimes it doesn't. But that people have the right to try at all, according to Justice Holmes, is the essence of our Constitution. By the 1880s, the "experiment" of granting state lawmakers the authority to regulate major industries was something corporate leaders refused to see set in stone. Not surprisingly, they found many obliging attorneys prepared to take up their fight for justice.

The legal wrangling raged on for the better part of three decades. In the spring of 1907 the battle lines moved to Minnesota, where state attorney general Edward Young became embroiled in a constitutional tug-of-war with broad implications. For many years the Minnesota State Legislature had led the movement to pull the railroads into line by mandating reasonable rates within its borders. A state Railroad and Warehouse Commission was formed back in 1885 to prohibit "'unjust discriminating' as to passenger or freight rates, as to terminal facilities, or as to persons, towns, villages, cities or stations." For a time at least, railroad owners and farmers were able to maintain a sort of unsteady peace with one another so long as the economy reaped rewards for both.[14]

But as the years passed, corporate profits soared, commodity prices continued to fall, Minnesota's farmers began to once again rail against extortionate rates, and lawmakers felt the pressure to respond. Ongoing negotiations between the railroads and state authorities offered the hope of compromise—a settlement that would demonstrate the state's desire to control rates and the railroads' interest in maximizing profits to please their shareholders. In early April of 1907 discussions broke down and the state legislature moved decisively. On April 4—less than a fortnight before Harold Stassen was born—legislators passed an act fixing two cents per mile as the maximum passenger rate to be charged by railroads in Minnesota. (The rate had previously been three cents per mile.) Failure to heed the statute was classified as a felony by the legislature, with violators incurring a fine up to five thousand dollars and/or as many as five years imprisonment per infraction. Obviously, the state meant business and expected railroad employees to abide by the new law. But the question of limiting the much more lucrative freight rates remained, and state lawmakers feared a legal challenge from deep-pocketed magnates like James J. Hill or J. P. Morgan. Two days later the *Minneapolis Tribune* reported, "Every effort is being made to secure the commodity freight rate reductions without the necessity of the expensive and long drawn out suits in the federal courts."[15]

Enter Minnesota attorney general Edward T. Young. As a Republican serving alongside a newly elected Democratic governor—John A. Johnson—Young ("E. T." to his intimates) found himself in a compromising position. During his multiple terms in the state house and senate, Edward Young had rarely been out of favor with the railroads. But times were changing. Governor Johnson was a reformer who quickly galvanized support in the legislature to get more railroad rate restrictions on the state statute books. Perhaps with an eye toward the 1908 gubernatorial race, Young sensed the shifting political winds. He also knew that his constitutional duty was to enforce the law in Minnesota.

Regardless of his motives, the attorney general girded himself and his assistants for the legal challenge that seemed inevitable. As early as February, Young was asking his former house and senate colleagues for increased appropriations to deal with impending litigation. He sounded more like a reluctant warrior than a reformer when he testified, "I will do my best under any circumstances; but if you want the state's interests protected there must be more help for the attorney general's office. If the legislature wants to take this off my hands, I will be delighted." Then in a statement that would prove more prophetic than he could possibly have imagined, Young added for good measure, "We are going in against an army of attorneys, and we don't want the people to ask why we were not prepared. I want the people to know, and intend to have them know, the true facts in the case."[16]

The "army of attorneys" Young envisioned eventually included some of the sharpest legal minds ever to grace Minnesota's or for that matter the nation's courtrooms. Representing the stockholders of several railroads affected by the Minnesota rate regulations were men of such future national prominence as Frank B. Kellogg (U.S. secretary of state under Calvin Coolidge), William D. Mitchell (Herbert Hoover's attorney general), and Pierce Butler (associate justice of the U.S. Supreme Court). Kellogg incidentally had been partners in a prominent St. Paul law firm with his cousin Cushman Kellogg Davis and was subsequently elected to Davis's old U.S. Senate seat during World War I. All of that, of course, was on the distant horizon in 1907. For the time being Frank B. Kellogg and his associates were earning their stripes as tenacious litigators. Kellogg had already developed a reputation as a trust-buster, having successfully prosecuted several monopolies on behalf of the Roosevelt administration. Now he found himself on the side of railroad shareholders. Needless to say, Edward Young had his hands full.

In December of 1907 the U.S. Supreme Court heard oral arguments in the case that became known as *Ex Parte Young*. Minnesota's attorney general denied the existence of any legitimate federal question by contending that the Eleventh Amendment required challenges to Minnesota statutes to be raised in state court. The people of Minnesota had spoken through their legislature in order to get the rate regulations passed in the first place, and the railroads would have to seek redress in the Minnesota court system. In writing for the majority nearly four months later, Justice Rufus Peckham acknowledged the controversial nature of the issues at hand: "We recognize and appreciate to the fullest extent the very great importance of this case, not only to the parties now before the court, but also to

the great mass of the citizens of this country, all of whom are interested
in the practical working of the courts of justice throughout the land, both
Federal and state, and in the proper exercise of the jurisdiction of the Federal courts, as limited and controlled by the Federal Constitution and the
laws of Congress."[17]

With that Peckham quickly dispensed of Edward Young's assertion that
the federal courts had no jurisdiction. He essentially supported the shareholders' argument that based upon the severity of the consequences for
violating Minnesota's rate regulations, the railroads had been denied their
Fourteenth Amendment right to due process and equal protection under the
law. In other words, the unreasonable penalties consigned by the legislature
and enforceable by Edward Young meant that the very survival of the railroads might be at stake. In that case, the state had overstepped its constitutional bounds and now posed an unwarranted threat to private enterprise.
Ironically, it was the sort of defense of "the sacred rights of property" that
would have caused Cushman Davis to wince a generation earlier. The pen-
dulum appeared to be swinging back toward the side of industry. Clearly
angered by this unmitigated defeat, E. T. Young charged that the Supreme
Court's decision "allows the enforcement of any state law to be prevented
by a federal injunction, and it makes state laws as useless as the resolutions
of a town caucus."[18]

But once again, victory for the railroads was fleeting. The changes that
politicians like Cushman Davis and Theodore Roosevelt and Edward Young
and Governor Johnson anticipated were not long in coming. To be sure they
arrived in waves, but by 1912 the high tide of progressivism was definitely
in as Democrats, Republicans, and a startling number of Socialists scrambled to carry the banner of reform at all levels of government. Conservative
businessmen who wanted to see government stay on the sidelines were out
of step with the prevailing attitudes of the day and risked winding up on the
wrong side of history. Such fears prompted one of New York's more astute
Republicans, Henry L. Stimson, to write his good friend Theodore Roosevelt in 1910:

> To me it seems vitally important that the Republican party, which contains,
> generally speaking, the richer and more intelligent citizens of the country,
> should take the lead in reform and not drift into a reactionary position. If,
> instead, the leadership should fall into the hands of either an independent
> party, or a party composed, like the Democrats, largely of foreign elements

and the classes which will immediately benefit by the reform, and if the solid business Republicans should drift into new obstruction, I fear the necessary changes could hardly be accomplished without much excitement and possible violence.[19]

Stimson's words amounted to both a diagnosis of and a prescription for the developing clash of wills among his fellow party members. He foreshadowed the split between Old Guard Republicans and enthusiastic supporters of Teddy Roosevelt's progressive candidacy, which spelled victory for the Democrats in the 1912 election. With that win Woodrow Wilson essentially co-opted the reform impulse in America and proceeded to steer the ship of state on a remarkably middle course. Change was needed indeed. But according to Wilson, the people—through their state legislatures—should first and foremost be the source of that change. In not so many words, this epitomized the *middle way*. Wilson had no interest in creating a socialist state to remedy the ills produced by rapid, unregulated industrialism. Nor did he resist the urge to empower responsible progressive reformers, campaigning in 1912, "I am, therefore, forced to be a progressive, if for no other reason, because we have not kept up with our changes of conditions, either in the economic field or in the political field."[20]

During the first few years of Harold Stassen's childhood, Minnesotans were well ahead of the curve when it came to walking the fine line between revolutionary and reactionary impulses. Where radical changes were threatened, reason ruled the day. Even Minnesota's controversial attempts to rein in the railroads would in time be viewed as measured and moderate by none other than the U.S. Supreme Court. Litigation continued back and forth between the railroads and Minnesota for six years after *Ex Parte Young,* with millions of dollars spent by both sides to determine the constitutionality of state regulations. Finally, in 1913, Justice Charles Evans Hughes drafted a monumental opinion in what were now collectively referred to as the *Minnesota Rate Cases.* In a startling departure from precedent and citing the commerce clause of the Constitution, Hughes deferred to Congress the ultimate responsibility for determining how "to alleviate any adverse effects of the state regulation on interstate commerce." Minnesota's lawmakers and citizens were finally vindicated. They could rest assured that their legitimate attempts to regulate trade within their borders did not require a special fiat from the federal courts. It amounted to a resounding victory for state authorities in general and for progressive reformers in particular. The nation's highest court at long last appeared to be a potent supporter of change rather than an impenetrable barrier set against it.[21]

But law of an entirely different sort was on the minds of many Americans in the summer of 1907. At The Hague in the Netherlands, preparations were already under way for a second great international peace conference. In 1899, representatives from twenty-eight nations had drawn up plans to mitigate the most inhumane effects of modern warfare, and now, eight years and three major conflicts later, expectations remained high for peace advocates. They had secured the active support of one of the world's richest men, Andrew Carnegie, and hoped that this round of meetings would significantly advance the cause of world peace. In 1905 Carnegie had offered a haunting portrayal of what the new century would bring if world leaders did not act to forestall the momentous pull toward war. He said, "We should delude ourselves if we assumed that war is immediately to cease, for it is scarcely to be hoped that the future has not to witness more than one great holocaust of men to be offered up before the reign of peace blesses the earth." Carnegie donated $1.5 million to build a colossal Peace Palace to facilitate future conferences and used his influence to encourage even greater participation than in 1899. This time forty-four nations obliged. When the editor of the *New York Times* publically disparaged Carnegie's efforts to achieve international cooperation, he responded in kind: "This seems the easiest and most direct road to the abolition of war, which decides not who is right, but only who is strong, exalting might above right. It is a path which the nations have already trod for some distance successfully and are familiar with. The will may be lacking, but the way is clear."[22]

On the very day Harold Stassen was born, the *New York Times* informed its readers that a veteran American diplomat would lead the U.S. delegation at The Hague. Joseph Hodges Choate, the former ambassador to England, was chosen by President Theodore Roosevelt to represent American interests at the peace conference perhaps precisely because he was a realist. Though Roosevelt supported "the whole Hague idea" in principle, he privately told advisors that he couldn't stand "the fantastic visionaries who are crazy to do the impossible." Choate—conservative, dignified, and stately— would doubtless have both feet planted firmly on the ground while negotiating with other world leaders. At seventy-five years of age, he was not prone to wild bursts of idealism. In that respect, the American representative was to find his European counterparts remarkably accommodating.[23]

As he had done in 1899, Russia's Czar Nicholas II took credit for proposing the international conference and was careful to outline what would and would not be open for discussion. Arbitration of disputes and defining the laws of war were suitable topics for debate, but Russia's leader, like Germany's kaiser, had no interest in even broaching the subject of disarmament. The British prime minister, along with the U.S. secretary of state, hoped that reduction of armaments would be given a chance at The Hague, but they were clearly in the minority. Strength through arms remained the order of the day. Even President Roosevelt, winner of the Nobel Peace Prize in 1906, had written to a friend that the navy was an "infinitely more potent factor for peace than all the peace societies."[24]

Over 250 delegates to the second International Peace Conference gathered for the opening session on June 15, 1907. Russia's ambassador to France, Alexander Nelidoff, led the czar's contingent and was quickly elected to preside over the proceedings. The aged Nelidoff delivered an uninspired keynote address, and "the round of applause at the conclusion of his remarks seemed cold and perfunctory." The response to Nelidoff's comments was to be expected. Those who were attending the conference in an official capacity—that is, as the representatives of sovereign states—held few illusions when it came to settling serious international disputes peacefully. Miracles were not on the agenda at The Hague. For the vast majority of participants, just negotiating with past or potential rivals signified a step toward peace, though a small one at that.[25]

What remains most remarkable about Nelidoff's speech is the extent to which he captured the essential spirit of the times in so few words and with such little fanfare. Perhaps the truth hurt more than anyone in attendance was willing or able to admit. If the nineteenth century had given birth to the potent political ideology known as nationalism and all of the destructive energy that comes with modern, industrial states in competition with one another, then the twentieth century was destined to be the era of internationalism. So theorized the professional peace advocates for whom the dream of a world without war was still very much attainable. And though he was clearly not in league with such visionaries, Nelidoff was willing to give voice to their objectives as well as to the enormous challenges with which they had to contend. He said, "Let us above all not forget that there is a whole class of questions in which the honor, dignity, and essential interests of individuals as well as nations are engaged, and in which neither party, whatever the consequences, will recognize any authority than that of its own judgment and personal sentiments." Then, as if to breathe life into the proceedings, he continued, "But that should not discourage us from dreaming of the ideal of universal peace and the fraternity of peoples, which are, after all, but the natural higher aspirations of the human soul. Is not the pursuit of the ideal toward which we must always strive, without ever reaching it, the essential condition of all progress?"[26]

The Russian minister closed with a flourish by revealing his own diminutive expectations, which descended like a pall on the entire assemblage: "Excelsior is the motto of our program. Let us set bravely to work. Our path is lit by the bright star of Universal Peace, which we shall never reach, but which will always guide us for Humanity's good. For whatever within the modest limits of our means we can do for individuals by lightening the burdens of war, and for States by preventing conflicts, will entitle the Governments we represent to the gratitude of humanity." Nelidoff had thus dispensed with utopian visions of peace and those who dared dream them.[27]

But still the dreamers persisted. One of them was the American social reformer Jane Addams. Known primarily for her efforts to spread the settlement house movement at the turn of the century, Addams published *Newer Ideals of Peace* in early 1907 and therefore solidified her reputation as a peacemaker as well. Social justice and the prevention of war were inextricably linked, according to Addams. Providing for the former necessarily led to the latter because war is the most bloody, irrational, and uncivilized form of injustice known to man. Such reasoning represented a progressive, enlightened view of human institutions that attracted adherents from the most unexpected quarters. Though he certainly approached the problem with different tools at his disposal, Andrew Carnegie shared Addams's enthusiastic desire to make peace a reality. It may very well have blinded him to the facts. In June of 1907, Carnegie set his sights on personally convincing Germany's Kaiser Wilhelm II to pave the way to peace. In what could go down in history as the greatest example of misspent flattery, Carnegie went so far as to inform the German leader if he would lend his full-fledged support to The Hague idea he might well earn the title "apostle of peace."[28]

By the end of the summer it was becoming clear that best intentions had given way to inertia at The Hague. Nations spent the bulk of their time agreeing to complex rules for a war they simply presumed already lay on the horizon. They developed dozens of international laws—none of which were enforceable of course—concerning neutral territory, naval tactics, the launching of projectiles or explosives from balloons, underwater mines, contraband, arbitration, and countless other messy details of war. They congratulated themselves on a job well done and made tentative plans to convene again in 1915. That never happened.

It is tempting to focus on both the naïveté of those who arrived at The Hague in 1907 with great expectations and the cynicism of those who intended to do no more than go through the motions. But taken as a whole, the attendees at the first or second great international peace conferences (including nineteen-year-old John Foster Dulles) helped advance the notion that individual nations should and could place some collective goals above their sovereign interests. Historians John Garraty and Peter Gay provided the most succinct and contextualized description of that work when they wrote, "The Hague Conferences of 1899 and 1907 successfully codified the laws of war and gave birth to the idea of an international court. That they failed to secure the peaceful settlement of all international disputes should not reduce them to aberrations in a world bent on war: they grew out of an experience of peace unparalleled in the history of Europe and from a desire to prolong and improve it." It would be left to the next generation, including the newly born Harold Stassen, to continue those efforts. Stassen decided at a relatively young age to make world peace his life's ambition, and his commitment to making it a reality never wavered. While others continued to dream, the politician-turned-statesman would in time get down to the difficult business of building a workable mechanism to prevent war.[29]

~

Nearly two hundred miles directly north of William Stassen's truck farm, another type of war erupted in July of 1907, the implications of which would have just as much influence on young Harold Stassen's future as the peace talks in Europe. Since the discovery of iron ore in 1890, northeastern Minnesota's Mesabi Range had attracted the attention of several wealthy businessmen, including John D. Rockefeller and Andrew Carnegie, and thousands upon thousands of immigrant laborers. For a decade and a half, ever-increasing amounts of ore extracted from open pits and underground mining operations on Minnesota's Iron Range helped fuel the nation's industrial growth and sent corporate profits soaring. Meanwhile, a hodgepodge of foreign miners—Finns, Italians, Poles, Slovenes, Greeks, Bulgarians, Croats, and Serbs—struggled to survive beneath the crushing weight of declining wages, hazardous working conditions, and the constant threat of termination. By the summer of 1907, tension between management and labor had reached a breaking point, and communities braced themselves for possible violence.

Much of the anxiety on the Iron Range that year developed after the Western Federation of Miners (associated with deadly conflicts in places like Coeur d'Alene, Idaho, and Cripple Creek, Colorado) attempted to unionize workers in northeastern Minnesota. In 1906 the WFM sent an Italian Socialist named Teofilo Petriella to the Mesabi Range with instructions to organize union activities. Petriella quickly recruited immigrant miners for leadership positions and consolidated the local unions into three ethnic groups—Italian, Slavic, and Finnish—each with their own chosen leader. Radicalism was about to rear its head on the Iron Range, and mine owners instructed their company managers to resist the emergence of collective action on the part of laborers.[30]

Anger had been fomenting among miners on the Mesabi Range for several years. The specific sources of their frustrations were many and varied, but as labor historian Philip Foner discovered, "The despotic tyranny of the bosses, mine captains and foremen was a complaint most frequently voiced by the miners." A new immigrant often had to pay a bribe to the foreman just to get hired in the first place. Then in order to keep his job or to earn a coveted spot in the mine from which he might extract a larger quantity of ore than his coworkers, the miner would have to keep up a steady stream of bribes to any number of bosses in whose hands his future rested. The bribes could involve money, food, liquor, or even "in some cases, submitting to propositions made to his wife and daughters."[31]

When union officials called a strike on July 20, 1907, Petriella continued negotiations with company officials in Duluth. He asked for small wage increases on behalf of the workers he represented, an eight-hour workday, and "the ending of kickbacks to foremen who determined which men would work the seams of high-grade ore." An official strike notice issued by the Minnesota district of the Western Federation of Miners declared, "strike but no violence."[32]

U.S. Steel, the largest ore producer in the world, responded forcefully. Corporate leaders directed managers on the Iron Range to "use any methods necessary to break the strike." Steel executives proved a great deal less squeamish about the use of violence to end the standoff than union leaders did. Special deputies and professional strikebreakers were quickly hired to descend upon the Iron Range in a show of force. For several days in late July and early August, an uncertain peace hung precariously over several Iron

Range communities. Striking workers marched several times in a show of solidarity and then dispersed when confronted by law enforcement officials. The August 10 edition of the Duluth *News-Tribune* declared, "Army of Deputies Overawe the Western Federation of Miners."[33]

For a short time the nation turned its attention to Minnesota and its beleaguered miners for fear the conflict would erupt into violence. Even Mary Harris "Mother" Jones traveled to the Iron Range as a representative of the Socialist party. Jones was a fiery, seventy-two-year-old activist who had gained a national reputation for her union work and for her outspoken criticism of child labor. In 1903 she attempted to gain a private audience with President Theodore Roosevelt, writing to him, "I have espoused the cause of the labor class in general and of suffering children in particular. For what affects the child must ultimately affect the adult . . . I know of no question of to-day that demands greater attention from those who have at heart the perpetuation of the Republic."[34]

By the middle of September, order had been reestablished on the Iron Range. Cooler heads prevailed as Minnesota governor John A. Johnson resisted mounting pressure to use the state militia to suppress the strike. Johnson paid a visit to several Iron Range communities during the late summer of 1907 but refused to show impartiality so long as the state's laws were upheld. In this sense, Johnson's decision to follow a middle course at a crucial juncture in management-labor relations provided an important precedent for future governors, including Harold Stassen, and likely thwarted the intentions of those who welcomed a violent outcome.

～

Remarkably, the ending of a major economic crisis in Minnesota coincided with the beginning of a much larger one on Wall Street. The Panic of 1907 broadsided investors that autumn and sent shockwaves through the nation's entire credit system. For months John D. Rockefeller had been predicting that the Roosevelt administration's ramped-up regulation of business would bring about a depression, and by October such fears appeared to be coming true. Banks faltered, the value of assets traded on the New York Stock Exchange tumbled, and communities across the country prepared for the worst. Famed Kansas journalist William Allen White described the panic's effects on Middle America: "Factories that had been booming turned glassy-eyed windows to us. Inland towns in the Ohio Valley and Pennsylvania showed us crowds of idle workers on the streets . . . Cloth signs on store buildings in the little cities and villages advertised bankrupt sales.

The banks were closed. Commerce and industry stopped dead-still. It was a terrible time."[35]

Pressed for time and options, Roosevelt swallowed his pride and turned to financier J. P. Morgan for help. Morgan orchestrated a number of eleventh-hour business transactions (that is, he shifted much of his vast financial empire from one bank to another) in order to stem the tide of economic catastrophe. Before the crisis had subsided, the U.S. government bailed out a number of banks suffering from the strain of speculative fever to the tune of $150 million in treasury certificates and bonds. It was one of America's more painful economic debacles, but it contained many valuable lessons for the future—so long as people were willing to heed the warning signs.[36]

As summer turned to fall and fall to winter back in Minnesota, William Stassen and his family prepared to confront what challenges and opportunities the coming cold would bring. The harvest had been reasonably good, the local banks had weathered the late financial storm, and young Harold had survived the first critical months of his life. There was much to be thankful for, including hope. Hope for peace. Hope for prosperity. Hope for the future. In short, hope for the types of things every generation spends half its time on earth pursuing for itself and the other half desperately trying to preserve for its descendants.

It would be an exaggeration to suggest that Harold Stassen was a born politician. But ample evidence exists to confirm that he was raised on an intellectual diet rich in political discourse and fortified by an acute sensitivity to injustice. In 1947, already campaigning in earnest for the Republican nomination to be president of the United States, Stassen wrote *Where I Stand,* a candid, articulate, and no-nonsense collection of his political convictions in full-length book form. The dedication reads, "With affection and respect to my father who, in addition to all else, began my education in government at an early age." Indeed, for all his accomplishments in academia, law, diplomacy, and politics, Stassen's fundamental and abiding view of the world can be traced to a single thread emanating from his father's informal tutelage. Harold referred to his father as "my oracle, a fount of sense making who, to my mind, richly deserved his standing in our area, and with that standing such honors as being named the local Republican leader." Simply put, William Stassen was the original rock upon which young Harold placed his political faith and fortunes.[37]

The elder Stassen for his part reveled in civic causes and local politics. A truck farmer by trade, William Stassen mixed good old-fashioned horse sense with a firm conviction that the Republican Party had more than earned the right to lead Minnesota, and America for that matter, into the twentieth century. The combination earned him votes. Pa Stassen was elected mayor of West St. Paul three times, served on the local school board for fourteen years, and led the Dakota County Republicans as chairman from 1928 to 1932. His was a pragmatic and typically midwestern brand of politics—establish yourself as a hard worker, get to know the people in your community, and pay attention to the sorts of things a family needs to improve its lot in life. The vast farm fields just south of the Twin Cities of Minneapolis and St. Paul offered plenty of challenges for folks dependent upon the many moods of Mother Nature. But greater still were the dreams of progress: paved roads, electrical lines, public schools, and expanding county and municipal services. William Stassen spent his spare time helping to make those dreams come true.

Harold Stassen with his father, William Stassen, about 1939

Years later, when his youngest son had just been elected governor of Minnesota, Pa Stassen was still working hard. A newspaper reporter caught up with him at the St. Paul City Farmer's Market and asked him about Harold's childhood. Sitting on a sack of potatoes and sorting through a basket of vegetables, the old farmer didn't mince words: "You want to start at the beginning. All right. He didn't eat much when he was a baby. Later on he could put away plenty. Still does. He always held his own with other boys, but was not dominating. Co-operative, I'd say." And of course there were the inevitable questions about Harold's schooling. He skipped three grades in elementary school and entered St. Paul's Humboldt Senior High at the age of eleven. Four years later he graduated from high school second in his class. It was 1922 and he was fifteen years old. To what did Mr. Stassen attribute his son's academic prowess? "He could stay away a day or so and it didn't seem to make any difference in his marks. The whole thing was he had a wonderful memory. Guess he still has it. He could look into a book, examples and things, and explain it to the older boys. He could grasp things. That's what helped him."[38]

Harold Stassen at
high school
graduation, 1922

But it was more than that. Young Harold had a thirst for knowledge and a tremendous work ethic, no doubt finely honed on the family farm. He came by husbandry naturally and learned to master the thousand-and-one chores that go along with keeping a farm profitable. When his father was laid up after an operation, Harold took over the reins at the Stassen farmstead and hauled daily produce to the St. Paul market for the better part of a year. "Harold was always a guy to get things done, more than the other boys. Ambitious," recalled his old man. "You ask me straight what kind of boy he is. He's a square-shooter. He don't take anything from anybody. I don't mean he's a roughneck. He's not looking for trouble, but he can face it when he has to."[39]

On December 7, 1921, fourteen-year-old Harold Stassen learned one of the most important lessons of his life. Standing on a hillside overlooking the sprawling meat-packing plants of South St. Paul, he watched incredulously as hundreds of Minnesota national guardsmen fixed their bayonets and advanced upon what he later remembered as "a tense, miserably cold picket line." The striking workers, nearly four thousand in all, had walked off the job two days earlier to protest an eight percent wage cut. Now their steely resolve was being put to the ultimate test. The picketing workers stood shoulder to shoulder in a long line stretching from the entrance of the packing houses to the giant Stockyard Exchange Building on Concord Street. Harold took in the scene wide eyed and unable to fully comprehend what was happening. The soldiers closed in, and "the picket line stood there for a moment, as American as the men in khaki, but then at the touch of bare metal and the prod of a rifle butt here and there, the line sagged and broke."[40]

Harold walked home after the confrontation feeling dejected and bewildered. At dinner that evening he sought counsel from his father and older brothers, who tried to put the day's events in perspective. They spoke of horrible working conditions in the packing houses, low wages, and the right of workers to strike. Then they discussed falling prices, the pressures facing livestock owners, and the industry as a whole. Harold brought the conversation back to the scene of troops advancing on unarmed strikers, which continued to tug at his conscience. William Stassen, sensing a teachable moment, responded, "The Guards should be a last resort, but they were used today as if they were the only answer. Harold, you'll live to see many changes, and one of the changes will be in labor. Maybe you'll live to see the whole picture changed and the shoe very definitely on the other foot."[41]

The strike continued on well into the winter. A federal court injunction limited how much influence could be brought to bear by the American Federation of Labor's International Meat Cutters and Butcher Workers, the union representing the South St. Paul meatpackers. Hardship mounted for the workers and their families. After two months the strikers voted, as Stassen later put it, "to surrender in order to survive." The wage cut remained, and the disheartened packers went back to work. Harold had witnessed part of a troubling national trend. Falling wages led to strikes from one end of the country to another in the postwar years. In most cases the law sided with owners, and workers paid the price. Unions were broken, profits accumulated, and wages continued to tumble. A new era of prosperity was dawning in the United States, but so far farmers and laborers hardly shared its benefits. The Upper Midwest and Minnesota in particular soon hosted a clash of political wills destined to alter the lives of all Americans.[42]

Stassen began attending the University of Minnesota in 1923. Six years later he emerged with a law degree and a gargantuan reputation to match his imposing frame; Harold was six foot three, broad shouldered, and already betraying the telltale signs of a receding hairline and impending baldness. Author John Gunther chronicled Stassen's ascendency to national distinction years later and concluded that his success resulted from more than natural aptitude, which he possessed in spades. "He was an exceptionally brilliant and pertinacious student," wrote Gunther, "and his industry was colossal." To pay his way through undergraduate courses and law school he worked multiple jobs ranging from "grease boy" in a bakery to night Pullman conductor on the St. Paul–Chicago run. A crackerjack marksman, Stassen also captained the University of Minnesota rifle team that won three national championships in a row. He served as president of the entire student body, spoke out against a proposed tuition increase at the university, and earned the praise of university president Lotus D. Coffman. Still he managed to rack up an impressive series of academic accomplishments. Famed *New York Times* journalist Harrison Salisbury knew Stassen on campus and was still marveling at his exploits nearly sixty years later. Toward the end of his own distinguished career, Salisbury wrote, "I still regard Stassen as the outstanding young political figure of his day. Extraordinary for his hard work, a first-class student and debater, the winner of speech medals, strong and rugged, articulate, personable, shrewd, he built a political system which monopolized the Minnesota campus. For him, the university was a dry run for adult politics."[43]

Even as he made lasting impressions upon fellow students and faculty members at the University of Minnesota, one abiding passion stood out among Harold Stassen's many and varied interests—world peace. He came of age in the shadow of World War I. He kept close tabs on U.S. foreign policy during the 1920s, frequently finding it lacking in rectitude. And he was not shy about sharing his opinions. What made Stassen's observations all the more striking was that he presented them in public with such cogency that listeners were often convinced by his line of reasoning. One prominent example will serve to illustrate this point. On April 7, 1927, Stassen took first place in the university's annual Pillsbury Oratorical Contest. Though the victory was surely satisfying (it set the stage for many subsequent honors, and the one hundred dollars in prize money no doubt helped cover his tuition costs), the speech itself provided remarkable insight into Stassen's developing political outlook.* He used the occasion to criticize ongoing American intervention in Nicaragua, which he blatantly labeled "armed imperialism."

~

To understand the context of Stassen's speech, it is important to remember that American military intervention in Nicaraguan affairs had gone on virtually uninterrupted since 1912. It represented a classic example of "Dollar Diplomacy," a foreign policy primarily associated with Republican presidents Theodore Roosevelt and William Howard Taft. When U.S. businesses encouraged insurgencies in Latin American countries, the U.S. government usually responded in kind. That meant choosing sides in the internal disputes of sovereign nations and then sending troops to manufacture a resolution that satisfied American interests. The policy's foundations were set in the fall of 1903 when the United States supported a Panamanian revolt from Colombia. With Panama's independence secured, American officials quickly signed a treaty with the new government granting the United States

---

* One of the judges Stassen impressed that day was a young speech professor and law student named Wayne Lyman Morse. A native of Madison, Wisconsin, Morse was deeply influenced by the progressive ideas and reforms initiated by Wisconsin governor (and then senator) Robert La Follette. Morse would one day carry that very same political tradition back to the U.S. Senate as a middle-of-the-road Republican (and then Democrat) from the state of Oregon. And he would gain lasting notoriety for opposing American participation in the Vietnam War. But that was all in the distant future. In April of 1927, he was recognized as an expert in the fields of debate and elocution. It was in that capacity that Morse had a front-row seat for the culminating event of Harold Stassen's collegiate career.

exclusive rights to build a canal through the Isthmus of Panama. The threat of European intervention in a Venezuelan crisis at the same time prompted the United States to consider the use of force in South America as well. Theodore Roosevelt's brash new form of "gunboat diplomacy" was thus born. Within two years he had formalized the policy into what he called the Roosevelt Corollary to the Monroe Doctrine. The president reported to Congress, "Chronic wrongdoing, or an impotence which results in a general loosening of the ties of civilized society, may in America, as elsewhere, ultimately require intervention by some civilized nation, and in the Western Hemisphere the adherence of the United States to the Monroe Doctrine may force the United States, however reluctantly, in flagrant cases of such wrongdoing or impotence, to the exercise of an international police power."[44]

President William Howard Taft's diplomatic record made clear his willingness to follow Roosevelt's lead in foreign affairs. When American dollars traveled to distant shores in the form of loans and investments, American Marines frequently followed. In 1912 Taft and his secretary of war, Henry Stimson, approved a plan to send troops to Nicaragua to help bring about economic and political stability. That mission lasted nearly thirteen years and helped maintain a succession of conservative, pro-American governments. The last contingent of Marines sailed for home in the summer of 1925 as the new American administration, led by President Calvin Coolidge, seemed satisfied that less was more when it came to foreign policy. But within two years things had become unraveled again in Nicaragua, at least as far as the United States government was concerned. Leftist rebels threatened the fragile status quo, and a protracted civil war loomed large on the horizon. In early January of 1927, Coolidge's secretary of state, none other than Frank B. Kellogg of Minnesota, recommended that U.S. troops return to Nicaragua in order to calm mounting tensions. By mid-March nearly two thousand American soldiers were back on Nicaraguan soil, in part, hinted Kellogg, to counter "Bolshevik Aims and Policies in Latin America."[45]

This is precisely the sequence of events Harold Stassen was referring to in his April 7 speech. He began by highlighting how various nations around the world reacted to American military action: "When the news of our recent attempt to set a house in order by sending marines to Nicaragua travelled across the Atlantic Ocean, an outburst of caustic criticism swept thruout [sic] Europe and was received with additional bitterness in Central and South America." Recognizing that his audience was well acquainted with the so-called "war to end all wars," Stassen pointed out with great irony that the "European press characterized Uncle Sam as a swashbuck-ling saber-rattling bully." He cited specific selections from the *New States-man* of London and the *Berlin Vorwaerts* lambasting the United States for "the inconsistency between this action and our attempt to climb upon a high pedestal and preach peace sermons to Europe and uphold the Ameri-can example as ideal." For good measure, Stassen added that many of "our South American neighbors interpreted this military intervention as fur-ther evidence of the selfish attempt of the United States to gain complete control of the western hemisphere. Practically the entire civilized world pointed an accusing finger at the United States and sneered 'Imperialist.'"[46]

But that certainly was not the whole story. Coolidge had many defenders at home, and the American press generally applauded his resolve. According to Stassen, "the *Washington Examiner* informed its readers that the United States was the protector and big brother of this hemisphere, and as such it was our duty to maintain order and check all communistic tendencies." Find-ing evidence even closer to home, Stassen pointed to the *Minneapolis Journal,* whose editors warned critics of U.S. policy to remember that "our actions are for humanitarian purposes, and that we are merely playing the role of big brother to our less fortunate neighbors." Stassen thus set the stage for a pro-vocative discussion of American foreign policy in the 1920s, promising his listeners to help them decide which interpretation of U.S. motives seemed most plausible. By the end of his speech, little room would be left for doubt.[47]

"We claim to be a Christian Nation, and the press labels our actions toward our neighbors as those of a Good Samaritan," Stassen told his audience, "but our neighbors bitterly assert that in reality our role is that of a thief." He cited examples of recent U.S. intervention in Haiti and the Dominican Republic. He quoted State Department communiqués suggest-ing that the U.S. military take control of the Caribbean governments to protect American banking interests. And he went so far as to condemn "the repulsive nature of our policy and its inconsistency with our ideals and principles of government." To what did we owe such a blatant disregard for traditional American values like consent of the governed, rule of law, and self-determination? According to Stassen, it was plain and simple greed. "There is in this country today a group of capitalists who stand ready to reap the golden harvest resulting from armed protection of American prop-erty on foreign soil," he announced. "Thru [*sic*] their influence they largely control the press and profoundly affect the policy of the State Department. Publicity is so arranged that the true issues do not reach the people, and

they do not realize that the United States in this policy of armed imperialism is departing from the fundamental principles of her government."[48]

And he wasn't finished yet. Stassen ratcheted up the rhetoric with one
final, blistering indictment of American motives and methods with respect
to the Caribbean:

> Cleverly concealed behind this camouflage of propaganda, the foreign
> investment group, consisting of about two percent of our total population,
> is injecting the poison of armed imperialism into our foreign policy and
> causing the other 98% to suffer the resultant losses and dangers. Shall we
> permit this group to continue to deceive the great mass of Americans, or
> shall we snatch away this mask of propaganda and expose the facts of our
> dealings with these backwards countries? With our citizens riding easily on
> the inflated cushions of our prosperity, unaware of the danger involved, we
> are treading that fatal trail of armed imperialism that led Europe to the
> verge of destruction and ushered Imperial Spain and the great Roman
> Empire to their graves. The suspicion and hatred toward us in all sections
> of the world as Uncle Sam is pictured as a bully among nations, advancing
> his own interests irrespective of the rights of others, should be sufficient
> warning of the results of our present irresponsible national will.[49]

He had made his case. Now the budding politician inside of Harold Stassen emerged with a candid appeal for honesty and transparency. He clearly
understood that human nature, like Mother Nature, is stubbornly resistant
to change. But individuals possess the capacity to transform their ideas and
their subsequent actions. This incontrovertible fact, according to young
Harold Stassen, represented the world's last, best hope for enduring peace.
And so he closed his oration as a politician might end a stump speech: "Let
us present the truth to the American people and have faith in their decisions, instead of permitting our desires, as manipulated by a small group
of our capitalists, to lead us blindly on, thru [sic] armed imperialism, to
exploitation and hatred, competition and conflict, war and bloodshed."[50]

It was a typical performance for the twenty-year-old law student from
West St. Paul, Minnesota. Harold had always been wise beyond his years.
He grew up quickly, assumed a great deal of responsibility at a young age,
and consistently aimed high when it came to academics. Now his hard work
was paying dividends and turning heads. Harrison Salisbury knew that there
was something special about Harold Stassen long before his name became

synonymous with politics. His intelligence would no doubt take him far, but one crucial question remained: In what direction was he headed? No one knew for sure in 1927. He sounded like a liberal when criticizing his nation's foreign policy, but his family's loyalties were solidly with the Republican Party. Perhaps he was somewhere in between. Time would tell.

One month after Harold Stassen won the Pillsbury Oratorical Contest, events in Nicaragua confirmed his accusations. Frustrated with the prospects of a costly war, Coolidge and Kellogg sent Henry Stimson on a one-man mission to resolve the crisis quickly and quietly. On Wednesday, May 4, 1927, Stimson met secretly with General José Maria Moncada on a hill overlooking the Tipitapa River a few miles east of Managua. A leader of the opposition movement, Moncada was fighting to unseat the Conservative president of Nicaragua—Aldofo Diaz. Stimson got right to the point. He said, "My country has recognized President Diaz, and the United States cannot make an error." Moncada countered, "You have made one, and it will cause the American government to lose much prestige in the public opinion of Hispanic America." The State Department had already assured Stimson that he had "the widest discretion in handling the entire situation" and even authorized him to suggest that "forcible disarmament may prove to be an alternative to settlement by negotiation." Knowing that his threats were backed by the full force of the U.S. Marines, Stimson laid all of his cards on the table. "Peace is imperative," he declared. "I have instructions to attain it willingly or by force." Within thirty minutes the matter was settled. Both sides agreed that Diaz would finish his term in office unopposed and then the United States would supervise a new Nicaraguan election in 1928 that would be open to all parties. Stimson joyfully cabled Washington ten days later: "The civil war in Nicaragua is now definitely ended." In truth, however, it had only just begun. One of the opposition generals refused to sign the agreement. His name was Augusto César Sandino, and he vowed to fight on against the corrupt, American-backed government in Nicaragua. For nearly seven years he carried out a guerrilla war to wrest power from the Conservatives. Though he was ultimately captured and executed for his efforts, Sandino sparked a revolutionary movement in Nicaragua that inspired leftist rebels some four decades later.[51]

As for the United States, it paid dearly for helping to prop up unpopular governments in Latin America. By 1933 a new wind was blowing in Washington and with it came an overhaul of American foreign policy. Within a year of taking office, President Franklin Delano Roosevelt ordered the removal of American troops from Haiti and Nicaragua and instituted what he called the "Good Neighbor Policy." In announcing his new approach to relations with Latin American nations, FDR declared that "the definite policy of the United States from now on is one opposed to armed intervention." That's more or less what Stassen advocated in 1927.[52]

~

The supreme irony of Stassen's position in 1927—both physically *and* politically—is that his Middle West, Republican background should have produced in him a much less enlightened view of U.S. foreign policy. He was, after all, raised and educated in the most isolationist region of the country, and by the mid-1920s the typical midwesterner had come to view America's involvement in the Great War as an unnecessary aberration never to be repeated again. While Stassen opposed imperialistic motives in Latin America, he certainly did not have his head buried in the sand when it came to America's growing economic and political influence in the world. Fellow Minnesotans Charles Lindbergh (first person to fly solo and nonstop across the Atlantic) and Frank B. Kellogg (U.S. secretary of state under President Calvin Coolidge) both traveled to France in the late 1920s to lend their considerable reputations to the cause of peace. Neither man, however, demonstrated a great deal of foresight when it came to assessing the tremendous sway of nationalism and the limitations of good intentions. The much-heralded Kellogg-Briand Pact, which purported to outlaw war as an instrument of national policy, was eventually signed by over five dozen nations, including the United States, Britain, France, Italy, Germany, Japan, China, and the Soviet Union. The global conflagration that commenced a decade later revealed wishful thinking on the part of both men—Kellogg for believing that nations could will their way to peace and Lindbergh for assuming that naked aggression on the other side of an ocean lay safely beyond the physical and financial interests of America. The increasingly popular turn toward isolationism in the postwar era and particularly in Stassen's neck of the woods signaled, in journalist Richard Freund's words, "the tendency of the United States to withdraw from 'foreign entanglements' and consolidate her position on the American continent."[53]

That trend was not entirely new, but it gained substantial momentum in the wake of World War I. The man who had arguably the greatest influence upon America's foreign policy in that era was Senator Henry Cabot Lodge of Massachusetts. As chairman of the Senate Foreign Relations Committee (the same post held by Minnesota's Cushman Kellogg Davis two decades earlier), Lodge led the fight to oppose ratification of the Treaty of Versailles, much to Woodrow Wilson's dismay. Defending his position in 1919, Lodge said, "We are a great moral asset of Christian civilization . . . How did we get there? By our own efforts. Nobody led us, nobody guided us, nobody controlled us . . . I would keep America as she has been—not isolated, not prevent her from joining other nations for . . . great purposes—but I wish her to be master of her own fate." Whatever his original intentions may have been, Lodge prevented the United States from joining Wilson's League of Nations, and, in historian Alan Brinkley's estimation, "American foreign policy embarked on an independent course that for the next two decades would attempt, but ultimately fail, to expand American influence and maintain international stability without committing the United States to any lasting relationships with other nations."[54]

But those unintended consequences were as yet on the distant horizon and, for the time being at least, beyond the recognition of nearly everyone except Woodrow Wilson. The president's rapid physical decline paralleled the unfortunate demise of his vision for what he characterized as the "liberation and salvation of the world." Politicians whose philosophies spanned the ideological spectrum but who represented voters in the Midwest tended to support Lodge's contention that America must remain the "master of her own fate." They were men like Senator Gerald Nye, a Republican from North Dakota, who investigated the link between profits made by munitions manufacturers and America's involvement in the First World War. Or Robert La Follette, Wisconsin's fiery progressive senator, who rejected both Wilson's call for a declaration of war against Germany and his Treaty of Versailles. Or Minnesota's Senator Henrik Shipstead, a member of the Farmer-Labor Party, who opposed American's participation in both the League of Nations and the World Court. And the list goes on: Senator George Norris of Nebraska, Senator William Borah of Idaho, Senator Robert Taft of Ohio, Senator Burton Wheeler of Montana, and Senator Arthur Vandenberg of Michigan. All of them contributed in one way or another to the notion that America's interests would best be served by staying neutral in the event of war in Europe or Asia. Writing in 1936, the German-born journalist Richard Freund (he became a British citizen in 1935) wisely observed, "Although the trend of isolation is now uppermost in American policy, the United States cannot so easily cut the ties which link her to the outside world. There is, to begin with, her foreign trade." And despite President Franklin Roosevelt's assurances that "If we are faced with a choice of profits or peace, we choose peace," the concept of strict neutrality would in time prove neither practical nor profitable. Harold Stassen would eventually come to personify the following assessment of that era: "A later generation," writes historian David Cronon, "after suffering the horrors of another world war, would pay tribute to Wilson's ideals by creating the United Nations, and this time only a scattered few would question the wisdom of wholehearted American participation."[55]

~

Born just after the turn of the century, Stassen was undeniably a product of the Progressive Era. His subsequent record suggests that when it came to domestic affairs, he grew to admire Theodore Roosevelt's brand of progressive Republicanism that promoted the regulation of American economic, business, and labor interests for the good of the nation as a whole. However, Stassen's approach to foreign policy matters would soon begin to resemble the intellectual pragmatism of Woodrow Wilson, for whom lasting peace required adopting an internationalist outlook upon the world. So in addition to being wise beyond his years, Harold Stassen was already years ahead of his time when it came to assessing the vicissitudes of global politics. At the moment, however, he was in no position to do anything about it. Someday he would be. For now he had to focus on finishing law school and charting his future. Events closer to home were changing Minnesota's political landscape in ways some citizens found liberating and others considered menacing. The old populist movement had morphed into something far more powerful in Minnesota—a legitimate third party that threatened to upset the traditional balance of power in local, state, and even national politics. In the midst of all this change, Stassen prepared to graduate from the University of Minnesota with a law degree. And along with a classmate who also happened to be from Dakota County—a fellow by the name of Ryan—Harold Stassen set his sights on establishing a law practice of his own and then giving politics a go. He was about to find his life's work.

2 An Ordered Society

In order to comprehend the context within which Harold Stassen first rose to political prominence, one must appreciate the milieu of Minnesota politics in the early Depression years. Few states in the union could lay claim to such a remarkable convergence of political movements and personalities. The conventional rules regarding party affiliation and voter behavior were being rewritten frequently in Minnesota during the 1930s. By the time Harold Stassen graduated from law school, he identified himself as a Republican despite the fact that the GOP's fortunes were dwindling from one end of the country to the other. Republicanism was simply in his blood. But Stassen's evolving philosophy regarding the role of government in society would also take into account the profound political changes that were sweeping his part of the country.

The late-nineteenth-century populist movement, which had inspired numerous reforms and then run out of steam in many parts of the country, produced a more radical political response in the upper plains. In neighboring North Dakota, what started as a rural farm protest organization had turned into a full-fledged third-party movement during the century's second decade. By the time Harold Stassen graduated from college, many of those ideas and methods had taken root in western Minnesota as well. Their origins can be traced directly to the national Nonpartisan League, formed in 1915 by a former socialist named Arthur C. Townley. Townley grew up in Minnesota before heading to North Dakota to try his hand at wheat farming. Success in agriculture eluded him, but Townley quickly established himself as a golden-tongued orator whose message resonated with frustrated farmers, much as Ignatius Donnelly's had done. The theme was hardly new: farmers do all the hard work and fall deeper into debt while the middlemen—owners of railroads, grain elevators, packinghouses, and banks—reap huge profits by charging exorbitantly high prices for their services.

What made Townley's organization unique was that it offered a specific set of remedies and then galvanized farmers into a mechanism that could produce real political leverage. As historian John D. Hicks wrote in the 1950s, the Nonpartisan League's so-called North Dakota platform amounted to nothing short of "state socialism." It called for "state ownership of terminal elevators, flour mills, packing houses, and cold-storage plants; state inspection of grain and grain dockage; the exemption of farm improvements from taxation; state hail insurance on the acreage tax basis; and rural credit banks operated at cost." Once the organization gained widespread acceptance among farmers, it promised to support only those politicians—Democratic or Republican—who endorsed its radical plan for reform. By the early 1920s, Minnesota farmers were jumping on the bandwagon and making similar inroads in state politics. When the two major parties proved too slow in meeting their demands, farmers joined forces with industrial laborers to form the Farmer-Labor Party. It represented a major victory for the all-but-forgotten cause of populism. According to Hicks, "From this point forward, both in North Dakota and Minnesota, and to a lesser extent in many other northwestern states also, the League furnished a convenient rallying center for the forces of agrarian discontent." But the Farmer-Labor Party of Minnesota would in time accomplish something that the old-time populists had never been able to pull off; it successfully, if superficially, overcame the traditional animosity that had lingered for decades between rural farmers and urban workers. By merging the interests of two traditionally exclusive interest groups, the Farmer-Labor Party at long last offered a viable and electable alternative to Democratic and Republican candidates. Minnesota politics would never be the same.[1]

Enter one of the state's most extraordinary public figures. By the time Floyd B. Olson was making national headlines as a possible third-party presidential candidate in 1936, his reputation as a charismatic reformer had become the stuff of legend throughout the Midwest. His political rise represented the quintessential combination of striking personality and astute opportunism. Born and raised in Minneapolis, Olson pursued law as a career and managed to get himself appointed Hennepin County attorney when his predecessor was ousted for misconduct in 1919. Olson quickly endeared himself to voters by taking on the residual forces of corruption in Minneapolis, notoriously documented by muckraker Lincoln Steffens in *The Shame of the Cities* nearly two decades earlier. He was perceived as a friend of the common man and twice reelected to continue his campaign against graft and the rising tide of organized crime that accompanied Prohibition. According to his biographer George H. Mayer, Olson's support came from average citizens who liked what they saw in the young, aggressive, and incorruptible prosecutor. "To his admirers," Mayer writes, "he seemed like a kind of modern Robin Hood, dispensing rough and ready justice that conformed with the spirit if not the letter of the law. He refused to break lances over lost causes, but in a cautious and pragmatic way sought to improve the tone of municipal government."[2]

Olson was a shrewd Democrat in a state traditionally dominated by Republicans. A city boy at heart, he watched curiously as first the Nonpartisan League and then the Farmer-Labor Party transformed rural angst into a potent political movement. By 1923 both of Minnesota's U.S. senators were Farmer-Laborites. Sensing opportunity in the shifting political winds, Olson broke with his fellow Democrats and seized the Farmer-Labor nomination for governor in 1924 from Charles A. Lindbergh, the famed aviator's father. Olson lost to a Republican in the general election but managed in the process to greatly increase his cachet among the Farmer-Labor faithful, especially those in rural parts of the state who knew little about him. But personal charm can take a candidate only so far. Olson came out of the 1924 race convinced that his political fortunes, and those of the Farmer-Labor Party in general, would be determined first and foremost by organization. A newly constituted Farmer Labor Association (formed in 1925) became the backbone of a statewide effort that would in five short years carry Floyd Olson to the pinnacle of state government. The stock market crash in October of 1929 and nationwide disenchantment with Republican policies provided a perfect storm of economic and political conditions for those favoring a sharp turn to the left. Minnesota historian Russell W. Fridley credits Olson with forging "a broad coalition of farmers, workers, socialists, isolationists, and progressives" in the 1930 gubernatorial election that led him to victory by nearly two hundred thousand votes.[3]

~

Meanwhile, Harold Stassen and his business partner Elmer Ryan were hard at work launching their own legal careers down in Dakota County. The two

met during law school and became fast friends in spite of their differing
backgrounds and political views. Ryan, a Democrat, was the son of a saloon-
keeper from Rosemount, a largely Irish Catholic community located a dozen
or so miles south of the Stassen farm. In 1929 Harold and Elmer graduated
from the University of Minnesota, passed the bar exam, and quickly set up
a small law practice in South St. Paul, just up the hill from the stockyards
where Harold had witnessed that violent clash between striking meatpackers and the National Guard. The firm of Stassen & Ryan struggled initially
to make ends meet, but fortune soon smiled on the young attorneys. First,
they secured steady employment codifying the attorney general's opinions
for the Minnesota State Bar Association. It wasn't glamorous work, but it
did help pay for their twenty-five-dollars-a-month rented office near the
Stockyard Exchange Building. Then, as the 1930 election season drew near,
Stassen decided to run for Dakota County attorney. Fledgling lawyers in
that era frequently sought political office in order to drum up business
and supplement their meager earnings. Floyd Olson had done essentially
the same thing in Hennepin County, laying the groundwork for a remarkable political career. And while there is no evidence suggesting that Stassen
already held such lofty ambitions, during the spring of 1930 he threw himself headlong into the campaign for county attorney. It would be the first of
many successful political campaigns.

Initiating a strategy that would characterize his many subsequent runs
for office, Stassen campaigned early and often. His surname carried some
weight in the northern part of the county, particularly among Republican
faithful. But down south where farms were larger and towns fewer and farther between, Stassen realized he'd have to make himself known in stout-
sounding communities like Farmington, Northfield, and Castle Rock. So he
hit the road in earnest, hoping for an opportunity to make his case to folks
who took an interest in local and county politics. That's exactly how he met
Ed Thye, a civic-minded Northfield farmer generally regarded as a leader in
that neck of the woods. One day Thye was reading a newspaper out on the
road by his mailbox when he noticed an old Ford Runabout approaching his
driveway. Stassen cut quite a comical figure in the car, his knees nearly up to
his chin. The young lawyer asked if he knew where Ed Thye lived, and the
farmer replied, "Speaking." The two got acquainted right then and there,
and Thye apparently liked what he heard. By the time the impromptu "mailbox conference" wrapped up, Ed Thye had pledged his support to Stassen
for Dakota County attorney. He encouraged the candidate to visit a few

members of the Waterford Township Board and suggested that with their backing Stassen would have little need to spend much more time campaigning in that part of the county. It was personal politics at its best. And though neither man knew it at the time, the short exchange marked the beginning of a political relationship that would one day lead both of them to the Minnesota governor's office.[4]

Stassen's campaign nearly ended as quickly as it began that April when he discovered he had contracted tuberculosis. Effective antibiotics were not yet available, and conventional wisdom suggested that tuberculosis patients responded best to long periods of rest and close monitoring by trained medical personnel. Pokegama Sanitarium in Pine City, midway between Minneapolis and Duluth, became Stassen's temporary home, and the 1930 federal census lists the facility as his residence in late April, right after his twenty-third birthday. With the primary election scheduled for early June, time became Stassen's greatest adversary that spring as he tried to regain his strength in the great north woods. Fortunately, his friends and

Harold and Esther Stassen, about 1939

relatives quickly mobilized to carry on the campaigning in his absence. Elmer Ryan kept their law office afloat and traveled from one end of the county to the other seeking support for his partner's candidacy. As president of the Dakota County baseball league, Ryan even enlisted young and enthusiastic ballplayers to canvass the entire county promoting the Stassen-for-County-Attorney movement.

Harold had another secret weapon to aid him in his first campaign for elected office. In November of 1929 he had married his longtime sweetheart, Esther Glewwe. Stassen first laid eyes on Esther during a Sunday school picnic at the Riverview Baptist Church many years earlier. He was only twelve at the time, so his initial impressions of her were far from romantic. She "ran like the wind" he later confided to friends and family members whenever the subject of their lifelong love affair came up. Esther's father owned a grocery store in the neighboring town of South St. Paul, where Esther and her siblings were raised and attended school. By the time she and Harold became newlyweds, Esther was an experienced legal stenographer and began to codify the attorney general's opinions for a salary of fifty dollars per month, thus giving her husband time to rest and his partner time for politicking on his behalf. Even Harold's older brother Elmer, a grocer by trade, got in on the action. He traveled to political meetings and made campaign appearances alongside Ryan, who introduced him simply as Mr. Stassen, which of course he was. Neither of the Elmers—Ryan nor Stassen—went out of his way to point out that the actual candidate was still bedridden and simply passing along ideas via frequent correspondence. The makeshift strategy worked. When the primary votes were tallied, Stassen came in first among four candidates despite the fact that he hadn't set foot in Dakota County for nearly two months.[5]

Stassen returned to his parents' West St. Paul home in July. He was far from fully recovered, but now that he had advanced to the general election, his candidacy was beginning to receive greater scrutiny. Someone tried to tag Stassen as anti-Catholic, but his campaign headquarters responded with a news release showing that Stassen had campaigned for Al Smith—a Democrat, but a Progressive—in a 1929 mock political convention at the University of Minnesota. And that his best friend was Irish-Catholic probably helped set the record straight. When rumors popped up that Stassen was deathly ill and practically had one foot in the grave, the young candidate rallied to make several public appearances in the fall. Mustering all of his energy and on strict orders from his doctor not to overdo it, Stassen

attended a few important political functions and then rushed back to bed
and to the crucial rest his six-foot-three-inch frame so badly needed. By
early November Stassen had managed to get himself elected Dakota County
attorney and to exhaust himself in the process. On the day after the election, he went back to bed and remained there until he took office.[6]

~

For the next eight years, Harold Stassen performed his duties as Dakota
County attorney with remarkable skill and determination. He demonstrated
an indefatigable work ethic and an unwavering commitment to upholding
the law, maintaining order, and ensuring justice for the nearly forty thousand residents of Dakota County. His responsibilities varied widely—from
prosecuting criminals and heading off labor strikes to representing frustrated farmers and arguing an important tax case before the U.S. Supreme
Court. The versatility Stassen demonstrated as county attorney no doubt
served to increase his standing in Republican ranks, which, taken as a whole,
fared none too well during the 1930s. But politics was not his chief concern
or interest at the time. Through the darkest days of the Great Depression,
Harold Stassen cut his teeth on criminal law and honed his administrative
skills from an office inside the impressive Dakota County Courthouse located
on Vermillion Street in downtown Hastings. A grainy black-and-white pho-
tograph from the summer of 1932 shows Stassen among several county
employees assembled in two rows at the courthouse's north entrance for a
formal portrait. They number twenty-five in all, including a probate judge,
five county commissioners, six administrative clerks, a manager of the county
poor farm, and the Dunn brothers—Jim and Larry—sheriff and deputy
sheriff respectively. Stassen stands just left of center in the back row, to the
right of and nearly a foot taller than assistant county engineer Al Kranz.
These county officials were about to be tested.

~

Less than a month later, in the early morning hours of Friday, August 5,
1932, an alarm system tipped Louis Fischer off to an attempted burglary on
his farm along Dodd Road at the northern edge of the county. Fischer was
owner of the Riverview Golf Course (known today as Mendakota Country
Club), and he had recently converted his large barn into a clubhouse. Once
he discovered that intruders were fast at work inside the building, he called
his brother Rudolph, who lived nearby in West St. Paul (just down the road
from William Stassen's farm) and worked as a Dakota County sheriff's deputy. Rudy Fischer arranged for fellow deputy Joe Heinen of Rosemount to

meet him at his brother's farm as soon as possible. Shortly before 3 AM the lawmen converged on the clubhouse, arrested two armed burglars without incident, and then proceeded to the county jail in Hastings. Summoning Larry Dunn, who lived next door to the jail, all three deputies began the routine process of booking and incarcerating the two suspects, identified as Harold Wilder and Dewey Sharpe. A few minutes later, Dunn removed the prisoners' handcuffs and started leading them toward the first jail cell. It was about half past three in the morning.[7]

Then all hell broke loose. Harold Wilder, the larger of the two prisoners, made a sudden "lion-like leap" upon Deputy Heinen, who was seated behind a desk. Wilder quickly overpowered the officer and grabbed his standard-issue .38-caliber pistol from its holster. In one swift motion, Wilder swung around and fired at point-blank range into the side of Rudy Fischer's chest. A split-second earlier Fischer had been sort of half-seated on a nearby desk, but now he "slowly slumped to the desk and then fell to the floor

County officers at the Dakota County courthouse, July 11, 1932. Stassen is standing, third from left.

without a word." He died instantly. Deputy Larry Dunn stared helplessly at the drama unfolding before him. He had neglected to bring his sidearm because, he later recounted, "We are waked up at all hours of the night to take in petty thieves and other criminals and I never thought of arming myself." Dunn hadn't anticipated dealing with cold-blooded killers early that Friday morning, but suddenly the tables had turned with fatal consequences. Dewey Sharpe grabbed Fischer's pistol from the dead man's holster and pointed it back and forth at the two remaining officers, both of whom were unarmed and entirely defenseless. Wilder demanded that they hand over the keys to Deputy Heinen's car, warning, "Better tell me where those keys are or I'll drill you too." Heinen quickly misled the two bandits into believing that the keys were still in his car. With that the gunmen darted out of the sheriff's office and fired one last shot in Deputy Dunn's direction.[8]

Phones began ringing at the homes of law enforcement officials all over the region within minutes of the shooting. Word spread like wildfire as police officers and several ordinary citizens from surrounding communities began a desperate search for the two fugitives, who were rightly considered armed and extremely dangerous. Wilder and Sharpe failed to commandeer a getaway car—thanks in part to Joe Heinen's intentional misdirection—so they headed north toward downtown Hastings on foot. The authorities picked up their trail after they crossed over to the east side of the Mississippi River on the Milwaukee railroad bridge. Investigators soon determined that the men were likely hoofing it along the railroad tracks back to St. Paul, a distance of nearly ten miles. Dakota County Sheriff J. J. Dunn took charge of the manhunt and dispatched a car north along State Highway 3, which at that time ran parallel to the Mississippi River and the Burlington line between Hastings and St. Paul. His office also alerted the St. Paul Police Department and the Washington County Sheriff's Office in Stillwater in an effort to mobilize additional resources to the north. With dawn fast approaching, authorities hoped that the combination of daylight and fatigue would force the assailants to expose themselves. With that prospect in mind, Dunn's deputies warned a storekeeper in the tiny town of Langdon, just south of Cottage Grove, to be on the lookout for two men walking in the vicinity. By now nearly two hours had passed since Rudy Fischer's death.

One of the first men to receive the shocking news was County Attorney Harold Stassen. Though he lived west of the river in South St. Paul, Stassen raced to the scene to help Sheriff Dunn organize what amounted to a posse of professional lawmen and outraged civilians. Henry Hallberg, the storekeeper in Langdon (now part of Cottage Grove), spotted the fugitives stopping at a water pump near his home shortly before 6 AM. He watched them cross to the east side of Highway 3 and continue on toward some cornfields. Hallberg contacted the telephone exchange operator in Cottage Grove, who passed the information on to local law enforcement agencies. Within minutes the heavily armed posse, which now numbered nearly forty men led by Dunn and Stassen, fanned out among the surrounding farm fields in all directions. The pursuers fired two or three rounds at Wilder and Sharpe, who darted in and out of a nearby cornfield. That proved enough for Sharpe, who gave up once he realized the posse meant business. Wilder continued to evade his captors for a few more tense minutes but eventually ran out of tall corn in which to hide. Officers from the St. Paul Police Department fired several more rounds in his direction, and Harold Wilder "finally threw himself on the ground and surrendered."[9]

With Deputy Fischer's murderers now in custody, Stassen turned his attention to interviewing the pair and preparing to prosecute them for a slew of offenses including murder in the first degree. He soon discovered that both men had extensive criminal backgrounds and connections to organized crime. Sharpe's record included a murder conviction in Chicago dating back to 1918. And Wilder, a Twin Cities native, had recently been implicated in a notorious kidnapping plot in St. Paul. When four shots rang out near their cells in Hastings on Friday evening, presumably fired by fellow gangsters for whom dead men tell no tales, the two prisoners were quickly relocated to the Washington County Jail in Stillwater. Stassen obtained signed confessions from each of the men and presented his findings early the next week to a grand jury, which returned identical nine-count indictments against both Wilder and Sharpe. On August 11, just three days after Rudy Fischer's funeral, Dakota County Judge W. A. Schultz signed off on a deal allowing Wilder and Sharpe to plead guilty to second-degree murder, which carried a mandatory life sentence. Harold Stassen avoided a costly trial and did well by his fellow citizens. The twenty-five-year-old county attorney had guaranteed "in record time" that the two cop killers would spend the rest of their lives "safely ensconced within the walls of the state penitentiary at Stillwater."[10]

~

Unfortunately for the residents of Dakota County, this tragic turn of events marked neither the first nor the last time that Stassen had to deal with organized crime and gangland violence in his jurisdiction. While it is true that

Minneapolis and St. Paul attracted most of the rumrunners and bank rob-
bers who ventured into Minnesota during the Depression, a handful of
criminals targeted smaller communities like South St. Paul, Farmington, and
Rosemount. Part of this was doubtless due to the fact that authorities in
St. Paul had struck up an informal bargain with criminal elements amount-
ing to "you're welcome here if you do your crimes elsewhere." According
to crime historian Paul Maccabee, the policy dated back nearly thirty years,
to the tenure of St. Paul Police Chief John O'Connor, who later boasted,
"If they behaved themselves, I let them alone. If they didn't, I got them.
Under other administrations there were as many thieves here as when I
was chief, and they pillaged and robbed; I chose the lesser of two evils."
Early in the summer of 1933, a bullet-ridden body was found in a car near
Farmington, and Stassen sought to extradite from a Kansas prison and question two gangsters authorities suspected of being involved. Investigators
connected the bullets from that murder to a sensational crime spree in 1931
that started with the pair of convicts escaping from Leavenworth Federal
Penitentiary, robbing a bank in Menomonie, Wisconsin, and finally kidnapping and killing the bank president's nineteen-year-old son. Then in the late
summer of 1933, South St. Paul was rocked by a brutal crime that sounded
like something out of James Cagney's 1931 film *The Public Enemy*. A local
newspaper reported the shocking details: "Slaying one policeman and critically wounding another, six bandits staged a reign of terror in South St. Paul
Wednesday morning as they robbed two bank messengers of $30,000, then
raked the city's main street with machine gunfire as they escaped."[11]

The brazen attack took place just outside of the South St. Paul post office
on Concord Street, not far from the law firm of Stassen & Ryan. The assailants clearly knew that the weekly payroll for the Swift and Company
meat-packing plant was scheduled for delivery to the Stockyards National
Bank and timed their assault accordingly. They shot and disarmed one
patrolman who was escorting the messengers and used his machine gun
to fatally shoot another lawman, South St. Paul police officer Leo Pavlak,
in the head. Though investigators, including Harold Stassen, combed the
scene for clues and interviewed several witnesses, the crime was never officially solved.

The plot thickened considerably that winter when another murder victim was discovered in rural Dakota County and Stassen started his inves-
tigation. The deceased was identified as forty-year-old Conard Althen, the
suspected bookkeeper for a major liquor syndicate based in the Twin Cities.

Because he was scheduled to testify before a federal grand jury, authorities quickly theorized that Althen was "rubbed out" by professionals to prevent him from fingering fellow members of the "alky racket." Or as the *Dakota County Tribune* put it, "Twin city gangsters, fearing an indicted rum suspect would talk too much, took their victim for a 'one-way ride' Monday night and left his bullet-riddled body lying dead at the side of Cedar avenue road four miles west of Rosemount." And as if the dramatic developments needed a more local angle, whoever wrote the story went on to editorialize a bit about the increasing burdens being borne by folks south of the river, adding, "Because of the fact that Dakota county is located just across the river from the Twin Cities, gangsters use this county for a dumping ground for their victims, causing additional work on the part of our county attorney, county coroner, sheriff and deputies, and added expense to county taxpayers."[12]

In fact, Althen had been shot no fewer than fourteen times, and investigators made a startling discovery when they examined the bullets removed from his body. The United Press reported that "ballistics tests determined that the slugs came from the machine gun stolen by six bandits who robbed two bank messengers of $30,000 and killed a policeman at South St. Paul." That suggested both killings were carried out by members of a criminal underworld whose reach extended far beyond Dakota County. In 1935 FBI agents raided the Chicago apartment of a notorious gangster named Arthur "Doc" Barker and discovered the Thompson machine gun used in the slaying of Officer Leo Pavlak. Suspicion then turned to Barker's criminal associate Alvin "Creepy" Karpis, a known killer wanted by the U.S. Justice Department "in 12 to 15 bank robberies, three kidnappings, and three mail robberies." Karpis was arrested, tried, and convicted on federal kidnapping charges in 1936 but never brought to Minnesota to face questioning in the deaths of Pavlak and Althen. It was one more reminder that justice then as now could be both delayed *and* denied despite the best efforts of honest lawmen and tenacious prosecutors.[13]

~

It would be a mistake, however, to conclude that Harold Stassen spent his entire tenure as county attorney trying to protect society from hoodlums, gangsters, and racketeers. Those sorts of cases did keep Stassen's name in the headlines during the early 1930s, but his reputation was growing in political circles because of his work to address the most pressing problem of the era—economic depression. As was the case in so many other midwestern states, farmers in Minnesota tried to keep pace with mounting debts even while the prices for their products plummeted. It all made perfect economic sense, of course, at least in the large scheme of things: increasingly efficient methods of farming coupled with rising unemployment in the nation's cities meant overproduction and decreasing prices. Or so the theory went. But farmers, known for their rugged individualism, do not typically live in the aggregate. And when things got bad enough, they began to take matters into their own hands. In neighboring Iowa, for instance, frustration gave way to the formation of a Farmers' Holiday Association under the leadership of Milo Reno. The idea was simple: collective action on the part of farmers could achieve what the free market could not—an increase in prices. Reno advocated any means necessary to slow the flow of farm products to market, including blocking highways and forcibly pouring milk into ditches if necessary. When the journalist Mary Heaton Vorse went to Iowa in 1932 to investigate the growing movement, she encountered an elderly farmer who said, "They say blockading the highway's illegal. I say, 'Seems to me there was a Tea Party in Boston that was illegal too.'"[14]

The movement spread north to Minnesota. Unrest among dairy farmers in Dakota County attracted outside agitators, most likely from Reno's circle, and milk ran in the streets. There was talk of blood running there as well. When farmers gathered at a large meeting to discuss additional courses of action, one of the attendees urged an escalation of violence. Someone said, "But what about the county attorney?" The answer came, "Lynch him!" Years later Stassen described what happened next as "the most difficult decision" of his life. He had entered unnoticed at the beginning of the meeting and was sitting quietly in the back of the room. Upon hearing the threat on his life, Stassen stood up and approached the platform, announcing as he moved forward that anyone who wanted to lynch the county attorney was welcome to do it right then and there. Once he had their attention, Stassen spoke directly to the farmers, pledging to prosecute any lawbreakers, as was his sworn duty, but offering to represent the dairy men pro bono in an effort to negotiate better prices. Cooler heads prevailed as the farmers, sufficiently impressed with the young attorney, took him at his word. Stassen eventually reached an agreement in eleven counties and raised the price of milk by 25 percent.[15]

The episode demonstrates one of Harold Stassen's particular strengths. His keen political instincts allowed him to size up a difficult situation quickly and work out a solution that placated all parties involved. Some called it pragmatism. Others described it as a broad middle way between two

opposing extremes, both of which were typically impervious to sound reason and the art of compromise. In Stassen's mind, those who tried to present such inflexible positions as commitments to principle did little more
than impede the political process at a time when the nation yearned for
expediency. The key was to know what truly motivated people when they
were stretched to their limits. As historian Frederick Lewis Allan sees it,
those who organized protest movements in the Midwest during the Great
Depression were acting far more reasonably than twenty-first-century readers might care to admit. He writes, "These farmers were not revolutionists.
On the contrary, most of them were by habit conservative men. They were
simply striking back in rage at the impersonal forces which had brought
them to their present pass."[16]

Stassen met several men of the same ilk down in Dakota County. Among
them was twenty-one-year-old Walter Klaus of Empire Township. Klaus
lived with his parents on their sprawling farmstead along the Vermillion
River, not far from Farmington. The family had fared well once upon a
time, earning enough to buy up more acreage and expand their production. But that was before the Depression. By the summer of 1933, they were
behind on their mortgage payments and in danger of losing everything. In
August of that year the Klaus family retained Stassen for the purposes of
avoiding foreclosure and almost certain eviction from their home. (At that
time it was not uncommon for county attorneys to also practice private
law to supplement their incomes.) That was the first time Walter Klaus
ever met Harold Stassen, and he clearly remembered it over three-quarters
of a century later. Klaus recalled attending a Saturday afternoon hearing at
the county courthouse in Hastings. Judge William A. Schultz was presiding,
and he gave his approval to a temporary payment plan, in lieu of foreclosure,
worked out by Stassen and a representative of the eastern insurance company that held the Klauses' mortgage. Stassen charged the family fifteen
dollars for his services, and the farm remained in its possession for the next
three-quarters of a century. It's no wonder Walter Klaus was among the first
group of young Republicans to jump on the Harold Stassen bandwagon.[17]

The Klaus family's ordeal was an all-too-familiar story during the worst
years of the Great Depression. And as it turns out, Minnesota was at that
very moment on the front lines of a constitutional battle to determine
how far state legislatures could go to protect privately financed mortgages.
Stassen's seemingly simple solution to the Klauses' predicament was made
possible by a state law passed earlier that spring. To stem the growing tide

of mortgage foreclosures, the state legislature enacted in April of 1933 what became known as the Minnesota Mortgage Moratorium Act. The law allowed homeowners to petition judges to temporarily halt foreclosures on their mortgages under terms considered "just and equitable" by the court. That is precisely what Stassen managed to do on behalf of the Klaus family when he stood before Judge Schultz in the Dakota County Courthouse.

But another couple from Minnesota faced a much more daunting legal process when they sought the law's protection to prevent eviction from their Minneapolis home. When Mr. and Mrs. John H. Blaisdell argued that the new law applied to their unfortunate economic circumstances, the Minnesota courts agreed and ordered that foreclosure of their home be temporarily suspended. The holder of the Blaisdells' mortgage, Home Building and Loan Association, appealed the decision, and the case went all the way to the U.S. Supreme Court. Given that many other states had already enacted or were considering similar acts of legislation to deal with the problem of mortgage foreclosures, the case garnered substantial attention nationwide. Attorneys for both sides delivered their oral arguments in early November of 1933, and the Court announced its decision just after the first of the year.

Writing for the 5–4 majority, U.S. Supreme Court chief justice (and former Republican nominee for president) Charles Evans Hughes upheld the Minnesota statute as constitutional, thus vindicating the state's efforts to deal with one of the most vexing consequences of the Great Depression. Hughes dismissed the notion that the Minnesota law violated the contract clause of the Constitution, declaring that "while emergency does not create power, emergency may furnish the occasion for the exercise of power." He affirmed Minnesota's authority "to protect the vital interests of the community" and added that the legislation in question "was addressed to a legitimate end; that is, the legislation was not for the mere advantage of individuals but for the protection of a basic interest of society."[18]

What remains most remarkable about Hughes's opinion in hindsight is how strikingly consistent it was with the spirit of the times, much to the chagrin of his opponents in the judiciary and most Old Guard Republicans. Less than one year earlier at his inauguration, President Franklin Roosevelt had boldly declared that "it may be that an unprecedented demand and need for undelayed action may call for temporary departure from that normal balance of public procedure." Listeners needed only wait until the new president had completed his first hundred days in office to comprehend fully what he had in mind for battling the effects of prolonged economic depression.

By then his earlier allusions to the "power to wage a war against the emergency" seemed perfectly in line with what Roosevelt had characterized as "action in this image and to this end." Several states, including Minnesota, were quick to embrace the New Deal and its broad implications, but the results struck some observers as downright revolutionary. Hence the need for judicial clarification. Though they did not win every constitutional battle, reformers like Harold Stassen of Minnesota who envisioned a broad middle way between inaction and state socialism were proving time and again that history was on their side.

Ironically, just one day before hearing oral arguments in *Home Building and Loan Association v. Blaisdell*, Chief Justice Hughes delivered another opinion that represented the highlight of Harold Stassen's legal career. Three weeks earlier, Stassen had traveled to Washington, DC, to argue a case before Hughes and the other eight justices of the U.S. Supreme Court. It was the thrill of a lifetime. Stassen was only twenty-six years old and had practiced law for fewer than five years, but none of that seemed to matter on Wednesday, October 11, 1933. That was the day he stepped forward to address the nation's nine most powerful judges in the matter of *State of Minnesota v. Blasius*.

The case had its origins in the spring of 1929, right about the time Stassen graduated from law school. The issue in question was centered upon the very same South St. Paul stockyards around which Harold Stassen's entire life seemed to be revolving. On April 30 a livestock trader named George Blasius purchased eleven head of cattle that had been transported to Minnesota from another state. Unfortunately for Mr. Blasius, May 1 was tax day in Minnesota, and the cattle he purchased the day before were assessed for taxation as his personal property, under the state's general tax law. Blasius refused to pay taxes on the cattle that he intended to resell, "arguing that they were only passing through the stockyard in the course of interstate commerce and were not subject to state taxation." A district court judge originally ruled against Blasius and ordered that he pay the taxes in Dakota County as prescribed by law. Blasius appealed the decision to the state supreme court, which agreed with his argument that the cattle were exempt from state taxation and overturned the district court's ruling. The Dakota County attorney's office, which Stassen now led, challenged that decision all the way to the U.S. Supreme Court, and he took personal charge of the case. Everything now hinged on the oral argument he prepared to present in early October of 1933.[19]

So as Harold Stassen gathered himself and approached the lectern to address the nine members of the nation's highest court, he could be forgiven for being a bit nervous. Years later he recounted the experience to a local newspaper reporter with vivid detail. He remembered "having trouble catching his breath and keeping his poise before the imposing, black-robed justices. His tongue stuck to his mouth." The justices fired one question after another at Stassen, making it difficult for him to find his bearings and make his argument. Then, as Stassen recalls it, Chief Justice Charles Evans Hughes leaned forward, looked the young attorney squarely in the eyes, and asked, "Do I understand that you were the prosecutor in the county where this case first arose?" Finally, an easy one.[20]

"His question was like a shot of adrenaline because he knew it was a question I could obviously answer," Stassen said. "It gave me a break, and I've always been thankful to him for that." Stassen went on to make a convincing case. The Supreme Court voted unanimously to overturn the state court's decision, with Chief Justice Hughes preparing the opinion. "There was no federal right to immunity from the tax," Hughes wrote, confirming the high court's view that the circumstances in this particular case did not qualify as interstate trade. Transportation of the cattle had ceased in South St. Paul, he added, "and the cattle were sold on that market to Blasius, who became absolute owner and was free to deal with them as he liked. He could sell the cattle within the state or for shipment outside the state." For Blasius the ruling meant that he needed to pay his fair share to the State of Minnesota. But in a larger sense, the case set an important legal precedent by closing a loophole through which individuals and corporations might try to avoid the payment of legitimate state or local taxes. And for Harold Stassen the entire experience represented another fine feather in his legal cap. On the Saturday after the Supreme Court's decision was made public, Stassen was back to work at district court in the familiar Hastings courthouse where the Blasius case originated. The presiding judge, who had first ruled against Blasius years before, pointed directly at Stassen and said, "Counsel?" Stassen replied, "Yes, your honor." The judge kindly declared, "I've always said that when those judges up there in the [state] Supreme Court reverse me they are wrong and I am right, and you just proved it."[21]

Earlier that year, Governor Floyd B. Olson had begun his third year in office by sounding an alarm that might have made even Franklin Roosevelt blanch. In his second inaugural address, delivered on January 4, 1933, Olson boldly asserted, "We are assembled during the most crucial period in the history of the Nation and of our State . . . Just beyond the horizon . . . is rampant lawlessness and possible revolution. Only remedial social legislation, national and state, can prevent its appearance." Under Olson's leadership the legislature passed a state income tax law to help fund public schools, enacted that temporary moratorium on mortgages, established a system of old-age pensions, and banned the use of injunctions in labor disputes. Indeed, Minnesota's Farmer-Labor Party was keeping pace with and in many instances outdistancing the New Dealers who were churning out fast and furious reforms from the nation's capital.[22]

But as the 1934 elections approached, Olson engaged in a dangerous political game with rhetoric as his weapon of choice. Words and phrases originally intended to rally Minnesotans around an ambitious reform program were used more frequently and with greater emphasis, as when he proclaimed to the Farmer-Labor faithful, "I am not a liberal. I am what I want to be—I am a radical . . . I want a definite change in the system." The more extreme elements of the Farmer-Labor Party—including avowed Communists—interpreted such language as a clarion call for revolution. Olson was inadvertently sowing the seeds of his own party's destruction by putting his seal of approval on a platform that pledged "to abolish capitalism." As historian John Gunther once observed, "Minnesota is a state spectacularly varied, proud, handsome, and progressive . . . It is a state pulled toward East and West both, and one always eager to turn the world upside down." But turning the world upside down figuratively and attempting to do so in a real political, social, or economic sense—as the phrase "abolishing capitalism" implied—are two very different things indeed. While most ordinary Minnesotans approved of the legislation coming out of St. Paul during Olson's tenure as governor, a growing number of them feared how far the party might go to establish "a new sane and just society." State ownership of banks, factories, packinghouses, mines, public utilities, and transportation and communication systems was beginning to be discussed as a real possibility. Then, as if to confirm people's unspoken fears of impending crisis, a violent truckers strike broke out in Minneapolis. The four-month ordeal claimed four lives and led Olson to invoke martial law. Subsequent recognition of the teamsters union seemed to suggest that labor violence could now be considered a means to an end rather than an end in and of itself. It represented a watershed in labor relations and the future of the Farmer-Labor Party.[23]

The ultimate beneficiary of Olson's words and actions amid a background of repeated crises was Minnesota's Republican Party, which was undergoing a crucial transition of its own. Floyd B. Olson's reelection in 1934 led to the formation of a political organization that would in time reinvigorate the GOP and return it to a position of prominence in Minnesota politics. Formed in the fall of 1935, the Young Republican League was established to "provide a rallying point for young persons of a Republican inclination, a training ground in practical politics, and a source of new personnel and fresh ideas in the Republican Party." In March of 1936 Harold Stassen was elected the first chairman of the organization and under his leadership membership soared. Youth and vigor had a great deal to do with it. For men and women of Harold Stassen's generation and political persuasion, the Grand Old Party was down but not out. If the Old Guard Republicans were unable or unwilling to accept certain realities about governing in the midst of economic depression, then the younger members of the party would take it upon themselves to pave the way forward. For the better part of the next decade, young Harold Stassen of Dakota County stood at the forefront of that movement.[24]

3 Freedom for Himself and Others

Harold Stassen was elected chairman of Minnesota's Young Republican League in 1936, a watershed year of sorts. The brutal civil war raging in Spain may have seemed remote and inconsequential to most Americans at the time, but its causes were rooted in the same brand of political extremism that was threatening democracy all over the world. With fascist regimes on the move in Europe and Asia and communism safely entrenched in the Soviet Union, the steady march of freedom that had characterized western civilization since the French Revolution seemed to be coming to a halt. From West St. Paul to Washington to the Wilhelmstrasse in Berlin and back again, tried and true systems of government were bending to the will of people or tyrants whose moods ranged from desperation to demagoguery. Everything, it seemed, was up for grabs.

And so it was with politics in Minnesota. As the 1936 election cycle approached, Governor Floyd Olson resisted those urging him to run for president at the head of a third-party ticket. While he criticized several aspects of the New Deal, Olson publically backed FDR for reelection and believed that a Roosevelt second term was essential for the continued success of liberalism in America. When radicals did nominate a third-party man for president—North Dakota congressman William Lemke—Governor Olson went so far as to cable neighboring senator Robert La Follette, Jr., of Wisconsin to declare that "liberals must unite in 1936 to re-elect Franklin Roosevelt to prevent the election of reactionary Alf Landon." Such conciliatory gestures on the part of Minnesota's Farmer-Labor leader were later reciprocated by the state's Democratic leadership, which paved the way for a permanent alliance down the road. In the meantime, however, Olson set his sights on the U.S. Senate seat held by Republican Thomas Schall. There was no love lost between the two, and the coming campaign promised to offer a series of blistering exchanges by a couple of old political pros. But when Senator Schall died after being struck by a Washington, DC, motorist just before Christmas in 1935, Olson found himself in the unenviable position of having to appoint someone to the very Senate post he hoped soon to hold.[1]

That process revealed a growing schism among Minnesota's Farmer-Laborites. The responsibility for actually governing a state was taking its toll on the Farmer-Labor Party, which had to contend with the "spoils" of victory. At the heart of the matter was political patronage—an age-old problem for the two major parties but a relatively new challenge for Farmer-Laborites, who now found themselves on the inside looking out. Olson biographer George Mayer described it as "the frenzied struggle within the reform movement for control of the patronage dispensing machine." Some party insiders hoped to assure the survival of their radical agenda (not to mention their personal political fortunes) by quickly infiltrating the state bureaucracy. But for all his rhetoric, Governor Olson was a pragmatist at heart who understood that his reform proposals depended upon the support of Democrats and Republicans in the state legislature (his party failed to win a majority of the seats in either house during the 1934 election). Alienating potential allies on either side of the political spectrum did not strike Olson as good governance. "Time and again," according to Mayer, "he warned Farmer Laborites that the party would never gain its economic objectives if its crusading spirit evaporated in a rush for jobs." The governor's warnings went unheeded.[2]

Now a showdown loomed over the greatest plum of them all—a vacant U.S. Senate seat. The professional "kingmakers" within the Farmer-Labor Party lobbied hard for Elmer A. Benson, Olson's commissioner of banking. They had two solid arguments for doing so. First, with Olson planning to run for the U.S. Senate in 1936, they hoped to nominate Benson for the gubernatorial race in his stead. Serving in the U.S. Senate, albeit temporarily, would most certainly provide Benson with the name recognition and prestige needed to secure the nomination for governor at the 1936 Farmer-Labor Convention. Secondly, appointing Benson to the Senate when he already intended to run for governor the following year insured that Olson would not have to face his own appointee in a contested primary election.

But the governor had several reasons of his own for not wanting to appoint Elmer Benson to the seat. Though he spoke highly of his banking commissioner publically and in private, Olson thought Benson lacked the requisite experience and independence worthy of a U.S. Senator. More importantly, Olson was fed up with the pressure applied by party insiders who seemed interested only in securing and then selling the spoils of victory. This was the proverbial last straw. He had no intention of caving to the demands of political professionals who, in his opinion, put neither the party nor the people before their own petty interests.

But despite his protests, Floyd Olson was in no shape for a political fight—or any fight, for that matter. Recurrent stomach ulcers had plagued him for over a year, and in the past four months the governor had lost nearly forty pounds. Just days before Senator Schall's accident, during the second week of December, Olson reluctantly agreed to visit the Mayo Clinic in Rochester for a full examination. Politics were about to become the least of his problems.

Dr. William Mayo informed the governor that tests revealed a growth in his abdomen, and the clinic's top physicians recommended immediate surgery. Olson made plans to return for the procedure after Christmas and headed back to St. Paul, where news of Schall's sudden death and the ensuing vacancy were about to engross his administration. When Benson's supporters eventually caught wind of Olson's reluctance to name their man, they took matters into their own hands, utterly confirming the governor's nagging suspicions regarding their motives and methods. They told the editor of the party's newspaper, the *Minnesota Leader,* that Benson's appointment was a foregone conclusion and instructed him to issue a special edition to that effect. When Olson saw the headline the next morning, he was infuriated. But by day's end it was clear that the preemptive strike orchestrated by party professionals had achieved its desired results. Olson's back was against the wall, and he knew it. According to his biographer, "If he had repudiated the Benson appointment, he would have split the party wide open. With election year approaching and his stomach insistently demanding attention, Olson lacked the stamina to rebuild the Farmer Labor organization from top to bottom." So with one swift signature he made Elmer Benson a senator, doubtless hoping that 1936 would portend better news for his own health and that of his party.[3]

Neither was meant to be. Cancer was eating away at Olson's pancreas, and Dr. Mayo told the governor that he had at most eight months to live. Suddenly the best-laid schemes of the Farmer-Labor men were about to go awry. Throughout the spring and summer of 1936, politicians on the left jockeyed for support at nominating conventions and among their party faithful, all the while slinging mud at one another and diluting the liberal vote in Minnesota. Floyd Olson's untimely demise on August 22 foreshadowed a similar slide into oblivion for the state's most successful third-party movement. With the benefit of hindsight, Farmer-Labor spokesman Karl F. Rolvaag blamed his party's downfall on the "forces of internal confusion, disorganization, and collapse" following the governor's death. For better or worse, Floyd B. Olson had, in the eyes of most Minnesotans, come to embody the spirit and substance of the Farmer-Labor movement. To whom his torch would now pass became a source of bitter resentment for Farmer-Laborites, but it also brought a gleam of hope to young, disaffected Republicans like Harold Stassen. They sensed a change in the prevailing political winds and intended to make the most of it.[4]

Franklin Roosevelt and the Democrats, however, had other plans for Minnesota. With the Farmer-Labor Party's future now very much up in the air, the prospects for a mutually beneficial arrangement with the Democrats never seemed more promising. Having already earned Olson's endorsement for reelection, Roosevelt and his political strategists now set out to unify Minnesota's liberals before the November 3 general election. A Republican resurgence (not to mention a Lemke long shot) could come about in the North Star State, they reasoned, only if Democratic and Farmer-Labor candidates campaigned *against* each other while conservatives collected votes.

The case of Patrick J. Delaney seemed to confirm this theory. On June 15, 1936, Delaney won the Democratic Primary for Schall's old Senate seat, the one Elmer Benson now held temporarily, by a two-to-one margin. He campaigned actively during that summer for what would essentially be a three-way race between Delaney and two other candidates—a Republican and a Farmer-Laborite. The state's gubernatorial race was shaping up the same way. And then during the first week of October, Delaney and the Democratic nominee for governor, Fred Curtis, suddenly withdrew from their races. Newspapers from one end of the country to the other pounced on the announcement. "New Deal leaders evidently want the Democratic strength behind the Farmer-Labor organization, which is pro-Roosevelt," declared the *Niagara Falls Gazette*. The *Snohomish County Forum* in far-off Washington State reported that "Political expediency brought about a strange state of affairs in Minnesota" and quoted a prominent Minnesota Democrat who characterized the surprising developments as "an absolute sellout" by party leaders.[5]

Veteran political correspondent Arthur Krock wrote extensively of what he termed the "Minnesota Fusion" in the *New York Times*. Krock noted that "Minnesota Democrats and the President have strange bedfellows in the Farmer-Laborites" but conceded that, with only three weeks until the election, "The President's chance of carrying the State is much improved."[6]

Krock stopped short of implying that Roosevelt had personally orchestrated the entire turn of events, but the president's own correspondence suggests just such a scenario. On October 6, Minnesota's Democratic headquarters in St. Paul received the following telegram addressed to Patrick Delaney:

I WANT YOU TO KNOW HOW MUCH I APPRECIATE THE FINE SENSE OF LOYALTY WHICH PROMPTED YOU TO WITHDRAW FROM THE SENATORIAL RACE STOP PERSONALLY I AM DEEPLY GRATEFUL THAT YOU WERE WILLING TO SACRIFICE YOUR PERSONAL AMBITIONS ON MY BEHALF AND FOR THE GOOD OF THE PARTY*

FRANKLIN D ROOSEVELT.[7]

All of this provided choice fodder for Roosevelt's critics on both the right and the left, but the speculation did little to change one overriding fact: the 1936 election was essentially a referendum on the New Deal, and on November 3 President Franklin Delano Roosevelt and the Democrats coasted to the most lopsided victory in American history. Five million more Americans voted for Roosevelt than had done so four years earlier. He carried every state in the nation except Maine and Vermont, earning himself 523 electoral votes to Landon's eight. Beginning in January, Democratic lawmakers would now hold over three-quarters of the seats in both houses of Congress, a remarkable mandate for what had been a dizzying array of New Deal reform

---

* To the best of my knowledge, this telegram was not made public in 1936, nor has it been written about since. I was given a copy of the original telegram by Patrick Delaney's granddaughter several years before I understood its larger significance. Her son happened to be a student in my American history course, and she thought I might be interested to know that his great-grandfather once ran for Congress. It wasn't until I began looking more closely at the 1936 election that I discovered the newspaper article announcing that Delaney had withdrawn from the race shortly before the general election. Coupled with Arthur Krock's "strange bedfellows" comment, the telegram provides compelling evidence to support the theory that FDR cut a deal with Minnesota's Farmer-Labor Party to assure his own victory in 1936.

legislation since 1933. But it really came as little surprise to those who understood Roosevelt's appeal among those whose burden was made heaviest by the Depression. Historians Arthur Link and William Catton put it this way: "Republican leaders must have surveyed the political scene during the early months of 1936 with considerable dismay. Not since Andrew Jackson's day had the Democratic Party been so firmly entrenched and so popular with the masses."[8]

~

Harold Stassen and fellow members of the Young Republican League counted themselves among the dismayed and disheartened. In addition to the Democrats' overwhelming victories, the Farmer-Labor Party racked up wins with Ernest Lundeen headed to the U.S. Senate and Elmer Benson easily carrying the gubernatorial race "by the largest plurality in Minnesota's history" up to that point. The only thing Republicans could do in the immediate term was wait and see whether or not Benson would manage to fill the enormous shoes Floyd Olson left behind. As it turned out, many Minnesotans were soon wondering the same thing. Historian Carl H. Chrislock observed that "the marked difference between Olson and Benson is aptly expressed in an often-repeated tale, possibly apocryphal but nevertheless illuminating. It tells of a businessman discussing militant Farmer-Labor rhetoric shortly after the 1936 election. He complained that 'Floyd Olson used to say these things; but this son of a bitch [Benson] *believes* them.'"[9]

Benson's administration floundered from the start. The new governor's perceived radicalism attracted "leftist" elements to the party and to positions within the state government. Benson's outspoken support for Popular Front causes—an umbrella term for "antifascist" crusades led by any number of left-leaning political organizations—only fueled speculation that he was in cahoots with the American Communist Party. Labor violence and public unrest were at an all-time high, and Governor Benson proved unequal to the task of restoring confidence in the state's democratic and capitalistic traditions. Or, his most conservative critics argued with conspiratorial zeal, perhaps he was disinclined to do so. Either way, Minnesotans continued to lose faith in the Farmer-Labor Party.

Then, just three months into his two-year term, Benson's actions and words suggested that he was either pro-communist or at the very least hopelessly naïve about communist infiltration of his own party. In early April, with the 1937 legislative session headed toward gridlock, Popular Front leaders organized a rally that drew over fifteen hundred marchers to the state capitol to pressure legislators. Benson addressed the crowd, saying, "In a fight like this it's all right to be a little rough once in a while." While no one knows for sure what the governor meant by that statement, the more extremist demonstrators entertained little doubt. "They broke into a locked room where the Senate Tax Committee was meeting" and, according to historian Steven Keillor, "The senators beat a hasty retreat. The mob-in-the-making took over the Senate chamber for the night." Fifteen hours later the protestors vacated the chamber and order was restored at the capitol, but lawmakers and the general public were shocked at such a brazen attack upon the legislative process. The Minnesota senate passed a resolution criticizing "the failure on the part of the chief executive of the state to take such action as may have been necessary to quell this mob." That no direct condemnation of the demonstrators and their heavy-handed tactics ever came from the governor's office greatly diminished Benson's hopes for reelection in 1938. It was becoming all too clear that the governor was losing the confidence of the majority of the people both within and outside the ranks of his own party. A drastic change was in order.[10]

All of this was proverbial grist for the political mill as Minnesota's Republicans geared up for another season of campaigning. But under the leadership of thirty-year-old Harold Stassen, this time would be different for the GOP. At the annual meeting of the Young Republican League in late April of 1937 (just three weeks after the debacle at the capitol), Stassen delivered a

Harold Stassen, 1937

keynote address that set the stage for a new and improved Republican strategy. He laid claim to the widening middle road by criticizing extremists on the left and the right, whom he characterized as "the twin obstacles to progress in Minnesota." On one side, Stassen declared, "is that small group of selfish reactionaries, who short-sightedly seek to stifle constructive efforts . . . and cling tenaciously to their accumulated wealth and improper privileges." And with obvious reference to Benson's administration, Stassen further lambasted "that small group of irresponsible radicals now in high positions in this state who are destroying honest business, undermining sincere labor unions, defeating constructive efforts of our farmers, and sentencing for life those now upon the rolls of the unemployed." His message struck a chord with the four hundred or so Young Republicans gathered that evening, and soon it would be transforming Minnesota's entire political landscape.[11]

~

On November 17, 1937, Dakota County attorney Harold Stassen stood before an assembled crowd of nearly one thousand people packed tightly into the Hastings High School gymnasium and auditorium. Speaking additionally to "the unnumbered thousands of radio listeners throughout the state," Stassen officially announced his intention to seek the Republican nomination for governor. It was a heady move given his youth and lack of name recognition outside of Dakota County, but Stassen's affable and honest tone resonated with his audience from the start. Taking a page straight out of Abe Lincoln's political playbook, Stassen led with purposeful humor:

> At the beginning of my remarks I wish to make it clear that I feel that this is not a time for the weasel words of politicians. It is a time for plain speaking, straight from the shoulder. So often our politicians try to keep their feet on one side of the fence and their tongues on the other. They remind me of the story of the justice of the peace in the mountains of Kentucky who listened to the long, eloquent but pointless arguments of the attorney from the big city at great length, and then, finally interrupted and said, "Mr. Lawyer, you argufy, you critify, you edify but you does not specify." Let us approach the problems of our state tonight directly, frankly, and openly.[12]

So began Harold Stassen's campaign to become Minnesota's next governor. Many significant obstacles still stood in his way, including opposition from Old Guard Republicans who were understandably less than enamored with the upstart county attorney. True to form, Stassen intended to win with or without the support of older, more traditional Republicans. He believed that they had taken power for granted after decades in office and virtually ran the party into the ground, holding desperately to policies better suited for the Gilded Age. He never expected conservative stalwarts to support him. Rather, he hoped, perhaps naïvely, that they would step aside and permit a new generation of Republicans to take up the mantle of leadership. America had changed, and it was time for the Grand Old Party to do the same.

Stassen's first test came a month after he announced his candidacy. At the state Republican Party Convention in St. Paul, Stassen-for-governor delegates managed to push through the adoption of a new party constitution, thus paving the way for "an immediate re-organization through election of new state officers and an executive committee." The *South St. Paul Daily Reporter* described the coup in terms that would have elicited a toothy smile from Teddy Roosevelt: "Progressive younger republicans who have been demanding that the G.O.P. awake from its long sleep and that the way be cleared for definite action in the coming campaign, swept to victory like a tidal wave in the state convention." *Bully* for them! But the real payoff for Stassen came when the convention voted to endorse no one for governor, opting instead to let the voters make their wishes known through the primaries. That's exactly what Harold Stassen was counting on. His father had raised him to value a democratic tradition that rewarded hard work and honesty with the honor of serving one's fellow citizens. Stassen believed through and through that if he placed his trust in the people and leveled with them about the issues that mattered most to Minnesotans, then he would earn their trust and support as well.[13]

According to a remarkable document tucked deep inside the state historical society's archives, Harold Stassen likely provided the most candid and accurate appraisal of the coming general election months before it actually occurred. The typewritten assessment, filed in Stassen's papers and titled simply "Memorandum of State Political Situation" (1938), bears no author's name but was undoubtedly written by or expressly for Stassen, who was by then campaigning in earnest for the state's highest office. The document begins with a description of several possible strategies to DEFEAT BENSON AND HIS IRRESPONSIBLE AND UNSOUND GROUP IN THE STATE LEGISLATURE. The first, which amounts simply to running a Republican candidate and hoping for the best, is quickly dismissed as foolhardy:

It is impossible to accomplish this by the sole means of the Republican Party. Careful analysis of the situation shows that there are now approximately 450,000 Farmer Labor voters in the State; 400,000 Republicans; 250,000 Democrats. The Farmer Laborites have control of most of the officials of the Democratic Party and of the organization so that if things are permitted to take their natural course, we will again have a Democratic withdrawal, and approximately 90 percent of the Democratic votes will in that case go [to] the Farmer Labor candidate. It is impossible to overcome this handicap by any type of straight Republican campaign. Furthermore there unquestionably remains considerable antipathy toward the Republican label.[14]

The next possible scenario involves encouraging a primary fight between Elmer Benson and another prominent Farmer-Labor man—Hjalmar Petersen of Askov. Petersen had been Olson's lieutenant governor and therefore served out the final four months of Olson's third term. He was also an outspoken critic of Governor Benson's iron-fisted control of the Farmer-Labor Party. The memorandum points out the advantages to a contested primary between the two, including "If he [Petersen] is not nominated, his primary candidacy will have two important effects. First it will divide the Farmer Labor Party and supply considerable ammunition against the Benson Administration. Secondly, it will keep the Farmer Laborites within their own primary, and keep them out of the Democratic primary."

The 1938 memorandum ends with a brief summary that best captures Harold Stassen's unique combination of pragmatism and populism. His was to be a campaign for the broad center of Minnesota's volatile political spectrum. The secret to winning over a majority of the voters rests in talking sense to all the voters. Stassen wanted to end the political polarization that had characterized Minnesota for the better part of a decade. As stated in the memo, "The entire campaign should be directed at the winning of voters whom we do not have in our column. The easy and most agreeable campaign is one directed at your friends. It seems to be successful but actually misses the objective. All publicity, speeches, literature, types of meeting, radio programs, should be weighed from the standpoint of the effect upon voters who do not intend to vote Republican, or are undecided."

~

Undecided voters. That's where Harold Stassen found his traction in the 1938 campaign. The old guard remained skeptical while the youthful Stassen

The New Leader Minnesota Needs

STASSEN
for
GOVERNOR

THE REPUBLICAN CANDIDATE

Prepared and circulated for Harold E. Stassen, South St. Paul, by Stassen All-Party Volunteers, Dr. George O. Orr, Chairman, 365 Robert Street, St. Paul.

Campaign poster, 1938

crisscrossed the state in his old Ford Runabout, talking sense to folks who admired his vigor and veracity. What he lacked in money he more than made up for in good old-fashioned politicking. Historian John Gunther recorded the impressions of an older Republican who caught the Stassen bug at a campaign dinner in Sauk Centre, hometown of Sinclair Lewis. "Stassen's speech was superb," Gunther wrote. "He ran away with the performance. Then photographers came with the coffee. Young Stassen couldn't be found to be photographed. He was at the front door, shaking hands with the crowd outside. The next day, practically every citizen of Main Street boasted of having met him 'personally.'"[15]

Even though he had not yet secured the GOP nomination, Stassen continued to hammer away at what he called "the false mask of liberalism put on by the present administration." He characterized Benson's regime as "radical in its encouragement of violence in strikes, in its inciting of class hatred and intolerance, in its fomenting of disrespect for law, in its attitude of opposition to all private business, and in its cooperation with radical activities from New York to California." Two days after his thirty-first birthday, Stassen was at the Spalding Hotel in Duluth to deliver a "hard hitting address" broadcast statewide on WCCO radio. He called for "a labor relations act modeled after the laws of Norway and Sweden which he declared had recognized and defended the rights of labor and avoided the caveman tactics of lockouts and strikes." (American journalist Marquis Childs performed an exhaustive study of the Swedish political and economic systems during the early thirties and produced a book heralding their successes in 1936. He titled his work *Sweden: The Middle Way*. The book also caught the attention of President Franklin Roosevelt, who soon after formed a committee to research the consumers' cooperative movement in Europe.) Addressing what had already become a major issue of his campaign—civil service reform—Stassen added, "It is significant that this administration claims to be a friend of labor but refuses to give its own employees the security of tenure, the seniority rights, and the fair treatment that all labor should have and that only a civil service bill can give to state employees." Then he let loose with a blistering critique of what the Farmer-Labor organization had reverted to since Floyd Olson's untimely death:

> There can be no progress in Minnesota as long as that small group of selfish political bosses pull the strings on Capitol hill. They are not building. They are tearing down. They are not conserving. They are wasting. Theirs is not

a true liberal program, it is a vicious political mixture of policies that are reactionary, radical, and racketeering. We had ample proof of this in the recent machine controlled convention held here in Duluth. It was not a convention. It was a puppet show. A handful of men held the strings that controlled the movements and even the vocal chords of a majority of the delegates. The convention could just as easily been held in a St. Paul hotel and all the furniture they would have needed was seven chairs and a table to pound on.[16]

Stassen was of course engaging in a shrewd double game. He was simultaneously mocking the Farmer-Labor state convention, which had just handed Elmer Benson its endorsement for governor as expected, and, in not so many words, encouraging Hjalmar Petersen to challenge Benson in the upcoming primary. It was the precise scenario laid out in the aforementioned "Memorandum of State Political Situation." Benson found himself increasingly under siege from all sides, and he had to spend inordinate amounts of time and energy fending off criticism levied by members of his own party. Petersen was in effect helping the Stassen campaign every time he charged Benson with coddling Communists, stifling opposition, alienating moderates, or dabbling in machine politics. Then, to add insult to injury, thousands of Republicans crossed over into the Benson-Petersen primary race in an all-out effort to put Petersen over the top. According to Gunther, "Even Republican money went into the Farmer-Labor primaries to beat Benson, who was thought of as anti-Christ at least."[17]

The strategy failed and succeeded at the same time. Benson defeated Petersen in the primary by a slim margin—51 percent to 49 percent. On the same day, Stassen trounced his opponents in the Republican race. Stassen carried 48 percent of the vote while his closest challenger—Martin Nelson—received only 28 percent. That Nelson was the GOP's nominee in the previous two gubernatorial elections made the victory even sweeter. Young progressive Republicans had bucked the party establishment and chosen their own candidate. Now that Benson had survived the primary scare from Petersen, albeit battered and bruised, the Republican establishment had little choice but to line up behind Stassen and support his campaign financially.

It didn't take long for the state's more conservative newspapers to jump on the Stassen bandwagon as well. The *Anoka County Union* declared, "Harold Stassen is the hope of the people of our state. He is the one man who has the chance of being elected over the powerful Farmer-Labor machine. He is a sound, logical, fearless, honest candidate, with a clear record and no strings. He is the man that Minnesota needs." The *Kerkhoven Banner* left little doubt of its position on the upcoming election: "Harold E. Stassen, candidate for Governor, in his address at the Swift County Fair at Appleton, made a fine impression on his audience. Governor Benson, who spoke the previous day, remarked that all voters who failed to vote for him were ignorant. Perhaps he will find after the November election that Minnesota has a good many ignorant voters." And to critics on the left who balked at Stassen's youth, the *Fairfax Standard* delivered a devastating blow: "Mr. Stassen, according to certain politicians, is an 'upstart' just because he is young, but Mr. Olson, though equally young, was a 'budding genius' because he belonged to the said politicians' party."[18]

In mid-August Stassen announced that he would not oppose his good friend and law partner Democratic representative Elmer Ryan, who was running for reelection in the state's second congressional district. The implications of that decision were not lost on Joseph P. O'Hara of Glencoe, who had earned the Republican nomination for the very same seat and naturally expected to receive support from all fellow GOP candidates. Stassen explained his position in this way: "When a personal decision is required, it is my custom to speak for myself and to speak frankly. The issues in this crucial campaign in Minnesota rise above party lines. We need and invite men and women of all parties to join with us." Ryan had made a similar announcement the week before, and grumbling could be heard among leaders in both parties. Postmaster general James A. Farley, a close friend and advisor to FDR, told an audience of faithful democrats in Duluth that "No democrat who has any regard for the future of the party will give the republican leaders any aid." Congressman Ryan quickly responded (with a delightful twist of irony): "The time to show that concern (for the party's future) was two years ago when the democratic candidates for governor and senator were withdrawn." Ryan added that defeating Elmer Benson was the top priority for Minnesotans and reiterated that he would help in that effort by supporting "a young, able, liberal candidate who can win, even though he be on the republican ticket." Responding to all the hoopla raised by the surprise announcements, H. E. Wolfe of the *Deer River News* probably spoke for the vast majority of independent-minded Minnesotans when he penned the following editorial: "For scores of years, American voters by the thousands have prided themselves that they vote 'for the man and not the party.' Messrs. Ryan and Stassen have given them a new mark to shoot at. It took real intestinal fortitude on the part of both to make their declarations. The old guard leaders of their parties may think them both guilty of treason. But if so, it is a kind of treason that makes for political progress. Real Americans will admire them."[19]

Stassen's campaign appealed to a broad and diverse coalition of potential voters. A colorful campaign brochure produced by the "Stassen All-Party Volunteers" made the most of their candidate's background and experience. It quoted the *Baudette Region* newspaper, which observed, "The farmers need have no fear of getting a rough deal from Stassen. A boy who was born on a farm and was a weed grabber during his boyhood and whose parents still conduct that farm, is sure to be friendly to agriculture." Stassen's popularity in rural parts of the state was undoubtedly aided by the fierce support of South St. Paul's Hook 'Em Cow gang, a horse-riding booster organization that claimed nearly eight hundred members in 1938. In late October the *Minneapolis Journal* reported that "more than 50 Minnesota cities and towns have stared pop-eyed at the rootin',' tootin' spectacle of horses and guns and drums and bugles." The paper added that all of the riders "are from Stassen's bailiwick" and confirmed that "The Hook 'Em Cows are in on the vote roundup for the duration."[20]

On Saturday, October 29, a procession of 650 cars stretching for nearly seven miles passed through most of the towns in Dakota County on its way to Hastings. Led by the Hook 'Em Cows on horseback and Mr. and Mrs. William Stassen in the lead car, members of the gigantic parade converged on the high school for one final rally in support of Harold Stassen. In the very auditorium where he had announced his candidacy nearly a year earlier, Stassen thanked his friends and neighbors for all their hard work and promised to follow through with his plan to reform the state government. "We have submitted to the voters of Minnesota a constructive, liberal program to build Minnesota and advance the welfare of its people," he said. "Everywhere it has been received with a warmth that is assuring." He repeated his pledge to pursue genuine civil service reform, open competitive bidding for state contracts, an improved old-age pension plan, less state spending, a fair and just tax system "based on one's ability to pay," a constructive labor policy, and a substantive labor relations act. According to the *Dakota County Tribune,* "Stassen declared he has made no trades or deals" and that "he is free and independent and no special privilege strings are tied to him." The fact that congressman Elmer Ryan was seated on the platform right near the man of the hour served to remind all in attendance that a Stassen governorship would be anything but politics as usual.[21]

A week and a half later, the voters went to the polls. Harold Stassen won Minnesota's gubernatorial election by the greatest margin in state history. He received 59 percent of the vote while Benson polled 34 percent and the Democratic candidate earned a meager six percent. Minnesotans had heeded the call to turn the rascals out, and in doing so they presented Harold Stassen with a resounding mandate for change. Voters from one end of the country to the other registered a similar sense of dissatisfaction with Franklin Roosevelt and the Democrats. As one historian summarized the midterm elections of 1938, "Overall, the GOP, which only two years earlier had seemed to be on its way to joining the extinct Whigs, had picked up a dozen governorships, eighty-two house seats, and eight new Senate seats. Republican incumbents had not lost a single race." The Democratic majorities in Congress were still intact, but the election had gone a long way toward proving that Republicans were on the rebound nationwide. Governor-elect Harold Stassen was most definitely in the vanguard of that movement. More importantly, he had helped to put his state's political house in order. According to Steven Keillor, by voting for Republicans, Minnesota had essentially "rejoined the national two-party consensus and repudiated its unique Farmer-Labor identity of the past eight years."[22]

At thirty-one years of age, Harold Stassen would soon be sworn in as the nation's youngest governor. He had helped revitalize his party, rally the people, and run a successful political campaign. But all of that was prelude. As the end of the year approached, Stassen prepared himself for the awesome responsibility of governing a state still very much in the throes of economic depression. He promised reform, and his fellow citizens expected him to deliver. What they didn't expect, however, was that the threat of war would soon overshadow the many challenges that awaited them in the new year. Despite their good intentions and best wishes, Minnesotans would in the not-so-distant future join their governor and their fellow countrymen in the greatest struggle this nation has ever encountered.

4 Struggle

Pressed to identify the most critical decade for America in the twentieth century, one might well choose the turbulent ten-year period stretching from 1936 to 1946. No single span of time during the last hundred years represents a more perilous, uncertain, and consequential era in what *Life* and *Time* publisher Henry Luce famously dubbed "The American Century." Shortly before America's reluctant entry into the Second World War, Luce characterized his nation's precarious position in this way: "As we look toward the future—our own future and the future of other nations—we are filled with foreboding. The future doesn't seem to hold anything for us except conflict, disruption, war."[1]

Indeed, crises typified most of the thirties, and as the decade reached its climactic conclusion, the prospects for peace, at home and abroad, never seemed more distant. Labor violence was on the rise in many American cities. Fascist dictators were on the march throughout Europe, and of all the conflicts brewing in the world, the Spanish Civil War perhaps best epitomized the bloody consequences of clashing rhetoric and will. Democracy there seemed doomed. In places where political extremism thrived, war invariably arrived to settle old scores or pave the way for new ones. And though he articulated it well, Henry Luce was not the only American who sensed the enormity of the gathering storm. Human suffering en masse loomed large on the horizon.

The decade preceding 1946 also represents Harold Stassen's transformation from small-town attorney to governor to presidential contender. And even while working to improve the lives of his fellow citizens, Stassen never lost interest in his one abiding passion—world peace. He did his duty at home and then enthusiastically joined the cause of freedom overseas. He fought against political intolerance, communist infiltrators, and right-wing ideologues at both the state and national level before girding himself to help combat the rising tide of Japanese aggression in the Pacific. Through it all, Stassen held firm to his fundamental belief that people are meant to be free.

～

On January 2, 1939, the day before Harold Stassen was to be inaugurated as Minnesota's twenty-fifth governor, political reporter Joseph H. Ball reminded his readers that Republicans faced a number of challenges in the coming days and weeks, not the least of which were high expectations. Writing for the *St. Paul Dispatch,* Ball suggested that voters had registered an overwhelming mandate for change in the November elections. Now they wanted results. The opening of the legislative session and Stassen's corresponding inaugural held both symbolic and substantive importance for Minnesotans. "To the general public," Ball wrote, "it will mean a new set of names in the news, a more temperate tone around the Capitol, possibly better government and, above all, they hope better business."[2]

Ball was on hand at 10 AM the next day when Stassen took the oath of office in the state capitol. It was a simple and relatively private ceremony attended by the new governor's family—including his two-and-half-year-old son, Glen—and a handful of government dignitaries, legislative leaders, newspaper reporters, and Republican Party officials. William Stassen looked on with pride as his son faced Chief Justice Henry M. Gallagher, right hand raised, and solemnly swore before God and a few dozen witnesses to faithfully discharge his duties to the best of his judgment and ability. At thirty-one Harold Stassen had just become the youngest governor in Minnesota history. Only time would tell if he had the administrative skill and temperament to be a successful one as well.

Later that day Stassen delivered his inaugural address before a joint session of the Minnesota house and senate. A cynical reading of that speech might lead some to assume that with the election behind him, Governor Stassen now struck a conciliatory tone in the hopes of healing wounds inflicted by a hotly contested campaign. But of course he already had a majority of lawmakers on his side. He brought with him a coattail legislature dominated by like-minded reformers, many of whom no doubt expected the young governor to savor the spoils of victory as had so many of his predecessors. Stassen's campaign, however, had emphasized the need for cooperation above all else, and that is exactly the sort of message he carried with him into office. "It is a rare occasion," he said, "when the people of a state, from the factory, the farm, the office and the home, of all parties, creeds and nationalities are united on a program of progress in the manner that the people of Minnesota now stand together." And in an effort to forestall politicking at the people's expense in the upcoming legislative session he added, "We must never permit narrow partisanship, the pressure of day to day problems, or minor differences of opinion, to cause us to lose sight of this broad fundamental fact, or to dim our vision of the future." Then Stassen got down to specifics. He proposed several pieces of reform legislation, including the state's first civil service law, a groundbreaking labor relations act, the establishment of a state department of social security and public welfare, and a massive reorganization of the Minnesota Commission of Administration and Finance. He challenged his fellow citizens to unite for the purpose of finding common solutions to difficulties that neither discriminated nor showed any signs of diminishing on their own—unemployment, low farm prices, labor unrest, and government inefficiencies. Governor Stassen declared,

> It is my conviction that after our difficult years of depression, and the uncertain days of experimentation and trial, we have now reached the point where, with an attitude of mutual understanding and cooperation between government and its citizens, with a spirit of encouragement to business, but a firm protection of the citizens against abuse, with the development of tolerance of one toward another, we can set out on a steady progress toward a future of better conditions and more jobs for our people, of a higher income and an approach to parity for agriculture, of a sound and well administered social security program—all under an enlightened democracy.[3]

Joseph Ball liked what he heard from the new governor and called his proposals "far more sweeping than had been expected." Stassen's hometown newspaper was even more effusive in its praise, pointing out that "a most encouraging sign of the situation is that the administration is headed by a tireless and level-headed young man whose background, experience and training have given him unusual opportunity to study and know the problems and needs of both agriculture and labor." But Stassen's position held possible perils of its own, far different from the ones demonstrated by the Farmer-Laborites. Whereas Benson had been vulnerable to the charge

Governor Stassen speaking at the dedication of the 4-H Building, Minnesota State Fairgrounds, 1939

that he was an extremist, Stassen's opponents on the right *and* the left could potentially execute a squeeze play on the governor. Political scientist Ivan Hinderaker, writing in 1949, summed up that scenario when he suggested that Old Guard Republicans might oppose Stassen because they fundamentally disagreed with his progressive instincts. Members of the Farmer-Labor movement, however, could stand in his way on principle simply because he called himself a Republican. According to Hinderaker's appraisal of the situation, "the Governor might be caught in the middle."[4]

What few political observers realized at the time was that Harold Stassen never intended to be "caught" anywhere but the middle. This was not politics as usual. Stassen, like so many of the Young Republican Leaguers who rallied around his campaign, had grown weary of the partisan divide that year after year resulted in either legislative gridlock or a no-holds-barred power grab. Stassen was interested in neither. He believed that the time had come to face the problems plaguing his state squarely. And no matter the issue at hand, he would use his best efforts to end what he called the "perennial schism brought about by stubbornness on both sides." To the astonishment of his detractors, Governor Harold Stassen seemed more concerned about doing right by the people of Minnesota than furthering the interests of his party. By the end of his first term in office, he had managed to do both.[5]

~

Stassen's adherence to the "middle way" was never more evident than in his efforts to bring about the Minnesota Labor Peace Act in 1939. From the Iron Range in the north to meat-packing plants in the south, Minnesotans had witnessed more than their fair share of work stoppages—either by strike or by lockout—during the 1930s. Reflecting a nationwide trend toward violence, the 1934 Minneapolis truckers strike had illustrated that the growing animosity between management and labor could have very real and very deadly consequences.

Governor Stassen was determined to reduce such onerous threats to Minnesota's productivity and peace. The key, he believed, rested in completing two equally important tasks. The first required diminishing the suspicion that existed between owners and workers. The second and perhaps more challenging job involved building a legitimate mechanism, backed by the force of law, to increase the likelihood of conciliation before either side had the opportunity to engineer a devastating work stoppage.

The new governor's party affiliation complicated his efforts to find common ground in industrial matters. "It is easy for a Republican Governor to find out what the employers are thinking about," Stassen openly asserted, "because they are always inviting him to lunch. But he soon learns that there is a wall between him and labor." To counter such assumptions, Stassen created a new executive office—state labor conciliator—and then appointed an honest-to-goodness union man to the post. The governor also made a concerted effort to get out and meet with labor leaders to demonstrate his genuine desire to understand their grievances. According to a feature story by *Life* magazine's Jack Alexander, the monthly meetings began as a goodwill gesture and soon, owing to everyone's candor, became a reliable means of anticipating conflicts before they turned into full-blown labor disputes. Alexander credited Stassen with making his presence known at the sessions and giving a long-overdue voice to labor. "His assets," Alexander wrote, "were his lumbering frame, a willingness to listen, an obvious desire to understand the worker's viewpoint and a feet-on-the-table informality of manner."[6]

This was hardly business as usual for a GOP governor. But Stassen had always charted a different course than his fellow Republicans—a more moderate, temperate, and at times downright progressive means of shaping public policy. Now he applied that "enlightened" philosophy to one of the most vexing problems facing Minnesotans. Stassen sought the legal expertise of several scholars with whom he had previously worked—members of the Minnesota Bar Association and professors at the University of Minnesota Law School. He consulted studies of labor-relations legislation developed in other countries, particularly Denmark and Norway. True to his word, Stassen demonstrated a willingness to search near and far for fresh ideas aimed at keeping Minnesota workers and business owners on the job.[7]

The plan that he and the legislature proposed and passed in April of 1939 required that before any strike or lockout could occur, the party intending to initiate a work stoppage in Minnesota had to file a written notice with the state labor conciliator and then wait ten days. During those critical ten days (often referred to as a "cooling-off" period), "production and work and wages and working conditions and the *status quo* in general must be maintained." Then negotiations under the direction of the state labor conciliator were to take place in earnest. Both parties had to attend and participate in good faith, and neither could legally walk out of the meetings before a settlement was reached or the ten-day waiting period expired. Furthermore, if the dispute involved "a major public interest" and no deal was struck, then "the governor could appoint a special fact-finding commission of three men, one representing labor, one the employer, and one the public." The commission had an additional thirty days—again with no change in the status quo—to investigate the matter, hear from those directly affected, and "make a public recommendation to both parties as to the basis on which their dispute should be settled."[8]

Though neither the labor conciliator nor the commission had the legal authority to compel the two sides to reach an agreement, Jack Alexander clearly recognized the benefits of such a law. "Negotiation," Alexander wrote, "is the heart of the Minnesota act. It takes place in the quiet atmosphere of the labor conciliator's office, and while it is in progress no wages or profits are lost." The experienced journalist had no illusions with respect to the conciliator's authority or lack thereof, but he also understood the value of facts. And by the time he began looking into the law's effectiveness, facts suggested it was working. The conciliator, Alexander clarified, "sits in merely as an interlocutor and a visible symbol of the public's interest in averting trouble. If no agreement is arrived at during the ten days, the right to strike or to lock out may be exercised in the usual way. It is being exercised less and less." The number of work days lost to strikes and lockouts in fact fell significantly during the years following passage of the Minnesota Labor Law.[9]

Governor Stassen later claimed that good old-fashioned horse sense made the difference. Looking back on the changes brought about by the law nearly a decade after its implementation, Stassen reflected, "In Minnesota we put our absolute faith in the inherent decency of man. It was not a faith misplaced. The people involved, whatever their political beliefs and whatever their estate in life, responded as only an enlightened and informed American can respond." And that of course had been Stassen's intention all along. In making the Republican Party a viable option for Minnesota voters once again, Stassen had essentially moved the tenor of political dialogue in his state back to the center. His progressive brand of Republicanism attracted a new generation of young leaders with bright futures, including Luther Youngdahl, Warren Burger, Elmer Anderson, Harold LeVander, and Albert Quie. More important, the success of Governor Stassen's first-term legislative agenda brought an end to the Farmer-Labor Party's radicalization of Minnesota. Forced to work within the framework of a new political landscape, Farmer-Laborites accepted the inevitability of a permanent fusion with Democrats, which in turn opened the door for aspiring liberals like Hubert Humphrey, Eugene McCarthy, Orville Freeman, and Walter Mondale. Harold Stassen made the middle an attractive destination, and politicians from both major parties scrambled to get there as well.[10]

~

And so began the building of Stassen's national stature. Journalists and politicians from around the country began taking note of Stassen's administrative prowess and his undeniably impressive poll numbers. In early September of 1939, as German Stuka dive bombers rained hell from above Poland, George Gallup put the following question to a representative sample of Minnesotans: "In general, do you approve or disapprove today of Harold Stassen as governor?" The results offered a stunning endorsement of the governor's leadership: 81 percent of respondents approved of Stassen's performance to that point. "Further breakdown of results was even more startling. Seventy percent of those who classed themselves as Democrats approved; 80% of those who classed themselves as Farmer-Laborites approved." He had earned broad, bipartisan support for his reform agenda before reaching the halfway point of his first term as governor. If such unprecedented cooperation could be achieved in Minnesota, surely it could happen in other parts of the country. Knowing full well that Democrats called the shots in Washington for the time being, Stassen urged his fellow Republicans to think of the future. "There has been too much quibbling over our share in the production of yesterday," he told an audience in Tulsa, Oklahoma, "and not enough concern for the production of tomorrow. I do not intend to say that I have all of the answers, but I shall present to you frankly some of my views."[11]

And that is precisely what he proceeded to do. Columnist Raymond Clapper became one of Stassen's earliest admirers as the young governor stepped ever so boldly onto the national stage. In 1939 Clapper was president of the famed Gridiron Club—Washington's most prestigious journalistic organization—which provided him a bird's-eye view of power and politics in the nation's capital. Originally a supporter of FDR, Clapper was growing disillusioned with both the New Deal and its architect. However, as the 1940 campaign season approached, Clapper scoffed at the notion that any modern Republican had as yet proven himself worthy of residing in the White House. "So cocky are the Republicans," he wrote, "that they are rapidly pulling to the right to a position of no compromise, feeling that—as in 1920—they can get away with anything."[12]

Such criticism of conservatives did not extend to Harold Stassen. The governor was making a name for himself nationally as a "boy wonder" of sorts due in no small measure to his relative youth and his proclivity for making sense, sounding reasonable, and getting elected. Stassen's fellow chief executives chose him to be chairman of the National Governors' Conference, and his stock continued to rise among the country's leading politicos. Clapper slated him to speak opposite former Indiana governor and Democratic workhorse Paul McNutt at the semiannual Gridiron Dinner on December 9, 1939. It was the first time Stassen ever met Franklin Roosevelt, and the young Minnesotan made a lasting impression upon the president as well as the other five hundred guests in attendance that evening.

In light of his midwestern background and Republican Party affiliation, Stassen offered a fresh perspective on foreign affairs, one that contrasted sharply with the ideas of fellow Minnesotan Charles Lindbergh, who would soon join the America First Committee and become its leading spokesperson. Most Americans, like Lindbergh, were neither ready nor willing to accept the notion that U.S. interests, to say nothing of humanity's interests in general, demanded positive action to avert a global catastrophe. But Stassen was already moving ahead of the curve and in the opposite direction. Toward the end of his remarks, Stassen announced, "Isolationism is dead, I hope the senior leaders of my party realize it before it's too late for my party and country. Furthermore, they must realize that we can only have one president at a time." By Stassen's own account, written fifty years later, what he did next caught everyone by surprise: "Then I turned to him at the head table, and I said: 'Mr. President, if the leaders of the Republican Party and the Congress do cooperate with you, you should make them co-pilots on foreign policy take-offs, as well as on the crash landings,' and the crowd just sort of exploded and stood and applauded, and when he [Roosevelt] appointed me five years later, after the war, to go to the United Nations, he said he'd never forgotten that moment in that speech."[13]

Judging by the rip-roaring display that followed Stassen's remarks, many in attendance were instantly smitten with the young governor. One "excited member of the club mounted the platform" and reported that Republicans in the room had "decided to dispense with the party's 1940 convention and draft Mr. Stassen as the Republican Presidential candidate." Raymond Clapper pointed out that there was only one problem with that idea: Stassen was not old enough to be president. The Constitution specified that the president must be at least thirty-five years old, and Stassen was only thirty-three.

At long last, former Republican presidential nominee Alf Landon of Kansas came to the rescue, doubtless with tongue in cheek. Remembering that Roosevelt had ignited a controversy the month before by officially moving the Thanksgiving holiday up by one week, Landon suggested the following solution: "If the President of the United States feels now as he did about Thanksgiving Day, maybe he will oblige the Republicans by changing the date of Governor Stassen's birth." Laughter ensued, but it was difficult to determine at whose expense it had come—Roosevelt's or Stassen's. With a pivotal presidential election just around the corner and war clouds gathering above, it's a wonder anyone in Washington was laughing at all.[14]

~

The scene was dramatically different halfway around the world. The Japanese were building their "New Order in East Asia," a harmless-sounding euphemism for replacing one form of imperialism with another while killing millions of people in the process. And the same could be said for Europe. By spring of 1940, Hitler was unleashing his *Blitzkrieg* upon Scandinavia and the Low Countries with devastating effects. France was next. What German armies had been unable to accomplish over the course of five interminable and bloody years just a generation earlier, they now dispensed with in six short weeks. Fascism had descended upon Europe like a curtain, signaling both an inglorious end to human advancement and the beginning of what Winston Churchill called "a new Dark Age." Now Britain stood alone.

Writing in the midst of it all, American historians Allan Nevins and Henry Steele Commager acknowledged that "it was indeed difficult for most Americans to understand the real nature of the threat that hung over them and over the whole world." Freedom itself was at stake, and not just freedom as an abstraction or a matter of principle. On the contrary, totalitarian dictatorships in Germany, Italy, and Japan threatened to destroy individual expression everywhere their tentacles reached. To believe that any democratic nation in the world was immune to such barbarity was at best shortsighted and at worst suicidal. For those who failed to see the issue for what it was—a struggle to the death for the future of humankind—Nevins and Commager offered a striking juxtaposition to underscore the danger at hand: "Democracy appeals to reason, Fascism to authority; democracy depends on co-operation, Fascism upon obedience; democracy has faith in education and in the ultimate triumph of truth; Fascism perverts education to propaganda and truth to national or party purposes; democracy exalts tolerance, Fascism exploits intolerance; democracy practices fair play, Fascism treachery and terror . . . The end of democracy is the free man in a free society, the well-being and happiness of the individual. The end of Fascism is the power, wealth, glory of the state or of the party or of the master race."[15]

Churchill and Roosevelt already knew how dire things really were. The two began corresponding regularly that spring, shortly after Churchill assumed control of the British government. In his first message to Roosevelt, dated May 15, 1940, the new prime minister highlighted the urgency of the situation: "I trust you realise, Mr. President, that the voice and force of the United States may count for nothing if they are withheld too long. You may have a completely subjugated, Nazified Europe established with astonishing swiftness, and the weight may be more than we can bear." Churchill's candid appeal suggests he understood, as least in part, the sensitive nature of FDR's political position. Given that Congress had legislated neutrality in the 1930s, the president had very little room to maneuver even if he were inclined to assist the British. The prime minister anticipated as much when he added, "All I ask now is that you should declare nonbelligerency, which would mean that you would help us with everything short of actually engaging armed forces." This sounded a lot like Roosevelt's "all aid to Britain short of war" policy, which was still in its germination phase. Americans were not yet ready to admit that their survival was directly tied to Britain's, and Roosevelt knew it. He needed time to cultivate public opinion and secure a third term as president. He was essentially managing two campaigns simultaneously—one to determine the fate of presidential power and the other to establish America's role in the world. And though no one could have anticipated it, FDR's ultimate success in each regard was about to be aided by two unlikely allies, both of whom happened to be Republicans.[16]

In the summer of 1940, Harold Stassen's star was rising rapidly and shedding considerable light upon a presidential hopeful by the name of Wendell Willkie. Together they were changing the future of the Republican Party and charting a less perilous course toward American participation in the war. The two formed an odd alliance, proving yet again that politics makes strange bedfellows. Stassen had essentially found his vocation in politics, while Willkie, a successful businessman who had made his fortune in utilities, was trying his hand at politics for the first time and aiming high. The pair would eventually incur the wrath of Old Guard Republicans, but on one glorious June night as thousands of GOP faithful gathered in Philadelphia's Convention Hall, the roar of "We Want Willkie" signaled a burst of enthusiasm as loud and clear as the ringing of the city's Liberty Bell in earlier days.

The two first met in late April of 1940 when Willkie visited St. Paul at the urging of John and Gardner Cowles, owners of the *Minneapolis Star-Journal*. The Cowles brothers were not exactly political kingmakers, but their publishing empire—which included *Look* magazine—certainly provided an efficient means of promoting candidates, especially before the advent of television. Willkie's appearance in St. Paul that spring marked an important step in his quest to secure the Republican Party's nomination for president. The gathering was designed to give Willkie an opportunity to woo influential Republicans in the Midwest. He read from a prepared text like a typical stuffed shirt for about thirty minutes and nearly bored his audience to death. Then Willkie suddenly tossed aside his script with a flourish and announced, "Some damn fool told me I had to read a speech. Now let me tell you what I think." His candor and common sense impressed everyone, including Governor Stassen.[17]

Willkie's campaign stop in Minnesota happened to occur at the same time Stassen was putting together the most important speech of his life. Because of his youth, popularity, and midwestern background, the Republican National Committee had chosen Stassen to be the keynote speaker at the party's upcoming national convention in June. On April 29, 1940, Minnesota's

Wendell Willkie, Republican presidential candidate, on whistle-stop campaign with his wife and Harold Stassen, 1940

governor was in Washington, DC, to discuss his ideas for the speech with Republican House and Senate leaders. The *New York Times* quoted Stassen as saying that the Republicans are "united on the fundamental questions and all determined to win." He further suggested that there were "shades of opinion in the party, but not enough difference between the East and West to confound him in his efforts to write a keynote speech."[18]

That, however, did not tell the whole story. In addition to regional differences among leading Republicans, there were serious ideological ones as well. The front-page story in the *New York Times* highlighting the governor's visit to the capital was headlined ISOLATION TO RULE STASSEN KEYNOTE. And when asked by a reporter if his speech would be "liberal," Stassen quickly replied, "I do not like that label. I do not know just what it means. But I can say that my speech will be forward and constructive and I think the platform will be that also." Stassen doubtless disliked the term because it was being used more and more often to describe his particular brand of Republicanism, specifically his enlightened and internationalist view on foreign affairs. It is probably what endeared him to Wendell Willkie, who shared a similar notion about America's role in the world. Isolationism had been the bailiwick of conservatives for so long, especially in the Midwest, that making any forthright statements to the contrary was considered tantamount to political suicide. Willkie avoided a direct confrontation on the issue and bided his time until the convention. And though he declined to discuss Republican presidential candidates during his trip to Washington, Stassen appears to have been leaning toward Willkie weeks before the delegates converged on Philadelphia. Raymond Clapper likely had something to do with that as well. The columnist traveled to Minnesota in May to have a long talk with the governor. When a friend later inquired what Clapper had asked Stassen during his visit, Clapper responded, "I didn't ask him a darn thing. I'm up to my neck for Willkie, and all I did was tell Stassen that Willkie ought to be the nominee."[19]

The scene was set for a contentious nominating convention in the city of brotherly love. The front-runners for the nomination included Senators Robert Taft of Ohio and Arthur Vandenberg of Michigan and a young up-and-comer from New York named Thomas Dewey. Willkie was still the dark horse. If Harold Stassen came to Philadelphia with his mind made up about which candidate he would support, he was keeping his cards close to his chest. That was to be expected. According to historian John Gunther, "By inflexible tradition, the keynoter at a national convention is a kind of neutral, and in particular is supposed never to support anybody himself until balloting has begun." For the time being at least, Stassen was playing the field. When someone asked a member of the Minnesota delegation where Stassen stood, the reply was, "He has one foot in Taft's camp, one in Dewey's, and a third with Willkie."[20]

The 1940 Republican National Convention convened on Monday, June 24. It was Harold Stassen's night to shine. After all of the preliminaries, Governor Stassen approached the eagle-blazoned podium with a copy of the speech in his hand, but he had already committed it to memory. As he surveyed the thousands of delegates and spectators who packed Philadelphia's Convention Hall, the sight must have given him pause. Perhaps he thought for a moment about how far he had come or where he still intended to go. At thirty-three years of age, Stassen was just catching his stride. Now he found himself in a unique position to boldly place his political ideals before the entire nation. He did not intend to squander the opportunity. "Our forefathers erected here a great lighthouse for liberty," he began.

> They showed us a new way for men to live. At last men and women could stand erect. They were free—free to think for themselves, to speak and to work and to worship for themselves. Free to use their hands and their brains to build homes for themselves. And free to choose from among themselves their own rulers.
>
> When those founders of our nation met in this historic city, a century and a half ago, the dark shadow of despotic government covered most of the earth. The wealth, the traditions and the power of the Old World all were arrayed against them.

Reminding his audience that the demise of democracies across the Atlantic had implications for all freedom-loving people, he added,

> For once again the black shadow of despotic force falls over the world. Fellow-Republican delegates, even as we meet lights are going out in Europe. Blackouts of dictators take the place of lighthouses of freemen. It is our grave responsibility to keep burning brightly the light of liberty . . .
>
> Let us announce here and now that we have faith in the future of this nation and its way of life. It is for us realistically to take inventory, to draw heavily from the lessons of the past, and resolutely to turn our eyes to the future.[21]

Stassen then took Roosevelt to task on several issues, particularly for presuming himself worthy of a third term as president. He criticized the administration for bureaucratic waste resulting from New Deal programs, though not for the basic economic philosophy that underpinned them. He said the nation was woefully unprepared to defend itself in the event of war, but he offered nothing that was even remotely reassuring to isolationists. In fact one line likely made the most conservative members of his party cringe. Stassen asserted, "It is the responsibility of government in its foreign policy to endeavor in every honorable way to create and nurture a world environment in which its people can proceed along life's path in peace, expanding their material well-being and developing their way of life." Might that include aiding the British?

Taken as a whole, his keynote address could not be characterized as either liberal or conservative. Stassen stuck to the middle ground, familiar territory for a man who spurned the radical and reactionary extremes in American politics. He finished by quoting George Washington, who had counseled his countrymen to steer clear of the ideological fringe: "If to please the people we offer what we ourselves disapprove, how can we afterwards defend our work? Let us raise a standard to which the wise and honest can repair. The event is in the hands of God." As he concluded that last line, Stassen raised both arms in the air and the audience roared with approval. He had spoken for nearly an hour.[22]

The most remarkable thing about Stassen's oration when viewed with hindsight is its statesmanlike quality. He said what needed to be said regardless of his political persuasion. Much of what he discussed that evening actually echoed the sentiments expressed by Franklin Roosevelt and Winston Churchill. When war broke out in Europe the previous September, FDR had assured the nation in a fireside chat, "As long as it remains within my power to prevent, there will be no black-out of peace in the United States." But things were rapidly deteriorating to a point where best wishes and good intentions could not forestall the menace of war. Inevitability was beginning to sink in. On June 4 the prime minister addressed Parliament knowing full well that his words would be heard in America as well. He promised that the British people "would carry on the struggle, until, in God's good time, the New World with all its power and might, steps forth to the rescue and liberation of the Old." Stassen's position—and eventually Willkie's— helped to make that realization less about politics and more about serving the nation's interest.[23]

But of course not everyone saw it that way, and what Stassen did immediately after his speech roiled Republicans for years to come. He met with
Willkie and pledged his endorsement as long as he could be Willkie's floor
manager at the convention. Stassen was preempting tradition, but Willkie
quickly obliged, no doubt recognizing the potential delegate draw of a
man "who symbolized the party's future and represented the Midwest." By
Wednesday morning news of Stassen's support for Willkie was in all the
newspapers. Additional endorsements followed as the Willkie bandwagon
gained momentum in the hours leading up to the nomination process. It
was now essentially a three-way race between Taft, Dewey, and Willkie.
George Gallup announced that his pollsters were tracking a definite upswing
in Willkie backers. Taft's followers dug in and raised doubts about the other
candidate's commitment to party principles, but that effort fell flat as a
pancake in the face of "We Want Willkie" chants emanating from the convention hall's balcony. Willkie had become the media's darling and now
the people wanted him, too. It took six ballots to accomplish, but by late
Thursday night Wendell Willkie had earned enough delegates to win the

Stassen taking the oath for his second term, 1941

nomination. He and Stassen had effectively wrestled control of the Republican Party from the conservative old guard.[24]

Not that it did much to improve Republican chances of defeating Franklin Roosevelt in November. On Election Day 1940, President Roosevelt and Governor Stassen were both reelected by sizable margins. The president pursued a foreign policy that justified arming Britain as an alternative to war. For the next twelve months phrases like "arsenal of democracy" and "lend-lease" became the common parlance of politicians who genuinely sought to keep America out of the war, while Charles Lindberg and the America First Committee saw their influence waning. When Wendell Willkie traveled to Britain in early 1941 to witness the devastating effects of the *Blitz* with his own eyes, citizens on both sides of the Atlantic could not help but see the symbolic importance of such a trip. Willkie carried a handwritten note from the president that read in part, "Dear Churchill, Wendell Willkie will give you this—He is truly helping to keep politics out over here." As if to remove any doubt of his allegiances, Roosevelt closed that note with a verse from Longfellow that he said "applies to you people as it does to us."

> Sail on, Oh Ship of State!
> Sail on, Oh Union strong and great
> Humanity with all its fears
> With all the hope of future years
> Is hanging breathless on thy fate.[25]

For his part, Harold Stassen recognized Roosevelt's victory as a clear mandate, like it or not, and urged his fellow Republicans to unite behind the president's policies. Speaking to an audience in St. Cloud, Minnesota, on Lincoln Day of 1941, he said, "We can best serve his [Lincoln's] memory and the people of our nation if we quietly resolve to make our Republican party the great humanitarian party . . . Further to do him honor, we should be the party that never loses sight of the fundamental need for union and unity." To be clear, Stassen's internationalist attitude was not typical; he was running far ahead of most Americans when it came to accepting the need for U.S. intervention in the global struggle. But all that soon changed. The rest of the country caught up to him on December 7, 1941.[26]

~

Governor Stassen was on his way to Washington, DC, to meet with legislators when he learned of the Japanese attack at Pearl Harbor. He rushed home immediately and issued a brief statement reassuring Minnesotans that they could and would do their part to help guarantee ultimate victory. In a statewide radio address broadcast ten days later, Stassen put the present struggle into perspective: "For there is being waged against us total war— war that arises from the perverted concepts in the minds of dictatorial groups, that brute force and decrees and slavery should take the place of a system of justice, of laws, and of liberties. Consequently, it is a war against free people as a whole and all they cherish. Thus it is clear that it is our duty to be prepared at home."[27]

That era was different from today in so many ways—some good and some bad. But one thing is certain: the collective sense of duty and sacrifice that pervaded American society after December 7 has not been equaled since. Looking back nearly sixty years later, Arlene Shramek, a homemaker from upstate New York, offered a typical explanation for what motivated her and millions of others to move into the workforce during the war. She said, "In those days patriotism was a virtue. Confidence in our leaders was strong. We were proud to be Americans and were willing to make the sacrifices necessary for our country to succeed and be safe."[28]

Speaking to the legislature, 1941

Stassen expected the same of all Minnesotans, and he led by example as the exigencies of war dominated his second term. He worked closely with the War Department to negotiate defense contracts and establish armament plants in his state, thus providing thousands of needed jobs. Midwestern farmers reaped a windfall for the first time since the Depression began, as demand for agricultural exports rose sharply. Cooperation and unity was the order of the day, so Stassen's chief concern shifted from practicing the art of compromise to maximizing war production and safeguarding the home front. Apparently the voters approved of his performance. In 1942 Stassen announced that he planned to seek a third term but if reelected he would resign after the first legislative session to serve in the U.S. Navy. He could have easily been exempted from active duty—as governor he qualified as an "essential citizen"—but he saw things differently, explaining, "The drive for victory against the totalitarian forces that threaten the future of free men will be conducted in the main by the young men of my generation. I want to be with them." That November Minnesota's electorate registered its support for his plan by keeping him in office with over a hundred thousand votes to spare.[29]

In the spring of 1943, *Time* magazine ran a brief story about Stassen's last few days as a governor and a civilian. His legendary work ethic remained undiminished. The article begins, "For a fortnight, the husky, serious, silo-tall young man who was Minnesota's Governor had been working 15 hours a day to clean off his desk. In & out of Harold Stassen's deep-carpeted office in the State Capitol went men on last-minute business: legislators, businessmen, labor leaders, Republican bigwigs. Harold Stassen listened to all of them, between interruptions plugged away at humdrum details. On the floor above the Legislature dragged to a close." Stassen's hand-picked successor was his old friend Ed Thye. The two fought side by side through many political battles over the years, and Stassen had convinced Minnesota's Republican Party to nominate the former farmer from Northfield to be lieutenant governor. Now, as he prepared to receive the torch, Thye expressed his gratitude: "Governor, if you hadn't staked all your chips on me, I wouldn't be where I am today, and I want you to know I appreciate it." Stassen replied, "You did it yourself, Ed." Five days later the former "boy wonder" officially resigned from office, enlisted in the navy, and boarded a train bound for the Great Lakes Naval Training Station in Chicago. The next two years at war would test his mettle as never before. But even as he followed his patriotic instincts, Stassen's commitment to achieving a just and lasting peace for all nations became stronger than ever.[30]

5 Free Man

Toward the end of the Second World War, when victory over the Axis seemed assured—a matter of *when* rather than *if*—American soldiers and sailors in the Mediterranean theater of operations were invited to participate in an essay contest. It was supposed to boost morale and get servicemen to think beyond the immediate demands and degradations of being immersed in war. First-place honors went to Isadora Rubin of Brooklyn, New York, for his composition entitled "What Victory Means to Me." Private Rubin was serving with a Fifth Army tank-destroyer battalion in Italy when he wrote, "If we can sweep aside untold obstacles to smash the most ruthlessly efficient machines of destruction ever devised, surely we possess the vision and practical genius to organize for peace, security, and a world designed for living." Rubin put to words what millions of his brothers-in-arms were thinking and feeling. He also articulated precisely the reasons for which Commander Harold Stassen helped write the United Nations Charter.[1]

Before he resigned as governor of Minnesota, Stassen voiced great enthusiasm for building an international mechanism to prevent war in the future. He wore it on his sleeve well before said sleeve carried the distinctive stripes of a U.S. Naval Reserve officer. He spoke to anyone who would listen about justice and tolerance and lasting peace. Many liberals, including CBS News correspondent Eric Sevareid, were inspired by the governor's candid appeal to reason. Sevareid had spent his formative years attending the University of Minnesota and still remembered Stassen's reputation as a political whiz kid on campus. Now he admired the pluck demonstrated by "Governor

Stassen, whom as students we had glibly written off as a 'power politician' and who was doing more for the intelligent cause than the rest of us put together."[2]

Sevareid was not alone. Poet Carl Sandburg visited Minnesota in the summer of 1942 and marveled at how folks there had replaced the false façade of isolationism with "pride and faith in a free man's way." A few months later Sandburg heard about a foreign policy address Stassen gave in Washington, DC, and lauded the up-and-coming politician's remarks. Sandburg wrote,

> A tough job with political tools and military arms Stassen sees ahead. If we can be sober, patient, and reduce anger and malice to a minimum, we stand a better chance at working out something new and good for a coming generation to build on. Some of us can hold only genuine affection for a political leader with malice toward none of his own political rivals and no odorous innuendoes, no carefully worded little stink bombs, meant for others who have different notions about how to reorganize and set going the shattered and burnt human world we face when this war ends.[3]

Even the Minnesota-born novelist Sinclair Lewis was on the Harold Stassen bandwagon by now. Nearly a decade earlier Lewis had written the critically acclaimed *It Can't Happen Here,* which offered readers a satirical look at the possibility of a fascist takeover in the United States. One of the most poignant lines of the novel came from a newspaperman: "More and more, as I think about history, I am convinced that everything that is worthwhile in the world has been accomplished by the free, inquiring, critical spirit, and that the preservation of this spirit is more important than any social system whatsoever. But the men of ritual and the men of barbarism are capable of shutting up the men of science and of silencing them forever." That was a remarkably prescient observation for 1935. Lewis soon pinned his political hopes on Harold Stassen, meeting with him on several occasions in the early 1940s and privately describing him as "a big young chap—thirty-five—who may some day be President."[4]

But during the war it was Stassen himself who embodied the words and deeds that reaffirmed Americans' faith in freedom. On the night before he left for military service, he told a gathering of friends and supporters, "I urge, therefore, that you carry on. Emphasize that the walls of isolation are gone forever. Join in the search for the best answers of the means and the methods of establishing a definite organization of the peace-loving nations of the world. It must be based upon the cornerstone of basic human rights wherever men are found."[5]

Wherever men are found. That phrase took on an entirely different meaning for Harold Stassen in late August of 1945 when Admiral Halsey ordered him to conduct the most important single mission of his life, one on which thousands of American lives depended. With little fanfare and even less concern for his own safety, Commander Stassen helped organize and lead Operation Swift Mercy, which offered redemption to nearly twenty thousand Allied prisoners of war. And just in time. Given the desperation of Japanese soldiers and civilians in the closing days of the war, no one knew for sure what would become of those brave American men whose great misfortunate it was to be a POW when surrender finally came. Stassen was among the first to find out, and the experience stayed with him for the rest of his life.

When Lieutenant Commander Stassen reported for duty in the South Pacific during the summer of 1943, many of his fellow sailors, particularly the regular naval officers, viewed his arrival with skepticism. That was probably to be expected. The former governor's political reputation preceded him, so the old seadogs naturally assumed that he was more interested in padding his résumé then fighting the war. Stassen dispelled that notion in a hurry by making a favorable and lasting first impression on Admiral William "Bull" Halsey. Their initial meeting lasted all of a few seconds, and, according to Stassen, the commander of the Third Fleet got right down to business.

HALSEY: *Are you here to work?*
STASSEN: *Yes, Admiral.*
HALSEY: *That's all I want to know.*[6]

Stassen became Halsey's flag secretary, charged with the responsibility of handling the admiral's correspondence. By all accounts Lieutenant Commander Stassen dispatched his duties with great efficiency and soon ingratiated himself with the admiral's other senior staff officers. Captain Doug Moulton said, "As soon as the staff saw how well Stass fit in, we began kidding him." They joked about Stassen becoming president of the United States someday and told him that they all expected cushy jobs once he made it to

Admiral Halsey and Stassen have coffee, November 13, 1945

the White House. Stassen reciprocated their good humor. "I wouldn't have a chance to fix you up," he said. "If I'm elected, I'll have the shortest term in history. I'll be inaugurated one day, I'll announce my cabinet the next day, I'll give a SOPAC [South Pacific Command] party the third day, and on the fourth day I'll be impeached for it."[7]

From there on out he was one of the gang. Technically speaking, however, he was an integral part of the command structure that would in short order lead history's most powerful naval fleet to, in Halsey's words, "absolute and unconditional victory." Though he joined the Third Fleet midway through the war, Stassen proved himself a capable naval officer whose loyalty to "Bull" Halsey was unflinching. For despite his brilliance, Admiral Halsey had his share of run-ins with controversy during the war, more often than not due to an intemperate remark. One such incident occurred on December 31, 1942, when Halsey told a group of journalists in the South Pacific that "we now had the initiative, that the Japs would keep retreating, and that the end of 1943 would see us in Tokyo." When asked a few days later in Auckland, New Zealand, if he stood by his rather bold forecast, the admiral doubled down. "That's right," he said confidently. "We have 363 days left to fulfill my prediction and we are going to do it."[8]

That was a hopelessly optimistic projection, and everyone knew it. Everyone, that is, except the Japanese. Two years later, when Halsey was still taking heat for the remark, Stassen told a *New York Times* reporter that the admiral's audacious assertion was meant to bolster Allied morale and befuddle the Japanese. The statement needed to be judged upon its pragmatic merit rather than its literal value. In other words, to what extent did Halsey's perceived overconfidence affect Japan's strategic and tactical planning? Stassen explained,

> He made it [the prediction] during the darkest period of the Pacific War. We had very little Navy afloat. Australia was very much concerned. The Japanese Navy was still strong. It was a pretty gloomy situation. Halsey knew that if the Jap Navy had attacked our force, it was doubtful if our fleet, even with its magnificent fighting spirit, could hold the line. So he made this bold, assertive statement both to mislead the Japs and to cheer up our force. It worked. The Japanese didn't attack for six months. Instead they tried to find out what in the world Admiral Halsey had that led him to make that statement.[9]

That explanation was both reasonable and convenient given two years of water under the proverbial bridge. One might even call it politically expedient. Stassen's attempt to justify Halsey's actions exemplifies the type of relationship that existed between the two men. Stassen genuinely respected the admiral for being a leader "whose confidence could clearly win battles." For his part, Halsey had long since abandoned any doubts he may have once entertained about Stassen's motives for going to war or his capacity for hard work. When Roosevelt offered Stassen the opportunity to participate in drafting the UN Charter, Halsey knew he would be losing a good man. Stassen recalls the admiral asking, "When you get through with this business for President Roosevelt, do you want to come back?" Stassen promptly answered in the affirmative, and Halsey wrote the orders out to make it official.[10]

For the next several months, the Third Fleet worked to bring about the final destruction of Japan while Commander Stassen focused on planning for a world that would, God willing, someday be at peace. Stassen's participation in the founding of the United Nations, described in the next chapter, must have seemed a surreal hiatus for him. But he returned, as promised, in time to be a part of the war's end.

That day finally arrived on August 15, 1945. While standing the eight-to-twelve watch on the bridge of the USS *Missouri*, Stassen witnessed an electrifying exchange of incoming and outgoing messages. He wrote it all down in the ship's log: "0804 Received news flash that President Truman had announced Japan's surrender . . . 1055 Received orders from Admiral Nimitz to cease offensive operations against Japan; but to continue searches and to beware of treachery. 1110 Broke out MISSOURI's Battle Flag and Admiral Halsey's Four Star Flag and began sounding ship's whistle and siren." Ever the professional, Stassen stuck to facts and simply reported what he observed—this is what we heard and when, this is what we are reporting to the fleet, this is what we are doing right now. But as his duty topside came to a close that fateful morning, Commander Stassen could no longer resist the temptation to throw objectivity overboard. His impromptu editorializing demonstrates both a profound respect for the admiral and a tremendous sense of history. Stassen concluded the log, "1113 Admiral Halsey ordered the signal 'Well Done' hoisted to fleet. So closes the watch we have been looking forward to, unconditional surrender of Japan, with Admiral Halsey at sea in command of the greatest combined fighting fleet in all history! As he stands on the bridge I can see a gleam in his eye that is unmistakable."[11]

News that the war had ended elicited a variety of emotions and reactions, all depending upon one's circumstances. Fear of Japanese kamikaze pilots who had nothing to lose but their lives, which of course was the point, kept the American navy on high alert. When Admiral John "Slew" McCain (grandfather of Arizona Senator John McCain) radioed Halsey to inform him that he intended to cease hostilities as ordered but would shoot down any enemy aircraft that approached his task force, Halsey concurred. "Affirmative," replied the Third Fleet's commander. "All snoopers will be investigated and shot down, not vindictively, but in a friendly sort of way." Halsey's instructions were quickly forwarded to his airborne fighters, prompting one pilot to ask his wingman, "What does the Admiral mean, 'not vindictively!'" The response came back short and sweet and sounding like a punch line from the *Jack Benny Show*: "I think he means for us to use only three guns instead of six."[12]

Halsey began reading his handwritten victory speech over the airwaves at 1:00 PM. Even as he spoke, "Men of the Third Fleet, the war is ended,"

Japanese kamikazes tried to zero in on the American armada in a last-ditch effort to avenge what remained of their vanquished empire. Halsey's gunners brought down a total of thirty-eight enemy aircraft that day. It was a fitting finale to a war in which, according to Halsey, "the forces of righteousness and decency have triumphed." Borrowing a phrase from Shakespeare's *Henry V,* the admiral praised his men for their unrelenting determination, saying, "We are, and shall always remain, a band of brothers, tried in the fire of the greatest holocaust this world has ever experienced, and because of this, indissoluble. That which we fought and bled and died for has become a reality. That reality cannot be, must not be transient, it must rest on firm foundations." For a man who had spent the past several decades of his life preparing for war and proving more than equal to the challenge, Admiral Halsey now appeared remarkably concerned with the future of peace. Sounding a bit like Isaiah beating swords into ploughshares, Halsey reminded his men to whom they were ultimately responsible: "Give praise to God Almighty for this and give humble and grateful thanks that He saw fit to use us as His instruments. Victory is not an end—rather it is but a beginning. We must establish a peace—a firm, a just, and an enduring peace. A peace that will enable all decent nations to live without fear and in prosperity. A peace that will glorify the inherent dignity and nobility of mankind."[13]

No wonder Halsey and Stassen got on so well with one another. They shared a vision that went far beyond the here and now. Both men hoped that humanity would learn from the mistakes of the past, bind up its collective wounds, and prevent a third world war. That is why Harold Stassen had worked so hard to produce a workable United Nations charter. And it was that same spirit, that same sense of inevitable redemption that doubtless inspired an unknown soldier in the North African desert to pen the following verse early in the war: *I knew that Death is but a door / I knew what we were fighting for; / Peace for the kids, our brothers freed, / A kinder world, a cleaner breed.* Soldiers everywhere could relate.

~

The war's end produced a different kind of response among the thousands of Allied POWs located in and around Japan. Omori Prison Camp was just a few hundred miles northwest of the USS *Missouri* on that fateful August day, but it might as well have been a world away. Built atop a man-made island and connected by a narrow wooden bridge to the western shore of Tokyo Bay, the camp measured roughly five hundred feet long by three hundred feet wide. A fence nearly three meters high formed the perimeter, and large pits near the water's edge were used for dumping human excrement from the latrines. Prisoners were also directed to take cover in the pits during air raids. Disease was rampant, torture frequent, and death commonplace at Omori. The Japanese considered it one of their first-rate prisoner-of-war camps. To the six hundred or so Allied soldiers imprisoned there, it was more like hell.

One of them was famed aviator Greg Boyington. Affectionately dubbed "Pappy" by his men, Major Boyington was the leader of an elite if eccentric group of marine corps pilots known collectively as the Black Sheep Squadron. In early January 1944, he scored his twenty-sixth confirmed kill of the war. Boyington's excitement at having tied the record held by fellow American "aces" Eddie Rickenbacker (WWI) and Joe Foss (WWII) was short lived: several Japanese Zeros shot Boyington's Corsair out of the sky just moments afterward. He ejected from the cockpit with seconds to spare and soon found himself drifting haplessly in the Solomon Sea toward New Guinea and the Japanese stronghold at Rabaul. Within hours he was picked up by a Japanese submarine and en route for what would become nearly nineteen months of brutal imprisonment. As far as the U.S. Navy was concerned, Pappy Boyington was almost certainly dead.

~

As Allied naval, air, and land forces approached the heart of Imperial Japan in early 1945, casualties increased dramatically on both sides. The cruel combination of Japanese fanaticism and American will had consequences far more deadly than anyone could have anticipated. And the killing was not confined to beachheads and battlefields. According to author William Craig, with the fortunes of war turning against them, many Japanese soldiers—particularly those guarding Allied prisoners—became ever more "callous, calculatedly inhuman and vindictive." As historian Malcolm Kennedy suggests in his study of Japan, published a generation after the war, those who committed atrocities were demonstrating a sort of self-fulfilled prophecy based upon a clearly outmoded but no less revered sense of tradition. "It had seemed as though," writes Kennedy, "they had reverted in outlook from twentieth-century soldiers to medieval warriors—equally courageous, tenacious, and ready to endure the greatest hardships, but lacking the restraints of the modern civilized fighting man." They had been raised, in short, on "the ineffaceable shame of surrender and an utter contempt of death." While it in no way excuses the crimes they carried out, Kennedy adds, "it helps to explain their treatment of prisoners, who in their eyes, had forfeited all right to be regarded as honorable human beings."[14]

Specific examples of Japanese brutality abound, and of course real stories passed along during the war fed imaginations already stretched beyond belief and back again on the home front. Veteran Paul Fussell demonstrates the phenomenon in his critically acclaimed work entitled *Wartime: Understanding and Behavior in the Second World War.* "A popular rumor during the war," Fussell writes, "told of a mother receiving a letter from her soldier son in a Japanese POW camp. He tells her that he is well and surviving OK and not to worry, and he adds that she might like to soak off the stamp on the envelope to give a friend who's a collector. When she does so, she finds written under the stamp, "THEY HAVE CUT OUT MY TONGUE." Given the notorious cruelty of the Japanese, in wartime that story could be received as entirely credible, making everyone forget that letters from captured soldiers bear no postage stamps."[15]

But truth was stranger—and involved far more danger—than fiction for thousands of American GIs held in Japanese prison camps. And while folks at home could not begin to fathom the harshness of their circumstances, scientists in the United States were trying to figure out what sorts of effects prolonged imprisonment was likely having on the POWs. Researchers at the University of Minnesota enlisted thirty-six volunteers to help them conduct their experiment. All were military-aged men, physically fit, and in good health. In fact, all thirty-six men were conscientious objectors who had chosen an alternative form of service. They agreed to follow a regimented exercise program for twenty-four weeks and a special diet consisting of two meals a day, mostly vegetables, with very little meat or dairy products. Researchers reduced the men's caloric intake until they reached semi-starvation, and then they were held there.[16]

For six months the men lived in relative freedom on the U of M campus. They were encouraged to attend classes, socialize, and spend their free time reading or writing. Few if any restrictions were placed upon their physical surroundings. They were, after all, free men; they had volunteered for this experiment. But the demanding workout program intensified in spite of the fact that each man had fewer and fewer opportunities to replenish his burned-up calories. It was all by design, and the study yielded disturbing results. By the end of the trial period, the subjects "finished down in weight 25 percent on average. Their clothes hung off them. Their hair was starting to fall out. Their level of fitness had dropped almost 75 percent, their work capacity almost 85 percent. Their coordination was bad. They were wobbly on their feet, clumsy and accident-prone."[17]

Eventually each individual man's physical deterioration began to negatively affect the group as a whole. Camaraderie went out the window. Men turned on one another and "squirreled away food" whenever they could, "torn between hogging and hoarding." They stopped bathing but smoked cigarettes incessantly. They grew more irritable and less sociable as time went on. They became obsessed with the thought of food, any food, even to the point of collecting recipes for dishes they had no chance of enjoying under the program's strictly reduced diet. And then some of them reached the point of hysteria. One man caught a cold and hoped that it would develop into tuberculosis so that he could finally eat and get some rest. "Late in the experiment he collapsed on the treadmill, and after that he tried to mutilate himself. He was going to cut off a finger, but he lost his nerve. Then he got hold of an ax and chopped three fingers off his left hand." This was obviously the most extreme case, but all of the men who participated in the experiment had become shadows of themselves physically, spiritually, and emotionally.[18]

None of this information would have come as a surprise to the Allied soldiers, sailors, and pilots held captive in Imperial Japan. They were living proof, and dying as well, that a biological law of diminishing returns could be manufactured in human beings. Thousands of POWs were being worked and starved to death, and still others met a swifter but no less hideous demise. In mid-December of 1944, on Palawan Island in the Philippines, 150 American prisoners were ordered into primitive air-raid shelters by their Japanese overseers. When a navy signalman named C. C. Smith refused to enter one of the crude, makeshift pits, a Japanese lieutenant "raised his saber high so that it gleamed in the midday sun, and with all his strength he brought it blade side down. Smith's head was cleaved in two, the sword finally stopping midway down the neck." While the other Americans huddled together inside the crowded trenches, several Japanese guards hurled buckets of high-octane aviation fuel into the openings followed by bamboo torches. The air-raid shelters quickly burst into flames, and the prisoners "squirmed over each other and clawed at the dirt as they tried desperately to shrink from the intense heat. They choked back the smoke and fumes, their nostrils assailed by the smell of singed hair and roasting flesh. They were trapped like termites in their own sealed nest." A few of the prisoners managed to escape the fiery grave, but the vast majority succumbed to what one of the Japanese guards later described in his diary as "a pitiful death."[19]

On August 11 of 1945, two days after an atomic bomb obliterated Nagasaki, a group of Japanese army officers met in their headquarters at Fukuoka. Payback was the order of the day. They arranged to have eight captured American airmen driven to an isolated area south of the camp and hacked to death with swords. The massacre was carried out ritualistically—one execution at a time—so that all but one of the prisoners had to watch his comrades die. Four days later the war was over, but none of the remaining American POWs knew it yet. The commanders at Fukuoka met again and prepared to endure the unendurable. After listening to Emperor Hirohito broadcast a surrender message to his bewildered subjects, the officers issued orders to eliminate sixteen more prisoners whom they "held responsible for indiscriminate bombing." The subsequent slaughter was described by one historian as "an orgy, a frenzied destruction of human beings. Shouts of triumph rose from the throats of the excited Japanese, who ripped and slashed the prisoners in the secluded forest."[20]

~

At Omori Prison Camp in Tokyo, Major Greg Boyington was suffering through a bout of yellow jaundice one morning when an elderly guard told him that the war had just ended. It was August 15. Boyington contemplated the news with skepticism but then observed several prisoners assigned to a nearby mine shaft returning to camp early that afternoon with all of their tools and light equipment. That had never happened before. Then a party of English POWs marched back through the camp's main gate singing. Also a first. Perhaps the end was at long last near.

That evening Boyington took his familiar post at the head of all the Allied prisoners standing in military formation. After saluting the Japanese officers, Major Boyington said to his men, "Hey, fellows, we don't know whether this is over, but I would like to suggest something. Let's stay in formation and all repeat the Lord's Prayer together." After they had finished doing so, one of the prisoners said, "Oh, Greg, that sounds so wonderful, why didn't we include that with every one of these formations?"[21]

Boyington was not an overtly religious man, but he sensed that deliverance was at hand one way or another. Offering up a simple prayer at such a precarious moment helped keep the surviving POWs united in body and spirit. The U.S. military had in fact provided its GIs with pocket-sized copies of the New Testament with the following message from President Roosevelt inscribed on the flyleaf: "Throughout the centuries men of many faiths and diverse origins have found in the Sacred Book words of wisdom, counsel, and inspiration. It is a fountain of strength and now, as always, an aid in attaining the highest aspirations of the human soul." Inspiration and strength, indeed. And also hope. The Lord's Prayer, which appears in the eleventh chapter of St. Luke's gospel, was a logical choice for Boyington on that particular day. Everyone knew it. But perhaps those with more intimate knowledge of the Bible recalled another string of verses from Luke's pen that, given the circumstances, might well have carried the enormous weight of prophecy for those waiting to be liberated: "Blessed be the Lord God of Israel; for he hath visited and redeemed his people . . . That we should be saved from our enemies and from the hand of all that hate us . . . Through the tender mercy of our God; whereby the dayspring from on high hath visited us, to give light to them that sit in darkness and in the shadow of death, to guide our feet into the way of peace."[22]

No one could predict what would happen to the POWs after Japan surrendered, but Admiral Halsey was not about to take any chances. Preliminary plans to evacuate the prisoners had been in the works since July, and after directing his planes to drop emergency provisions on the camps that were identifiable from the air, Halsey ordered Stassen and Commodore Roger Simpson to liberate the surviving POWs as soon as possible. "Speed was most essential," Stassen later wrote. "If no serious opposition developed we would proceed at once to get the prisoners out to the hospital ships where we could feed them, bathe them, and give them medical attention."[23]

But there were many logistical issues with which to contend. The official surrender ceremony would not take place for two more weeks, so forecasting how the Japanese military and civilian population would react to the sudden presence of armed American soldiers in and around Tokyo was difficult. There also remained the critical question of who was really in charge after August 15, 1945. The Japanese government had agreed to surrender unconditionally, which meant that ultimate authority for law and order in Japan would be vested in a supreme commander appointed by President Truman. But because the legal transfer of power was still several days away, it was anybody's guess as to who was making policy decisions on a day-to-day basis in Tokyo and how or if said orders were being carried out. To a large degree, everyone in Japan—friend and foe alike—was in a state of limbo.

That is certainly how it felt to the prisoners at Omori, at least the ones who were lucky enough to still be alive. All outward signs, particularly the expressions on the faces of the Japanese guards, suggested that the war was over, but nothing indicated that the prisoners could expect to be liberated immediately. For one thing, no American ships entered Tokyo Bay in those first few days after the war ended. But then carrier-born planes appeared like angels from on high, tipping their wings to let the prisoners below know that help was on the way. Soon giant B-29 bombers arrived from the Marianas, "dropping fifty-five-gallon drums of food and supplies from just a few hundred feet." Pappy Boyington was having none of it. Observing the chaos created by frequent airdrops, the major sought refuge in an air-raid shelter. A fellow prisoner asked him, "Why don't you stay out here and get some of this stuff? You can watch these things come down and they won't hit you." Boyington fired back, "Nuts to that. After living through all I have, I'm damned if I'm going to be killed by being hit on the head by a crate of peaches."[24]

On August 28 Boyington and the other POWs "saw salvation arrive in the form of a destroyer task group, led by Commodore Roger Simpson and Commander Harold Stassen. As the ships came closer and finally anchored off Omori at dusk, they knew, finally, that rescue was at hand." Prisoners had painted their roofs with messages to communicate with the pilots flying overhead. The huge "P.W." atop several buildings attracted even more parachuted care packages, but resulting injuries prompted prisoners to write DROP OUTSIDE CAMP!!!! on one structure. The next morning navy pilots returned to their carriers after filming the camp, and Halsey's staff was shocked to see PAPPY BOYINGTON HERE! clearly printed on one of the buildings at Omori. Despite the fact that Major Boyington had been a prisoner of war for nearly twenty months, this was the first indication anyone had that he was still alive. In March of 1944 President Roosevelt had awarded him the Medal of Honor in absentia, but the citation still sat in Washington, DC, while its recipient remained—officially at least—missing in action and presumed dead.[25]

Stassen and Commander Douglas Moulton had previously flown to Atsugi airport, located about fifteen miles west of Tokyo Bay, to make contact with the Japanese command and prepare for rescue operations at several prisoner of war camps in the area. Two weeks had passed since the shooting stopped, and the Japanese officers shed little additional light on the status of things at Omori or elsewhere. The Americans, it seemed, would have to find out for themselves. Satisfied that his men would not meet substantial resistance, Halsey radioed ahead to Simpson and Stassen: "Those are our boys—go and get them."[26]

Prisoners of war at the Omori camp celebrate the arrival of the American fleet, August 29, 1945

August 29, 1945, was liberation day. Simpson and Stassen and their men went as far into Tokyo Bay as they could aboard the USS *San Juan* and then proceeded the rest of the way on landing craft. They brought along Commodore Joel T. Boone, fleet surgeon, and several more doctors from Halsey's Third Fleet. Stassen was overwhelmed by the reception they received from the POWs: "When they saw our landing craft approaching, they waved their arms and cheered, and some jumped into the water and started swimming out to meet us . . . It was an extremely emotional scene as we were the first free men that these prisoners had seen, in some cases, since the fall of Bataan."[27]

A navy photographer captured the sight in what remains one of the most inspiring images of the war. Several dozen shirtless men are crowded together at the water's edge. Though clearly underfed as evidenced by their loose-hanging skivvies or the homemade belts holding their cut-off trousers to their waists, they are jubilant. Hands raised high and smiles broad and beaming for the camera, the men look as though they've just received word that their collective death sentence has been overturned. Several are holding large, improvised flagpoles bearing the official colors of Holland, Great Britain, and the United States, each unique in design but all fittingly red, white, and blue for the men who are there to take it all in. Electrical lines in the background suggest the existence of civilization on this manmade and godforsaken island, but it seems that was merely window dressing. Uncivilized things happened there. The prisoners had been to hell and back at Omori, but the expressions on their faces at this exact moment registered pure, unadulterated joy. And freedom as well.

Boyington approached Old Glory and gave her "the snappiest salute" of his life. Looking back many years later, he still referred to her with profound respect as the flag "which had released me, which had made me a free man." As he turned to survey his liberators, Major Boyington caught sight of Commander Stassen and vice versa. The two had briefly crossed paths earlier in the war when Admiral Halsey and his staff paid a visit to the Black Sheep's base of operations on the Solomon Islands. Now, two years later and under very different circumstances, Stassen approached with his hand thrust forward and said, "God sakes, Pappy, we didn't know you were alive until we saw that picture the plane took this morning. We couldn't stay out there anchored just a thousand yards from you boys and let you stay any longer." What happened next sounds like something out of a John Wayne movie, but several prisoners saw it with their own eyes. One of them was an army

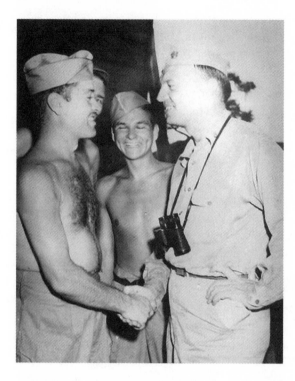

Major Greg "Pappy"
Boyington greets
Commander Stassen at
the liberation of the
Omori prison camp,
August 29, 1945

air corps pilot named Robert Goldsworthy. As Stassen's men began directing the prisoners onto Higgins boats for transport to hospital ships, a Japanese colonel intervened, saying, "You can't do it. I have no authority from
Tokyo to let any of these people go." Goldsworthy watched Commander
Stassen—all six foot three inches of him—grab the Japanese colonel by the
tunic and lift him off the ground. Stassen announced, "I have no need for
orders from Tokyo to do what I want to with these American prisoners."
This effectively ended the one and only interruption during the process of
evacuating nearly six hundred prisoners from Omori.[28]

There were additional camps in the vicinity and thousands more POWs
to liberate. Stassen quickly learned that prisoners at a hospital named Shinagawa were in desperate need of medical attention. He commandeered a
truck and drove a mile or so to the site along with Commodore Boone and
two Japanese guards. Stassen put his impressions of Shinagawa bluntly in a
report subsequently published by Captain Walter Karig, USNR. "It was a
hellhole!" Stassen wrote. "Most of the men were ill; the medical prisoners
had no mattresses. They slept on their bare bones in wooden bunks three

tiers high. In this hospital the men were bedridden but with no beds. Without exception they were all thin and emaciated wearing old tattered dungarees. They were bearded and dirty because there were no shower facilities. American PW doctors had not been permitted to care for the sick."[29]

Nearly three-quarters of the men Simpson and Stassen encountered were seriously ill, and, according to a report in the *New York Times,* "all of the rescued prisoners, except those recently captured, were suffering from malnutrition." Their specific physical ailments varied widely as did their psychological conditions. Some of the prisoners told Commander Stassen, "Thank God you came today. We might not have held out another week under the impact of emotion and uncertainty after the surrender." The liberators had to stay on their toes for fear of reprisals from either Japanese prison guards or civilians. But not surprisingly, some of the newly freed prisoners had blood on their minds as well. "One Marine," Stassen recalled, "who had been a PW for some time, asked 'When do we shoot the guards?'"[30]

U.S. Navy personnel began evacuating the men immediately. Once aboard the hospital ship *Benevolence,* which was aptly named and anchored in Tokyo Bay, the former prisoners received medical care, food, hot showers, and new clothes. They also began telling their stories. One of the first to see and hear from the prisoners directly was Julius Ochs Adler, a reporter for the *New York Times* who had sailed into Tokyo Bay with Stassen's advance team. Adler listened to several of the survivors describe their prison ordeals and swiftly wired a story to his editor in New York. He minced no words in trying to inform readers back home what their sons and brothers had experienced at the hands of an unmerciful enemy. Adler began,

> Having recently visited the political concentration camps in Germany of Dachau and Buchenwald with a group of newspaper and magazine publishers at the invitation of Gen. Dwight D. Eisenhower immediately after the capture of the camps, this correspondent believes on the basis of interviews with several score of American officers and men captured by the Japanese, that the treatment of our soldiers, sailors, airmen and marines by the Japanese was in many instances as horrible and atrocious as that meted out by the Germans. Brave and courageous scarcely describes these Americans, who have survived the bestiality and cruelty of their captors.

Stomach-churning details followed. Adler described men being "beaten with baseball bats, rifle butts, bamboo rods and belts" as well as several hideous

tortures designed to make prisoners suffer excruciating pain but not necessarily die. One particular version of the practice, Adler wrote, was "twisting
a bamboo with blunted point in the ears until profuse hemorrhage caused
collapse." Adler also quoted Commodore Joel Boone, the medical officer
accompanying Stassen the day before, who shared his observations after
visiting multiple camps in the Tokyo area. "I thought I had seen courage in
France," Boone said, "but I never saw anything displayed like this."[31]

Meanwhile, Simpson and Stassen kept the rescue operations running
around the clock until all of the Allied prisoners held in Japan were free.
Stassen flew to Niigata on the western coast to make contact with the
emperor's representatives and reassure the POWs there that they would
soon be evacuated by rail. Despite protests from Japanese officials who cited
"a severe shortage of equipment" to do the job, Stassen managed to get
several trains lined up to transport the prisoners to the east coast, where
hospital ships awaited their arrival. Then he traveled ahead to Yokohama to
oversee the final stages of prisoner repatriation. When it was all completed,
even Commander Stassen marveled at how smoothly things had gone given
what might have been. That the Japanese prison guards chose acquiescence,
however grudgingly, over mass slaughter no doubt saved thousands of lives
in those critical first few days after the war ended. But despite the operation's ultimate success, Stassen still regretted that they had not been able to
bring every single serviceman home safe and sound. He said, "The whole job
took us 17 days and we took out 14,000 men. Altogether there were 23,000
PWs evacuated from Japan. We lost only one PW, an Air Corps Major, and
we tried desperately to save him. He was put under an oxygen tent and
given blood transfusion, but he was too far gone."[32]

〜

Japan's formal surrender was scheduled to take place on September 2 aboard
the USS *Missouri*, Admiral Halsey's flagship, which was by then anchored
in Tokyo Bay alongside hundreds of other Allied ships. Theodore White, a
war correspondent for *Time* magazine, flew into Japan the day before and
gazed in amazement when he realized "there in the morning sun, stretching as far as we could see in the inner arms of Tokyo Bay, was Halsey's Third
Fleet—flattops and battleships, cruisers and destroyers, more ships than anyone had ever seen before in one place, or is ever likely to see again." It was
an awesome display of military might, but it was merely the opening act of
a drama-laced ritual designed for the entire world to see. There had been
little time to prepare for the official signing, the end of the war having come

sooner than most had expected or been willing to predict (except for Halsey, of course), but the Americans were determined to underscore both the substantive and symbolic nature of the ceremony. Case in point: on the morning of the surrender, White noted that "an old flag with thirty-one stars hung from one of the *Missouri* turrets, the same flag that Commodore Perry had brought to Tokyo Bay when he opened Japan to the West ninety-two years earlier." And then as if to close the histrionic loop, White and his fellow journalists were told that the flag atop Mighty Mo's mainmast was the very flag "that flew over the Capitol on December 7, 1941." That subtle touch of triumphant panache was not so easy to authenticate, but it made good copy.[33]

Even as the evacuation of Allied prisoners proceeded, Stassen hustled back to the *Missouri* in order to take part in the historic event. As Halsey's flag secretary, Stassen needed to help coordinate the arrival of dignitaries and work through the myriad details regarding protocol. One delightful example serves to illustrate just how strapped for time and resources they were on the morning of the ceremony. Navy lieutenant Robert Mackey ran into Stassen on the starboard side's quarterdeck as preparations were under way to receive the Japanese delegation. Commander Stassen looked like he was on a mission, so Mackey asked him what he was doing. "We're going to have a surrender," Stassen replied, "but the British sent us over this table and it's not big enough and I don't want it on a British table anyway. What do we have aboard?" Mackey surveyed the British contribution, which looked to be about the size of a card table, and then suggested, "Well, what about a general mess table?" Stassen quickly shot back, "We can't have a formal surrender on a general mess table." "Why not!" Mackey countered. "We put a ward room cloth over it and it would probably look all right." Stassen relented and a boatswain was sent to retrieve what amounted to a long dining room table from the mess quarters below deck. Meanwhile a steward mate searched the wardrobe for a green felt cloth the likes of which were often thrown over tables for late-night poker sessions. A couple of chairs were brought up from the ward room to complete the arrangement, and Mackay said, "Harold, it looks all right to me!" Stassen agreed. Within minutes the tattered old mess table and a coffee-stained green cloth had helped transform the *Missouri*'s quarterdeck into what one Japanese eyewitness would later proclaim "an altar of peace."[34]

At a few minutes after 8 AM, General Robert Eichelberger, commander of the American Eighth Army, was piped aboard and escorted by Commander

Harold Stassen to his place of honor among the Allied officers. Eichelberger's forces had successfully fought to regain the Philippines and were now charged with overseeing the occupation of Japan. War was his vocation, but he had been summoned by his superiors on this particular day to witness the supreme triumph of peace. As he walked along the glistening deck of the USS *Missouri* with Stassen at his side, Eichelberger sensed the enormity of it all, later writing, "I had the eerie feeling that we were walking through the pages of history." And he was not alone. Teddy White spotted enlisted men on every available portion of the giant battleship hoping to catch a glimpse of the ceremony. "Sailors in dress whites sat with their feet dangling over the long gray barrels of the sixteen-inch guns on which they perched," White wrote. "They hung from every line and rope. This would be a sight to remember, to tell their children, to tell their grandchildren."[35]

The Japanese delegation arrived at precisely 8:55 AM. There were eleven men in all per American instructions: three army, three navy, three government, and two members of the Japanese press. Led by the new foreign minister, Mamoru Shigemitsu, the emperor's representatives took up their assigned positions opposite the green baize and facing a wall of military brass—stars and bars and various brands of soldierly insignia from one side of the deck to the next. Enveloping the Japanese on three sides were generals, admirals, and marshals from England, Canada, New Zealand, Australia, Holland, Russia, and China, adorned in olive-drab, red-tabbed, or khaki dress uniforms and caps, standing at attention, ramrod straight, and wearing the solemn but satisfied countenances of victors about to be crowned with so many laurels. All the assembled men could do—conquerors and conquered alike—was stare at one another and wait.

At eight minutes past nine, General Douglas MacArthur emerged from an adjacent cabin and, in White's words, "took the curse off the savage moment." He was followed closely by Admirals Chester Nimitz and "Bull" Halsey. Here were the principal architects of Allied victory in the Pacific. It had taken their forces nearly four years of unrelenting sacrifice and hardship to complete the job, but now, under the general's leadership, they would declare and inaugurate total peace in just a matter of minutes. MacArthur approached the microphone with a single sheet of paper in his hand and began reading:

We are gathered here, representatives of the major warring powers, to conclude a solemn agreement whereby peace may be restored. The issues,

involving divergent ideas and ideologies, have been determined on the battlefields of the world and hence are not for our discussion or debate . . .
Rather it is for us, both victors and vanquished, to rise to that higher dignity
which alone befits the sacred purposes we are about to serve, committing
all our people unreservedly to faithful compliance with the understanding
they are here formally to assume.[36]

The terms of the surrender—unconditional—had been prearranged by
politicians. Nothing the military men said or did on the deck of the USS
Missouri could change that. But what struck at least one of the Japanese
observers who attended the ceremony was the absolute absence of rancor
and vindictiveness emanating from General MacArthur's speech on that
fateful day. Where was the bitterness and contempt, the abject humilia-
tion that they had come to expect from Japan's sworn enemy? MacArthur
continued, "It is my earnest hope—indeed the hope of all mankind—that
from this solemn occasion a better world shall emerge out of the blood and
carnage of the past, a world founded upon faith and understanding, a world
dedicated to the dignity of man and the fulfillment of his most cherished
wish for freedom, tolerance, and justice."[37]

It had been overcast when MacArthur began speaking. Now, almost prov-
identially, the clouds parted and the sun shined down brilliantly upon the
assemblage of peacemakers. The general invited his Japanese counterparts
to approach the ceremonial table and affix their names to the two instruments of surrender—one covered in leather for the Allies and a canvas-clad
copy for the Japanese. Then representatives from each of the Allied nations
stepped forward to do the same. MacArthur signed last, of course, to make it
official, and finally, rising from his chair, he announced, "These proceedings
are now closed." As the Japanese delegation departed, MacArthur stepped
over to Halsey, put an arm around his shoulders, and said, "Bill, where the
hell are those airplanes?"[38]

Here came the grand finale. They approached from the south, as if on cue,
immediately after MacArthur had queried Halsey. Teddy White remembered it starting "as a light buzzing in the distance, then a roar, then the
deafening tone of countless planes converging" over the USS *Missouri*. Four
hundred B-29s joined by fifteen hundred carrier-born fighters and bombers
were engaged in a coordinated flyover of monumental proportions. White
could hardly believe his eyes, but "there they were, speckling the sky in
flecks of scudding gray; it was American power at zenith. They dipped over

the *Missouri,* passed on over Yokohama, inland over Tokyo to brandish the threat, then back out to sea again." The curtain could finally come down on the most destructive, costly, and deadly man-made catastrophe in all of history.[39]

~

But General MacArthur was not finished. He stepped toward the microphone again, holding a second and much longer speech that would be broadcast to his fellow Americans. This time he was more retrospective and verbose. He used phrases like "holy mission" and "spiritual recrudescence" and "crucible of war." First he had extinguished the war; now he would light the peace. It was MacArthur's opportunity to caution his countrymen not to typecast him as only a conquering hero, which of course he was. But he was a visionary as well. His message almost got lost in the pageantry of it all, but not quite. One line resonated with his listeners because it had become a familiar refrain during the war. When MacArthur said, "Today, freedom is on the offensive, democracy is on the march," Americans from one end of the country to the other knew what he was talking about, just as they had known it on June 6, 1944, when General Dwight D. Eisenhower informed them of the great invasion of Europe with these stirring words: "The free men of the world are marching together to victory!"

America's collective conscience, if such a thing exists, had never been more confident in the righteousness of its ideals and its actions. Americans won the war, but democracy and the freedom it ensures were the victors. That's certainly how Harold Stassen felt when he contemplated his impending return to civilian life. But as in war, there are no guarantees in peace. The next several years would prove challenging for Americans in ways that no one could have predicted on September 2, 1945. For Harold Stassen, however, the future held risks and rewards beyond his wildest dreams and his darkest nightmares.

6 The United States of the Earth

O n the evening of Saturday, June 23, 1945, Senator Arthur Vandenberg prepared to record his thoughts for the day. It was an old habit. He sat down in the office of his fourth-floor suite at San Francisco's Fairmont Hotel, his temporary home since late April, and fed a sheet of paper into the well-used portable typewriter atop his desk. Then Vandenberg considered the enormity of what he and his close colleagues—not to mention representatives from forty-nine other nations—had just accomplished. For nearly two months the seven members of the American delegation to the San Francisco Conference, including thirty-eight-year-old Commander Harold Stassen, had struggled mightily to make the United Nations a reality. They had worked under enormous pressure and against considerable odds to help hammer out the UN Charter. Senator Vandenberg collected his thoughts and wrote, "Now that we are at the end of our labors and our tensions are relaxed, I look back upon what I believe to be a remarkable performance not only by our Delegation but by the Conference as a whole. To have obtained virtual unanimity under such complex circumstances is a little short of a miracle."[1]

For those who knew and admired Senator Vandenberg, a staunch Republican from Michigan, the formation of the UN was but an encore to Vandenberg's earlier conversion from ironclad isolationist to dedicated proponent of international cooperation. That miraculous change was brought about by both an avalanche of events and the persistent prodding of other influential Republicans—Harold Stassen, Wendell Willkie, and John Foster Dulles chief among them. Now, with the world at long last on the brink of peace,

Vandenberg could afford some time to ponder their endeavors. He was in a reflective mood as he continued to type:

> I have made some critical observations about Stassen . . . But, in retrospect, I want to put him down as one of the ablest young men I have ever known; with not only a tremendous capacity for hard work but also with an equal facility for going to the heart of difficult and complex problems; with a fine personality and a superb earnestness in pursuing the highly important assignments which he has carried here; and with the greatest tenacity in his fidelity to his ideals.
>
>   We have finished our job. I am proud of it. It has been the crowning privilege of my life to have been an author of the San Francisco Charter.[2]

The job to which Senator Vandenberg was referring helped create and was indeed the product of exceedingly high expectations. The most destructive war in human history had not yet concluded, but its ultimate result was a foregone conclusion. At tremendous cost in both lives and treasure, the Allies had cooperated in an unprecedented fashion to turn back the tide of fascist armies stretching to the farthest reaches of the globe. No longer would naked aggression be tolerated by the international community as an acceptable means of statecraft. On that point there was nearly universal agreement among the Allied nations in April of 1945. But soldiers and civilians alike also understood that sentimentality alone would do little to protect future generations from the scourge of war, particularly after the current crisis had moved out of the headlines and into the history books.

Few knew better what was at stake than famed American war correspondent Ernie Pyle. In late August of 1944, Pyle sat beneath an apple tree in northern France and dared to look beyond the fighting that encompassed him. "And all of us together," he wrote, "will have to learn how to reassemble our broken world into a pattern so firm and so fair that another great war cannot soon be possible." It was a beautiful notion, but Pyle knew that history had not been on the side of peacemakers during his lifetime. Nor did perfecting the art of war do much to further the odds of preventing it in the future. He added soberly, "Submersion in war does not necessarily qualify a man to be the master of peace. All we can do is fumble and try once more—try out of the memory of our anguish—and be as tolerant with each other as we can."[3]

Pyle might as well have been writing about Harold Stassen. Summoned to the White House in early 1945, Commander Stassen represented a critical element in President Roosevelt's plan for the postwar world. As a direct participant in the war, Stassen's presence at the formation of the United Nations assured that the sixteen million American men and women who fought the good fight would also have a symbolic seat at the San Francisco Conference. But appointing Stassen was no mere window dressing. Roosevelt clearly remembered that the former governor's progressive views on internationalism predated America's active involvement in the war. In short, the two men shared a fundamental belief in the need for an empowered world organization to provide justice and maintain peace once the war ended. In addition, as a nationally recognized Republican, Stassen would play a role in the American delegation that would help ensure that Roosevelt's push for international cooperation would garner bipartisan support in Congress. The president was keenly aware of the challenges Woodrow Wilson faced in 1919. The error that Americans had made after World War I, Roosevelt himself believed, "was that, having fought for liberty, the United States lost interest in the fate of the world." He had to convince the American people and their representatives not to make the same mistake again.[4]

As it turns out, Roosevelt began his search for allies across the aisle in the U.S. Senate by homing in on Stassen's home state. His most stirring appeal for the United Nations came just two weeks before the 1944 presidential election. Speaking at the Waldorf-Astoria Hotel in New York City on October 21, the president cast aside any doubts regarding his commitment to seeing a world organization through to the end: "The power which this nation has attained—the moral, the political, the economic, and the military power—has brought to us the responsibility, and with it the opportunity, for leadership in the community of nations. In our own best interest, and in the name of peace and humanity, this nation cannot, must not, and will not shirk that responsibility." According to Roosevelt speechwriter Robert Sherwood, that evening's address on foreign policy was designed in large measure to gain the backing of Minnesota senator Joseph Ball, a moderate Republican who was "a leader in the fight against isolationism on Capitol Hill." In 1940, Governor Harold Stassen had appointed Ball to fill the vacancy left by Senator Ernest Lundeen, who was killed in an airplane crash. Reelected in 1942, Senator Ball represented the independent wing of the Republican Party, which had grown weary of isolationist rhetoric. As the 1944 election grew near, Ball bucked his party's leadership by indicating "he would give his support to whichever candidate took the firmest, most unequivocal position on the cardinal issues relating to the postwar world organization."

When Republican nominee Thomas Dewey sidestepped the issue, Roosevelt seized the high ground, saying, "Peace, like war, can succeed only where there is a will to enforce it, and where there is available power to enforce it . . . The people of the Nation want their Government to act, and not merely to talk, whenever and wherever there is a threat to world peace."[5]

Sufficiently impressed with the president's candor regarding his foreign policy objectives, Senator Ball threw his support behind Roosevelt for a fourth term. FDR trounced Dewey in November and turned his full attention toward winning the war *and* the peace. Tapping Republican senator Arthur Vandenberg to represent the United States at the founding of the United Nations was a masterstroke. Vandenberg had been one of Roosevelt's fiercest critics during the New Deal, and as a member of the Senate Foreign Relations Committee in the 1930s, Vandenberg drifted deeper and deeper into isolationism while war clouds formed over Europe and Asia. Writing to a constituent on April 16, 1940, Vandenberg left no doubts as to where he stood on the subject of war: "I am opposed to American participation—directly or indirectly—in any of these wars; and since I do not intend to take the 'last step' in this bloody direction, I also do not propose to take the 'first step' or any other step which would lead in this direction—unless and until the American national interest has to fight for its own existence." Vandenberg had become the darling of midwesterners who considered themselves safely beyond the reach of foreign aggressors. There was even talk of running him for president. Though Vandenberg of Michigan and Ball of Minnesota belonged to the same party, the two senators held diametrically opposed views when it came to assessing America's role in international affairs. Old Guard Republicans pinned their party's hopes on the likes of Arthur Vandenberg and Ohio's Robert Taft while treating Joseph Ball and Harold Stassen like the black sheep of the family.[6]

And then the change began. Slowly at first and with much reluctance, but begin it did. In early March of 1941, Congress pushed through Roosevelt's Lend-Lease bill, which solidified America's role as the great "arsenal of democracy." Two months earlier Roosevelt had implored Congress to act with unmistakable urgency: "Let us say to the democracies: 'We Americans are vitally concerned in your defense of freedom. We are putting forth our energies, our resources, and our organizing powers to give you the strength to regain and maintain a free world. We shall send you in ever-increasing numbers, ships, planes, tanks, guns. That is our purpose and our pledge.'"[7]

Vandenberg fought Lend-Lease tooth and nail. When it became clear that the president's bill had cleared the House and the Senate, Vandenberg reflected upon the significance of the legislation in apocalyptic terms, typing in his diary, "I had the feeling that I was witnessing the suicide of the Republic. This is what I believe is the result. We have torn up 150 years of traditional American foreign policy. We have tossed Washington's Farewell Address into the discard. We have thrown ourselves squarely into the power politics and the power wars of Europe, Asia, and Africa." Histrionics notwithstanding, the senator from Michigan was essentially right about one thing— the world had changed dramatically since the early days of the Republic. Roosevelt, for his part, could not have agreed more and pursued a policy that took into account changing times and circumstances. Where Vandenberg's position represented the hopes and fears and sentimental longings of the typical American, Roosevelt's stand signified the stark reality of modern warfare. Isolationism was no longer a viable option.[8]

To Vandenberg's credit, he honored the rule of law despite his personal opposition to the law in question. He acquiesced to the will of the people as all true proponents of democracy must do in the end. Writing to a friend shortly after the historic vote, Vandenberg confessed, "I fought it from start to finish. I think it was wrong . . . I think it will *not* stop short of war. But it is now the law of the land. It is now our fixed foreign policy whether we like it or not." And so the shift was under way, not just for Vandenberg but for the nation as a whole. War raged in Europe and Asia, and Americans hoped against hope for a way to avoid direct involvement. But December 7, 1941, changed all of that. The Japanese attack on Pearl Harbor jolted the nation from its collective complacency once and for all. Looking back on that day, Vandenberg confided in his diary, "In my own mind, my convictions regarding international cooperation and collective security for peace took firm form on the afternoon of the Pearl Harbor attack. That day ended isolationism for any realist."[9]

In January of 1943, shortly before he resigned as governor of Minnesota to join the naval reserves, Harold Stassen spoke to the Twin Cities branch of the Foreign Policy Association. Like fellow Republican and 1940 presidential contender Wendell Willkie, Stassen already had something of a reputation as an internationalist. But now his ideas began to take shape and congeal into a concrete plan. He envisioned a permanent United Nations organization aimed at preserving what he called "an enduring peoples' peace." The key, Stassen said, was to be specific. "Perhaps the greatest present deterrent to increasing world cooperation is a tendency on the part of many people to admit its desirability, to acknowledge the correctness of general statements of the subject, but to say it is impossible to work out." Stassen scoffed at the naysayers. He loved to draw parallels between the challenges facing the framers of the U.S. Constitution and the immense but surmountable obstacles that awaited those who took up the cause of world government. Just as the founders had risen above regional and ideological differences to achieve a unity of purpose, so too, Stassen believed, would his generation make the United Nations a reality.[10]

The proposal he unveiled on that January evening was both revolutionary and conspicuously conservative, not unlike the Constitution itself. It was radical (perhaps ironic as well) in the sense that Stassen foresaw an era of unprecedented international cooperation coming on the heels of the most destructive war in human history. It was, however, conservative in terms of organization, structure, representation, and procedure. Stassen was also a realist. He understood that the ultimate success of any world government, no matter how inspired, would require the active support and participation of the four most powerful nations in the world—Britain, China, Russia, and the United States. Getting the major powers to see eye to eye after the war represented but one set of challenges. Finding a way to bring all other peace-loving nations to the table and giving them a share of the decision-making powers created yet another series of dilemmas. Stassen rightly anticipated that this basic conflict of interests would prove the greatest hindrance to international understanding and unity in the postwar world.

Harold Stassen favored a United Nations government made up of a single house parliament. Representation and voting rights in the parliament would be determined by a formula taking into account the percentage of literate citizens, the financial contributions, and the overall resources of member nations. Clearly, the larger and more advanced nations of the world would have the greatest influence because they would have the largest number of representatives. Democracy and equality would not necessarily mean the same thing. But that was the price Stassen believed individual nations would have to pay in order to secure long-term peace. In addition to organizing temporary governments in the Axis nations after the war, Stassen had high hopes for the types of activities the UN would oversee. Too high, according to some. Publisher William B. Ziff included a brief critique of Stassen's plan in a book entitled *The Gentlemen Talk of Peace,* published in 1944. Under a chapter sardonically labeled "Organizing Utopia," Ziff cautioned against giving the type of world government Stassen envisioned too much power. "The function of this authority though supposedly limited," he wrote, "would be potentially of unlimited power since it would administer the international airports, regulate the airways and direct interstate commerce, shipping and other business of global dimensions. Its ultimate influence is guaranteed by the fact that it would have at its disposal a United Nations army to enforce its decisions."[11]

Stassen had definitely gone way out on a limb. But his convictions demanded it. And despite what his critics claimed, he was not alone. Wendell Willkie had just returned from a goodwill trip around the world and was beating the same drum. In his much-publicized account of the journey, *One World,* Willkie declared,

> America must choose one of three courses after this war: narrow nationalism, which inevitably means the ultimate loss of our own liberty; international imperialism, which means the sacrifice of some other nation's liberty; or the creation of a world in which there shall be an equality of opportunity for every race and every nation. I am convinced the American people will choose, by overwhelming majority, the last of these courses. To make this choice effective, we must first win not only the war, but also the peace, and we must start winning it now.[12]

President Roosevelt was moving swiftly in a similar direction, and British prime minister Winston Churchill was already advocating "a postwar 'world organization' armed with 'overwhelming military power' to keep the peace." Few supporters of the idea, however, had offered much in the way of details. That is what set Stassen apart from the rest and what no doubt endeared him to Roosevelt. Though they differed in so many ways, both men adhered to the promise of the middle way—the notion that compromise and not extremism offered the last, best hope for human progress. When it came to organizing the world for peace, the soon-to-be ex-governor of Minnesota and the president of the United States were beginning to sound remarkably alike.[13]

～

Vandenberg came to the same basic conclusion later than Stassen, Willkie, and Roosevelt, but that he arrived at all and with great zeal is a testament to his strength of character. With Americans at war on two fronts, the senator threw himself headlong into the work of planning for the future. By the summer of 1943, with the Allies turning the tide in both Europe and the Pacific, Vandenberg was drifting closer to the middle way. With respect to the postwar world, he wrote to a fellow Republican, "I am hunting for a middle ground between those extremists at one end of the line who would cheerfully give America away and those extremists at the other end of the line who would attempt a total isolation which has come to be an impossibility." He was sounding more and more like Harold Stassen every day.[14]

Arthur Vandenberg's conversion was nearly complete. By early 1945, with Allied armies marching toward victory, policy makers in Washington turned their attention to winning the peace. Despite his failing health, FDR prepared for a grueling trip halfway around the world to discuss postwar arrangements with Winston Churchill and Joseph Stalin. Agreements made at the Yalta Conference would eventually complicate relations between the United States and the Soviet Union. For the time being, however, winning the war demanded and delivered Allied cooperation. Until their bombs forced Berlin and Tokyo into unconditional surrender, differences among the Big Three were conveniently swept aside.

On January 10 Vandenberg dropped a bombshell of his own. Standing before his colleagues in the U.S. Senate, he delivered his magnum opus, the greatest single discourse of his long political career. In what became known as the "Speech Heard Round the World," Senator Arthur Vandenberg made a frank confession. Looking dignified as ever, no doubt humbled by the weight of the occasion, Vandenberg addressed the president of the Senate with words clearly aimed directly at the American people: "Mr. President, there are critical moments in the life of every nation which call for the straightest, the plainest, and the most courageous thinking of which we are capable. We confront such a moment now. It is not only desperately important to America, it is important to the world. It is important not only to this generation which lives in blood. It is important to future generations if they shall live in peace."[15]

The senator from Michigan proceeded to make a heartfelt plea for embracing FDR's vision of a postwar world. He doubtless cringed at the irony. Vandenberg, the great defender of isolationism—or as he preferred to call it, "insulationism"—was now lifting the banner of internationalism. The man who had been so vocal and unrelenting in his criticism of Franklin Roosevelt before the war was now adding his voice to the rising chorus of supporters. The transition had not been easy, Vandenberg admitted, but changing circumstances made it necessary. As if to justify his conversion to a skeptical nation, he added, "I hasten to make my own personal view-point clear. I have always been frankly one of those who has believed in our own self-reliance. I still believe that we can never again—regardless of collaborations—allow our national defense to deteriorate to anything like a point of impotence. But I do not believe that any nation hereafter can immunize itself by its own exclusive action."[16]

He had reached the climax of the speech. There could be no question where Arthur Vandenberg's loyalties now resided—not with party, not with political expediency, but with peace. And he was willing to follow Roosevelt's lead. As he neared the end of his oration, Vandenberg humbled himself even more. In a gesture that must have made a lasting impression upon FDR—and the entire nation for that matter—the senator proclaimed, "I realize, Mr. President, in such momentous problems how much easier it is to be critical than to be correct. I do not wish to meddle. I want only to help. I want to do my duty. It is in this spirit that I ask for honest candor in respect to our ideals, our dedications, and our commitments, as the greatest contribution which government can now make to the only kind of realistic unity which will most swiftly bring our victorious sons back home, and which will best validate our aspirations, our sacrifices, and our dreams."[17]

Vandenberg was at last on board. Ernie Pyle had put it down in simpler terms, but it was the same idea. Something good had to come out of all the death and destruction that now encompassed humanity, and only unity—world unity—could make it happen. That is exactly what the Roosevelt administration hoped to demonstrate at the San Francisco Conference scheduled for the coming spring. In mid-February, on the last day of the Yalta Conference, Roosevelt authorized the State Department to announce the names of the seven individuals who would lead the American delegation at San Francisco. Secretary of State Edward Stettinius was chosen to chair the group. Fellow Democrats Senator Tom Connolly of Texas and Congressman Sol Bloom of New York also made the list, along with Virginia Gildersleeve, dean of Barnard College and dedicated UN activist. In a calculated but no less sincere effort to assure bipartisan support for the United Nations, Roosevelt named three Republicans to the delegation: Senator Arthur Vandenberg, Congressman Charles Eaton of New Jersey, and the thirty-seven-year-old former governor of Minnesota currently serving as assistant chief of staff for Admiral "Bull" Halsey in the Pacific.

Now it was Stassen's turn to help advance the ball toward the goal line. Though initially flabbergasted by the presidential appointment, he wasted little time accepting. Stassen realized that his participation could prove a political liability, but he embraced the opportunity, declaring, "It is as much my duty to take an assignment to work for a successful peace as to work for a successful war." *Time* magazine quickly applauded Stassen's appointment, reporting, "No one doubted Harold Stassen's sincere interest in international cooperation, nor his determination to speak his mind when events called for it. By the time the San Francisco conference opens, Harold Stassen will be out of uniform and free to talk."[18]

And talk he did. Stassen paid a brief visit at home before heading to Washington to confer with the president and the other members of the American delegation. On March 8 he delivered a remarkable speech to his fellow Minnesotans, reminding them that we are all "citizens of the world" and suggesting "that we do not subscribe to the extreme view of nationalist sovereignty, that we realize that neither this nation, nor any other nation, can be a law unto itself in the modern world, and that we are willing to delegate a limited portion of our national sovereignty to our United Nations organization." It was a radical concept and one that actually terrified most Americans who had been reared on the belief that limited sovereignty and national security were mutually exclusive. Stassen was seeking not to renounce American independence but to submit that "true sovereignty rests in the people, and the people know that for their own future welfare they must exercise a portion of that sovereignty on a world level in place of a nationalist level."[19]

This was precisely the fine line FDR tried to walk at Yalta and from which he had no intention of detouring. On March 13 the president formally received the delegation for the first time since making the appointments. Stassen was shocked at Roosevelt's physical condition, noting that when the president reached to pour a glass of water his hands shook uncontrollably. Few Americans realized just how ill FDR had become while managing the nation's, and to an ever-greater extent, the world's affairs. Roosevelt's doctors knew full well that the president was suffering from severe heart disease and desperately needed rest, but their patient did not always oblige. Before arriving at the White House for a brief meeting and photo with the president, the delegation convened at the State Department to confer with the secretary of state. Stettinius personally thanked all of the members in advance for their service, adding, "I am sure it would be difficult to find a more representative, a more highly qualified group in the country. Most of you have already had a prominent part in shaping the proposals which are to serve as a basis for the drafting of the United Nations Charter. We are all prompted by the same desire to succeed. I am confident, therefore, that while free in pursuing our personal views and convictions we shall be able to work as one team."[20]

The proposals to which Stettinius was referring were drawn up at the Dumbarton Oaks Conference in the late summer and early fall of 1944. Representatives from the United States, Great Britain, the Soviet Union, and China met just outside Washington, DC, to discuss plans for developing a permanent organization to maintain international peace and security. These preliminary proposals, discussed again by the Big Three at Yalta, provided the basic outline of a worldwide forum dedicated to peace. The San Francisco Conference, slated to begin on April 25, would set it all in motion. President Roosevelt had become consumed with the idea. It was to be the crowning achievement of his presidency. Nothing less than the fate of humanity depended upon it. In a speech that was to be broadcast nationwide on April 14, Roosevelt planned to say, "Today we are faced with the pre-eminent fact that, if civilization is to survive, we must cultivate the science of human relationships—the ability of all peoples, of all kinds, to live together and work together in the same world, at peace."[21]

The president had been haunted for so long by the failure of Wilson's League of Nations, but now those demons seemed to have been exorcised. Keeping the Grand Alliance together and winning the war augured good things to come in the way of cooperation and compromise. Roosevelt appeared more confident than ever that his dream of establishing a United Nations was about to be fulfilled. In mid-April at his presidential retreat in Warm Springs, Georgia, he privately told a few intimates that he wanted to be in San Francisco for the first meeting. He went so far as to suggest that he would consider resigning the presidency to become the head of the United Nations. No one knew if he was joking.[22]

But none of that was meant to be.

On April 12, 1945, Franklin Delano Roosevelt died of a massive cerebral hemorrhage. As the nation reeled and then mourned, the business of governing, of fighting, and of planning went on. President Harry Truman immediately confirmed that the San Francisco Conference would proceed as scheduled and the American delegation would remain unchanged. He was going to follow through with FDR's wishes. Few realized that the new president was just as committed to the idea of the United Nations as was his predecessor. In fact, since he was a young man, Truman had kept a portion of his favorite poem—"Locksley Hall" by Alfred, Lord Tennyson—tucked inside his wallet. It was with him the night he took the oath of office as the thirty-third president of the United States. A portion of it reads,

> Till the war-drum throbbed no longer, and the battle-flags were furl'd
> In the Parliament of Man, the Federation of the World.
> There the common sense of most shall hold a fretful realm in awe,
> And the kindly earth shall slumber, lapt in universal law.[23]

~

As delegates from around the world arrived in San Francisco, Harold Stassen busied himself assembling a crackerjack staff to assist him at the conference. He wired the presidents of Yale and Harvard looking for the names of students who "had shown great ability in international affairs and studies and had been off to war." He quickly chose Cord Meyer from a list of possible candidates. Meyer was a twenty-four-year-old veteran

Commander Harold E. Stassen, USNR, and pressmen at the Fairmont Hotel during a United Nations Trusteeship meeting on April 3, 1945

who had lost an eye and was soon to lose his twin brother during fierce fighting in the Pacific. A graduate of Yale, Meyer threw himself into the work at San Francisco and performed admirably. Before long he agreed with the press that Stassen had clearly "distinguished himself as one of the most able members of the American delegation." But by the summer of 1945, Cord Meyer would have serious misgivings about the UN's prospects for success. He harbored lingering fears that "the strength of nationalistic feeling and the deep-going ideological differences in the world" would prove fatal to the peacemakers' plans. Meyer drifted farther to the ideological left and served as a founder and president of the United World Federalists before pursuing a career with the CIA that lasted over a quarter of a century.[24]

Another aid to Stassen was furnished by the State Department. Ralph Bunche, a young foreign service officer, became the only African American to work on behalf of the American delegation at San Francisco. It proved the beginning of a long and distinguished career at the UN for Bunche, who would receive the Nobel Peace Prize in 1950. In the spring of 1945 he rolled up his sleeves to begin preparing for what he called "the hardest working conference I have ever attended." Bunche labored tirelessly providing information for Stassen, who took the lead on negotiating the thorny issue of trusteeship. "He is an easy person to work with," Bunche wrote of Stassen, "provided you don't mind working. He goes at a terrific pace and demands plenty of materials prepared for him—but he reads and uses it, and that is gratifying." Like Cord Meyer, Bunche became disillusioned at times. In a bout of frustration he wrote, "There is practically no inspiration out here—every nation is dead set on looking out for its own national self interest."[25]

This then was the fundamental challenge that Harold Stassen knew he and the other delegates—representing fifty nations in all—would have to overcome if they were to make the United Nations work. Stassen did his best to help with the public relations blitz surrounding the proceedings. He received hundreds of letters a day from fellow citizens who pinned their hopes for peace on the United Nations. Just as the conference began, Stassen penned an article in the *Rotarian* explaining exactly what the delegates intended to accomplish and how. He ended it with characteristic flourish:

> The San Francisco Conference is an opportunity, a golden opportunity, to win a beachhead in the battle for peace. Whether it will become the

jumping-off place on the long, hard drive toward winning the peace is a
question to which the people of the United Nations and their leaders hold
the answer.

Already the voices of the pessimist and the cynic are heard. They point
to the things that divide the peoples of the United Nations. But I believe
that the differences are less strong than the deep desire of human beings
around the earth that from the present conflict will emerge a peace that
shall last.[26]

By mid-May the United Nations committee on trusteeships, of which
Stassen was already a central figure, had become hopelessly bogged down in
semantics. The intended purpose of the Trusteeship System was to provide

All seven members of the U.S. delegation to the UN conference in San
Francisco. Seated from left to right: Virginia Gildersleeve, dean of Barnard
College (partially hidden); Sol Bloom, House of Representatives; Tom Connally,
Senate; Edward R. Stettinius, Jr., secretary of state; Arthur H. Vandenberg,
Senate; Charles A. Eaton, House of Representatives; Commander Harold E.
Stassen, USNR

a mechanism for administering and supervising territories that had not yet achieved—for various reasons—sovereign nation status. The committee was chaired by Mr. Peter Fraser, former prime minister of New Zealand. Despite Fraser's best efforts, it was clear that the traditional imperial powers—Britain, France, and the Netherlands—viewed the issue from a completely different perspective than countries like China, the Philippines, and the Soviet Union. While the various representatives generally agreed that "self-determination" should be the ultimate goal of all peoples, British and Dutch delegates balked at the inclusion of the word "independence" in the UN Charter. It simply hit too close to home. Many of the delegates doubtless remembered Winston Churchill's famous remark, "We mean to hold our own. I did not become His Majesty's first minister in order to preside over the liquidation of the British Empire." Maximo Kalaw, a delegate from the Philippines, perhaps best summed up the sticking point on May 10 when he declared, "If you want to do away with this bickering and animosity between the dependent peoples and the conquering powers, you cannot take away the position that whatever power is in control of the dependencies will look at the qualifications for self-government through the light that suits that nation best."[27]

Other delegates entered the fray. Dr. Hubertus van Mook of the Netherlands held that "the realization of self-government needs no trusteeship, no commissions, and no time-table as long as the intentions of both parties remain unsullied by greed, tyranny, or bad faith." The Chinese delegate, Dr. V. K. Wellington Koo, argued that "self-government alone, as a political objective to be obtained, will not be sufficient" and stressed that his nation attached "great importance to the introduction of this word 'independence' as well as 'self-government' as among the objectives of the territorial trusteeship system." After a few days of mulling it over, Lord Cranborne of Great Britain suggested that forcing the issue of independence would be counterproductive, using a classic colonial metaphor to compare the British Empire to a ladder: "On the bottom rung you will find the most primitive people, who are only fit as yet to take a very limited part of the administration of their affairs, and then, as you climb this ladder, you find territories where the people take an ever increasing part in the local administration . . . Independence, if it comes, will come as a natural evolution."[28]

At this point Harold Stassen began to assume the role of mediator between the colonial powers and those nations seeking independence. He announced that the U.S. delegation was endeavoring to formulate a working paper to help focus negotiations on a few key yet contentious issues. Propelled by the encouragement he received from the other committee members, Stassen formally introduced his "Proposed Working Paper on the Subject of International Trusteeship" the next day—May 15. The committee voted unanimously to make it the basis for further discussion. Two days later the Chinese and British delegates locked horns once again on the use of the word "independence." Stassen quickly intervened:

> It is our basic and general position that the Charter that we draft at San Francisco cannot successfully have a hope of attaining the great objectives for which we meet, the objectives of future peace and security and advancement and welfare, the objectives for which millions of people throughout the world are looking for accomplishment, unless it can start out, as we conclude our work in San Francisco, with the solid and combined support of the five major powers and of the maximum number of the other United Nations . . . We must seek the maximum area of agreement.[29]

He was characteristically searching for some sort of middle ground. Stassen only objected to the use of the word "independence" if its inclusion meant that the British and French would refuse to sign the charter. He was sympathetic to the pleas of smaller nations, but when push came to shove he did not want to see the entire United Nations derailed by a single word. He emphasized his point:

> Now then we have before us the proposal that we add some additional language, language which in different countries means different things . . . I say that on this direct basis, that we should not go beyond where the five Powers can agree on the things that should go in the Charter . . . nor should we go beyond the places where the majority of the other United Nations can agree. If we go beyond, then we draw a paper that will not have breathed into it the life of ratification and support and future use that will mean the real welfare and security and peace of the world.[30]

Representatives from several small nations, including Iraq, praised Stassen for his eloquence and then insisted on proceeding with the Chinese amendment anyway. Chairman Fraser, sensing that the committee had reached an impasse, directed delegates from the United States, China, Australia, the Soviet Union, and Britain to get together and work out exactly what was meant by the term "self-government" so that they could get to the bottom of the "independence" issue.

While other committees hammered out agreements on the use of the veto by permanent members of the Security Council, regional arrangements, an International Court of Justice, and the role of the UN secretariat, among other important issues, Stassen's committee continued to flounder. On May 31 another delegate from the Philippines took issue with the original language proposed by Great Britain in Chapter XI, Article 73, Section A of the charter, which began with "State members of the United Nations which have responsibilities for the administration of territories inhabited by people not yet able to stand by themselves." Carlos Romulo, a Filipino writer, soldier, and diplomat, questioned the meaning of the phrase. When Lord Cranborne of Great Britain suggested that it was quite obvious, Romulo begged to differ, saying, "I wonder if it is. I wonder if that doesn't mean ability to protect themselves. That is the way I interpret it. Perhaps my English is very poor. If that is the interpretation, how many nations during this world holocaust would have been able to stand by themselves without the aid of other nations?" Romulo's position was unassailable given the current state of global affairs, and everyone at the committee meeting realized it. Lord Cranborne did not know how to respond, and the debate ended abruptly. Stassen had been watching the exchange intently. He grabbed a piece of paper, scribbled a few words in pencil, and sent the note over to where Romulo was sitting. The message said, "Congratulations. We are proud of you." The original British wording never made it into the final UN Charter.[31]

But the fight raged on over the use of the word "independence." The delegate from Iraq weighed in with a passionate defense of what he phrased "Wilsonian principles and the Atlantic Charter," declaring,

> When we speak of equality, it should be for all. When we speak of independence, it should be for all. When we speak of the right of self-determination, it should be for all. Unless we leave this Conference with that view of universality, with that view of brotherhood, unless we practice that, the world will continue to suffer from pains and agonies, and wars will succeed one after the other . . . We see, Mr. Chairman, this Charter lacks greatly giving people some channel, some way of expressing their own feelings, their own rights, or participating in self-determination. The words we have are all weak and vague. We want clarity, Sir. We want definiteness.[32]

The committee on trusteeship convened for its twelfth session on the afternoon of June 1. Stassen presented his fellow delegates with wording he hoped would garner their collective support. He and his assistants had worked most of the previous night trying to craft language that satisfied all of the nations present. They essentially pursued the middle way. In Article 73 the Americans formally declared the UN's responsibility "to develop self-government, to take due account of the political aspirations of the peoples, and to assist them in the progressive development of their free political institutions." And then to meet the persistent demands of the Chinese and many of the smaller nations, they revised Section B of Article 76 (which covers the basic objectives of the trusteeship system) to read as follows: "to promote the political, economic, social, and educational advancement of the inhabitants of the trust territories, and their progressive development towards self-government or independence as may be appropriate to the particular circumstances of each territory and its peoples concerned, and as may be provided by the terms of each trusteeship agreement."[33]

The delegates accepted Stassen's revisions and several members went out of their way to praise his efforts. Carlos Romulo of the Philippines thanked "Commander Stassen to whom we owe so much for his patience and tact and skill in drafting, redrafting this working paper." And then, in a gesture that no doubt would have thrilled Harry Truman, Romulo quoted Alfred, Lord Tennyson by rejoicing, "The old order changeth, yielding place to new, and God fulfills himself in many ways, lest one good custom should corrupt the world."[34]

Stassen thanked his colleagues and insisted that many people had a hand in forming the final document on trusteeship. He referred to his role in the process as "a distinct honor" and said he hoped that "our document will live and will mean progress for the peoples of the world, including particularly those peoples who have not reached the stage where they can be directly represented at the United Nations Council table." That statement was greeted with applause. But perhaps the most gratifying note of praise came from the committee's chairman, Peter Fraser of New Zealand, who said,

I pay tribute—of course I hope to do it in public—to Commander Stassen's handling of this program—on this paper I mean. You talk about all the other committees. They had brick, they had clay and straw; they had all the materials. We had none. The children of Israel's task was small compared to ours. We had no guidance. We had a blank sheet of paper, and I think the

U.S. Secretary of State Edward Stettinius signs the UN Charter at a ceremony
held at the San Francisco War Memorial Opera House on June 26, 1945. President
Harry S. Truman stands at left; Stassen, the tallest man on the stage, looks on.

> method we adopted, that was to place the job, just like a bill in Parliament
> or Congress, in the hands of one man, I think that has been amply fulfilled,
> and the example of cooperation with him we have had is one of the most
> inspiring things about the conference and one of the best organs for the
> future of the conference.[35]

~

On June 26, 1945, President Harry S. Truman joined the American delegation to officially sign the United Nations Charter. "History will honor
you," he told a crowd of 3,500 people packed into the San Francisco Opera
House. This charter means, he explained, that "we all have to recognize—
no matter how great our strength—that we must deny ourselves the license
to do always as we please . . . This is the price which each nation will have
to pay for world peace." John Foster Dulles, serving as an advisor to the U.S.
delegation, enthusiastically declared, "I believe it can be a greater Magna
Carta." And Senator Arthur Vandenberg told the press, "In my opinion, our

intelligent American self-interest indispensably requires our loyal coopera-tion in this great adventure to stop World War III before it starts."[36]

As Commander Stassen prepared to rejoin Admiral Halsey in the Pacific, he could afford to bask briefly in the glory of a job well done. He had helped to accomplish what many people thought was impossible. The United Nations was a reality at last, and Harold Stassen had played a major role in bringing it to fruition. It may have pleased him to learn that a *Newsweek* poll of foreign correspondents queried at the end of the conference had ranked him as one of two delegates who had the greatest impact on developing the final text of the UN Charter. Even the folks back at home in Minnesota knew how hard Harold had been fighting to win the peace. The *Winthrop News,* published two counties over from William Stassen's farm, proudly announced, "It is little wonder that news men and others attending the con-ference from all over the world look to Harold Stassen as one of the great men of the day and whose star has but begun to shine."[37]

7 A Rare Bird

There was a two-year stretch leading up to the 1948 presidential election when Harold Stassen didn't just make the news, he *was* the news. His image graced the cover of every major news magazine in the country—*Time, Life, Look,* and *Newsweek*. They carried feature stories with titles like "The Case for STASSEN," and "The Man from Minnesota," and "Can STASSEN Win?" and "Stassen: Hard Work + Courage = Votes." The leading political columnists of the day closely monitored his speeches and travels as he began to look more and more like presidential timber. Joseph and Stewart Alsop wrote about him regularly. So did Walter Winchell and Arthur Krock. Drew Pearson lauded him for having "the courage to take a stand on almost everything" while "other candidates were being coy." Roscoe Drummond, writing for *Life* magazine, called Stassen a "careful, feet-on-the-ground internationalist" and offered this stunning appraisal during the run up to the 1948 Republican National Convention: "The plain fact is that Stassen's *total* experience excels that of any one of his opponents." He was an honest-to-goodness contender for the highest office in the land (or any land, for that matter, given American hegemony in the immediate aftermath of World War II).[1]

But it wasn't just political pundits for whom Stassen's name resonated. He was beginning to enter the nation's lexicon though not yet as a punch line unto his own. That would come much later. For the time being even Hollywood couldn't resist making the most of Harold Stassen's popularity. In the April 19, 1948, issue of *Newsweek* magazine, the one with Stassen on the cover, a new film by Frank Capra was featured as the picture of the month. Based upon a wildly popular and Pulitzer Prize–winning play by Howard

TIME

THE WEEKLY NEWSMAGAZINE

Boris Chaliapin

PRESIDENTIAL CANDIDATE HAROLD STASSEN
"If we are right, we will win."

Stassen on the cover of *Time* magazine, August 25, 1947

Lindsay and Russel Crouse, *State of the Union* was scheduled to hit theaters nationwide the very next day. Reviewers at *Newsweek* lavished the film with praise, writing "it emerges as about the most exciting movie ever made, as topical as today's newspaper, as comical as a circus with a plot, as intensely romantic as the elopement of a beautiful couple." Featuring an all-star cast (Spencer Tracy, Katharine Hepburn, Van Johnson, Angela Lansbury, and Adolphe Menjou), *State of the Union* pokes fun at professional politicos while honoring the undeniable durability of America's democratic traditions. When self-made business tycoon Grant Matthews, played by Tracy, decides to make a bid for the presidency, he is caught between the idealism of his adoring wife (Hepburn) and the cold, calculating ambition of an alluring newspaper heiress (Lansbury). Director Capra pulled no punches in mocking the nomination process and later acknowledged that it carried little risk given his audience. He wrote, "The great majority of Americans (Republicans and Democrats), whose politics lie in the middle of the broad political spectrum, will laugh at political lampoonery if the lampooning is even-handed. However, the closer their political hue shifts toward either end of the spectrum, the more they lose their sense of humor. Those at the extreme ends—Communists or Fascists—never laugh. They can't." Capra clearly understood the middle way as well.[2]

Stassen is mentioned frequently in the film because, of course, he was in reality considered one of the very few odds-on favorites for the Republican nomination in 1948. Van Johnson's character draws a clear distinction between businessman Grant Matthews and "the Tafts and Deweys and Stassens and Vandenbergs" who collectively represent the party establishment. And when Matthews arrives in Detroit to deliver an important speech, a newsman fishing for a scoop asks, "Is it true you're seeing Governor Stassen here?" Just six months earlier, real-life editors at *United States News* (later *US News and World Report*) wrote, "Mr. Stassen's stock is rising. Important Eastern Republicans are giving him a reappraisal. He is strong among young Republicans. He has a large following among veterans, backed by his own war-service record . . . In several States, Mr. Stassen is falling heir to remnants of the following of the late Wendell Willkie.[3]*

* The timing of that report and the subsequent release of *State of the Union* takes on an even more interesting twist when one adds another piece of information into the mix. Howard Lindsay and Russel Crouse cowrote the original play in 1945. It was a poorly kept secret at the time that the story's inspiration came from businessman Wendell Willkie's 1940 run for the White House and his extramarital

Perhaps the most telling exchange in the entire picture takes place between Grant Matthews and a big-time political conniver by the name of Jim Conover, played by Adolphe Menjou. Conover, the archetypical machine boss, tries to enlighten the politically naïve Matthews with a harsh dose of reality: "You're not nominated by the people; you're nominated by the politicians! Why? Because the people are too darn lazy to vote in the primaries." Undaunted, Matthews fires back, "Nomination or no nomination, they've got to know where I stand before they vote for me!" Coincidently or not, Stassen titled his 1947 book-length political tract *Where I Stand* and began with this bold proclamation: "I believe in frankness, and thus it was when the American press asked me pointedly whether I intended to be in the race for the Republican nomination for President, I answered directly, 'Yes, I do.' In the same spirit and with a candid statement that my views are subject to continuing study and future public adjustment in the light of new facts, I present with humility *Where I Stand.*"[4]

Harold Stassen's hat was definitely in the ring. He set out to prove in 1948, among other things, that presidential primaries could ultimately determine the future of American elections (they do) even if said achievement came at the expense of his own political fortunes (it did). In tracing the arc of Stassen's political journey after World War II, it is particularly useful to remember that among the many innovations we attribute to the ancient Greeks are democracy, tragedy, and comedy. Stassen's perennial runs for office would eventually and at various times come to embody those same three elements. Occasionally they occurred simultaneously.

~

When he returned to Minnesota after the war, Stassen conferred with several friends and associates before determining his next move. He would, of course, get back into politics; the question was when and where. Conventional wisdom suggested that a U.S. Senate seat was virtually his for the taking, particularly given his wartime experience and internationalist outlook. Senator Henrik Shipstead, Minnesota's elder statesman and one-time-Farmer-Laborite-turned-Republican, was up for reelection in November of 1946, and many considered him out of step with the nation's shifting foreign policy. In late July of 1945, while Stassen was drawing up preliminary plans

---

affair with a prominent New York newspaper editor named Irita Van Doren. The play premiered on Broadway in November of 1945, a year after Willkie's death and apparently beyond the reasonable bounds of recrimination.

Former governor Harold Stassen signing his book, *Where I Stand,* in
Minneapolis on November 13, 1947

to rescue Allied POWs in Japan, Senator Shipstead voted against ratification
of the United Nations Charter. Only one other senator, William Langer of
North Dakota, joined him in doing so. Their votes constituted a stunning
though ultimately meaningless repudiation of everything Stassen and the
other American delegates had worked so hard to achieve in San Francisco.
Justifying his position, Shipstead asked his colleagues in the Senate, "Have
we, through our diplomacy and our participation in international politics,
become so enmeshed that it is now impossible for us to maintain our political independence on a basis of justice and peace, or are we now at the end
of our rope as an independent nation?" It was the same old boogeyman that
isolationists, particularly those in the Midwest, had been using to garner
votes for the better part of four decades. By 1946 most Americans were having none of it. Ever steadfast in his conviction that America could still stand
alone, the senior senator from Minnesota would by year's end discover that
that ship had sailed.[5]

Harold Stassen quickly ruled out a run for the U.S. Senate, deferring to
his colleague Ed Thye, who had succeeded him as governor in 1943 and then

easily won reelection in 1944. Thye begged off, encouraging his old friend to challenge Shipstead in the primary himself and then coast to victory in November's general election. But Stassen could not be moved, explaining that his "talents are as an administrator, not a legislator." Stassen's detractors questioned his motives at the outset and continued for years to characterize his decision not to pursue the Senate as proof positive of his blinding ambition to be president. Even Ed Thye called it a "great mistake" at the time, the meaning of which took on that much more significance when two brand-new congressmen from the class of '46—John Kennedy and Richard Nixon—eventually went on to occupy seats in both the Senate and the White House. Stassen however, according to historian Barbara Stuhler, "thought he could better prepare himself for high office by improving his qualifications, especially in international affairs, through extended travel abroad."[6]

Motives are as difficult to nail down in the present as in the past, so the truth of what ultimately determined Stassen's course of action in 1946 probably lies somewhere between these two theories. But Harold Stassen's abiding passion and purpose continued to be, as it had been since his college days, working for world peace. Helping form the United Nations was just the beginning, and Stassen clearly understood this undeniable fact: senators do not make foreign policy; they approve or reject it. Only presidents possess the power and influence and creativity to link domestic policy with the elusive but all-important task of establishing lasting peace among nations, especially in the atomic age. So Senator Thye went to Washington in 1947 (he bested Shipstead in the primary election and then won easily in November), and Mr. Stassen traveled the world, later writing, "My journeys through fifteen war-torn countries earlier this year made it clear to me that the peace of the world and the very hope of mankind now depend primarily on the success of the American economic system at home."[7]

Stassen was not the only one who believed that talking to the Russians and their allies in Eastern Europe held the greatest promise for peace. David Lawrence, publisher and editor of the *United States News,* wrote an editorial entitled "It's Not Too Late" in October of 1947. Sounding much like candidate Stassen, the usually conservative Lawrence declared, "It is never too late for a man or a nation with a righteous cause to submit such a cause and the whole record to public scrutiny." If the intense rhetoric being lobbed back and forth between the United States and the Soviet Union could be replaced by civil discourse, Lawrence theorized that "there will be an era of unexampled peace." "The solution of today's crisis," he concluded, "depends on America's capacity to exercise the common sense of old-fashioned diplomacy—something to which Russia will respond because she can gain more that way than by any other. So will America." Harold Stassen expressed a very similar notion after meeting with and talking directly to Joseph Stalin in Moscow. "I believe that peace and co-operation between Russia and the United States are possible," Stassen wrote. "For all our differences, our grave mutual suspicions, war is not inevitable."[8]

Unfortunately, events in 1947 and the interpretations that followed them did not support such lofty optimism. The term "Cold War" was coined in April of that year (American financier and presidential advisor Bernard Baruch first used it), and the proverbial "Iron Curtain" was proving every bit as menacing as Winston Churchill had predicted one year earlier. It appeared as though the conciliatory measures that had sustained the great wartime alliance between the Americans and the Russians were giving way to confrontation with increasing frequency and friction. By the time George Kennan offered his essay entitled "The Sources of Soviet Conduct" for public consumption in the summer of 1947, President Truman and the State Department had already had over a year to review its contents and begin shaping American foreign policy accordingly. In his capacity as a diplomat and an astute observer of the Soviet Union since the 1930s, Kennan provided unique insight into the machinations of Russia's political leaders. He became convinced in the years following World War II that Stalin's unwillingness to cooperate with the West had more to do with the Soviet leader's image at home than his fear of threats from abroad. In other words, Kennan suggested that "the dictator needed to portray the West as evil in order to justify his own control over the Russian people." According to Stalin's view of the world, force was rewarded whenever and wherever it encountered weakness. The rule applied equally to both interpersonal and international relations. How then should America deal with the growing threat of Soviet militarism? The logical thing to do, Kennan hypothesized, was to "contain" or present a "counterforce" to all forms of Soviet aggrandizement. War had the potential to destroy the Soviet Union in 1947, and Stalin knew it. However, the gearing up for possible war with the West and the constant vigilance that accompanies such preparations made Stalin and his police state virtually indispensable.[9]

Kennan's analysis of Soviet-American relations could not have come at a more auspicious time. President Truman and his national security advisors grappled with several developing crises in Europe at that very moment.

The specter of communist takeovers in Greece and Turkey loomed large in 1947 as the British more or less passed the torch of global leadership to their American cousins. The cynics portrayed it more like leaving the United States holding the bag, but the result was the same in either case. The United States alone had the influence—militarily, economically, and morally—to stem the tide of communist expansion. The only real question was how to do it. Kennan's rational approach to the problem (i.e., Stalin *acts* like he wants to go to war even though he knows that actual war is clearly not in his nation's best interest) provided the Truman foreign policy team with the seemingly perfect solution—match the Soviet challenge step for step until Stalin comes to the conclusion that appeasement will never be an option for America. Wasn't that, after all, the great lesson of the late war? Never again would the Allies make the Munich mistake. Military preparedness and immense amounts of foreign economic aid—the likes of which culminated in the Marshall Plan one year later—represented a major departure from traditional American policy. Sensing that his fellow countrymen would rise to the challenge if they knew how high the stakes were, Truman implored the nation, "I believe that we have reached the point at which the position of the United States should be made unmistakably clear . . . There are times in world history when it is far wiser to act than to hesitate . . . We must be prepared to pay the price for peace, or assuredly we shall pay the price of war."[10]

There is an oft-repeated anecdote from those days that involves Harry Truman meeting privately with a few key members of Congress to seek their support for his get-tough policy with the Soviets. Truman and representatives from the State Department made their best pitch for sending millions of dollars in economic and military aid to anti-communists in Greece and Turkey. And that would likely be only a beginning. The legislators were noticeably skeptical. Undersecretary of State Dean Acheson pointed to a giant map on the wall and offered a metaphor regarding one rotten apple ruining every other apple in the barrel, a more organic but no less effective version of the as-yet undeveloped domino theory. According to one telling of the story, an awkward silence followed Acheson's presentation until Republican Arthur Vandenberg, chairman of the Senate Foreign Relations Committee, turned to President Truman and said, "Mr. President, if you will say that to Congress and the country, I will support you and I believe that most of its members will do the same." Another account of that meeting has Senator Vandenberg approaching Truman on his way out the door and remarking, "Mr. President, if that's what you want, there is only one way to get it. That is to make a personal appearance before Congress and scare the hell out of the country."[11]

No one who participated in the conference remains alive to set the record straight. But regardless of the exact words that were used to convey the sense of urgency surrounding the proceedings, Truman's subsequent actions are proof enough of Vandenberg's influence. Just a few days later, on March 12, 1947, the president stood before a joint session of Congress and declared in part, "I believe that it must be the policy of the United States to support free peoples who are resisting attempted subjugation by armed minorities or by outside pressures . . . In helping free and independent nations to maintain their freedom, the United States will be giving effect to the principles of the Charter of the United Nations." Thus the Truman Doctrine was born, at least in theory. Paying for it and putting the idea into practice would prove easier said than done. Despite Vandenberg's pledge of support, many conservative members of Congress were of the opinion that charity begins—and ends—at home. Representative Harold Knutson of Minnesota, who shared a first name with Stassen and little else, typified the opposition when he said, "I guess the do-gooders won't feel right until they have us all broke."[12]

Truman found himself in a quandary, and what happened next represents one of the greatest ironies in American history. By attempting to prepare the nation for the types of sacrifices one expects in wartime (i.e., massive outpourings of money, materiel, and perhaps even men), Truman was asking Americans to support an unprecedented policy designed to *prevent* war. But the ironical part did not end there. While ostensibly pursuing the defense of our most cherished ideals at home and abroad (i.e., liberty, opportunity, due process, and equal justice under the law), the Truman administration initiated a campaign to identify potential subversives in the United States, an effort that quickly, if inadvertently, took on a life of its own and made a mockery of the Constitution.

The first indicator came just nine days after President Truman addressed Congress regarding the crises brewing in Greece and Turkey. On March 21, 1947, he issued Executive Order No. 9835, which laid the foundation for "an elaborate Federal Employees Loyalty and Security Program." Truman launched the program to counter congressional claims that the federal government was harboring Communists. Members of the House Committee on Un-American Activities (HUAC), including first-term representative Richard Nixon (R-California), had already begun investigating alleged communist

Young Stassen supporters in Minnesota, 1947

infiltration of Hollywood, and they were about to set their sights on the U.S. State Department. With a presidential election year fast approaching, Truman essentially took their bait, hoping to deflect a campaign issue that already had some conservatives foaming at the mouth. At first glance it appeared to have worked. A reporter for *Time* observed that the president's "order to root out subversives from government employment hit a solid note with Congress, and further pulled the rug out from under his political detractors. The charge of 'Communists in government' and nothing being done about it, a favorite theme of the reactionaries, simply will not stick any longer." As Harold Stassen and the rest of the country were about to find out, nothing could have been further from the truth.[13]

By the fall of 1947, Stassen's campaign for the Republican presidential nomination was already in full swing. He was setting a swift pace early in the race and causing his competitors—most notably Thomas Dewey and Robert Taft—to get working on their campaigns far ahead of their intended timetables. In September Stassen met with James Forrestal, Truman's newly appointed secretary of defense. According to Forrestal's notes, Stassen suggested that "his tactics of discussing the issues of the day had forced both of his opponents into an earlier discussion of central issues than they had planned or wanted." Stassen then offered a remarkably progressive view of American foreign policy. "With regard to Europe," Forrestal wrote, "he felt that the country was ahead of Washington in its willingness to support a strong and constructive policy in Europe, but that more leadership and more facts needed to be given. The country would support the implementation of our Greek policy even to the extent of sending troops." Forrestal left no indication of whether or not he agreed with Mr. Stassen's rather rosy assessment of public opinion. The Truman administration was taking nothing for granted.[14]

That Stassen had his finger on the pulse of the nation in 1947 is debatable. Republican delegates meeting in Philadelphia the following summer to award the nomination would have much to say on that subject, but until then Stassen was in it to win it, and his "prodigious endeavors" to garner supporters never wavered. "Thus, in twenty-one months," *Time* declared, "the U.S. had almost daily opportunity to study Harold Stassen, the freewheeling political phenomenon, his plans, his thinking, his reaction to the crisis of the post-war world." That his efforts began to pay huge dividends in 1948 is beyond dispute. Journalist Irwin Ross, who covered the presidential campaign from start to finish, contends that "it was one of the many ironies of 1948 that Harold Stassen's candidacy was initially not taken seriously by his opponents." Author Jules Abels, writing ten years after the events in question, was even blunter. "The struggle for the [Republican] nomination is, in essence," Abels observed, "the chronicle of the rise and fall of Harold Stassen. This introduces the first 'if' of many in the 1948 story, since it is widely believed in the Republican Party that if Stassen had been nominated, he would have been elected." By the time Dewey and Taft got around to taking Harold Stassen's candidacy for what it was—one man's relentless crusade "to prove that his rhetoric moved the voters as well as headline writers"—they were no longer the clear front-runners. Stassen had become the man to beat, in spite of what the party establishment wanted to believe.[15]

It did not occur overnight. Stassen's strategy was calculated and forward thinking, and it addressed a fundamental problem facing Republicans then and now: that their appeal must reach beyond traditional Republican ranks

Robert Taft's entry into the crowded primary field, as viewed by cartoonist
Clifford Berryman of the *Washington Star* (October 23, 1947)

to win. It was the same approach Harold Stassen took in all five elections
that he had entered—and won—in Minnesota dating back to 1930. It was
what had inspired him to help create the Young Republican League and
then capitalize upon its growth to reclaim the political center of gravity
in his home state a decade earlier. Indeed, it was what prompted him to
proclaim to his fellow Republicans, "We must never permit the left wing
to claim a monopoly on humanitarianism." And given what eventually happened in the 1948 presidential election, no politician has perhaps ever been
more right. As syndicated columnist Roscoe Drummond put it in a feature
story for *Life* magazine dated March 1, 1948, "The Republican party must
nominate an electable as well as a capable presidential candidate. Stassen
supporters believe that his prospects of winning are better than those of

the other candidates. The pre-eminent reason is that Stassen has shown that he has a compelling appeal to the nonparty or independent voter. The independent vote, which the Republican party has lost in every presidential election since 1928, is obviously indispensable to a Republican victory. Only a few diehard Old Guardsmen now fail to see this."[16]

Come April, Stassen jumped out of the gate quickly, racking up impressive wins in three of the four earliest primaries and securing a considerable number of convention delegates. He struck first in neighboring Wisconsin, where his herculean efforts to drum up support set the tone for his entire campaign. As Irwin Ross put it with masterfully metaphorical flourish, "he cultivated Wisconsin with the assiduity of a Fuller Brush man canvassing a high-rise apartment house." Stassen visited the Badger state ten times in the run-up to the election, making speeches, taking questions, and shaking hands with voters from one end of the state to the other. He was energized by direct, candid discussions with the folks he encountered along the way and vice versa. Stassen was in effect integrating personal politics into the primary system to a degree that had never been done before. And it was working. On April 6 Stassen stunned the political prognosticators by besting all of his opponents and winning 19 of the 27 available delegates. The man who had been heavily favored to win—General Douglas MacArthur, who attended high school in Milwaukee—secured the other eight delegates, but the humiliating loss signaled the coming end of his presidential campaign. New York governor Thomas Dewey had the most disappointing showing of all in Wisconsin. He arrived late in the game, carried out a dignified campaign lasting all of two days, and when the final votes were tallied did not have a single delegate to show for his efforts. The *New York Herald-Tribune* summed up the election two days later: "The former three-time Minnesota Governor is no longer a dark horse. All at once Mr. Stassen has emerged from the fringe of interesting possibility. From now on he is in the first division of contenders for the Republican Presidential nomination."[17]

On April 13, which happened to be his forty-first birthday, Stassen made front-page headlines again when he out-polled six other candidates in Nebraska's primary election. This time he did it by helping produce a record turnout and garnering 43 percent of the total votes cast. MacArthur was now all but out of the running, and the leading contenders like Thomas Dewey and Robert Taft were reeling from such highly publicized defeats. Two weeks later Stassen mounted a last-minute write-in campaign in the Pennsylvania primary and was rewarded with seventy-four thousand votes—roughly a

A plea from the Republican Party during the Nebraska primary, as viewed by cartoonist Clifford Berryman of the *Washington Star* (April 13, 1948)

third of the ballots cast. That he once again bested Dewey of New York and Taft of Ohio, whose respective states shared borders with Pennsylvania, was hardly lost on political observers. In late April *Business Week* led off its Washington news pages with a stunning prediction: "Your Next President: Harold Stassen. Two months before Philadelphia, six months before election day, it looks as if you can say that."[18]

Other reputable sources were about to make similar pronouncements. Richard Wilson, head of *Look* magazine's Washington Bureau, wrote that the Republican Party's established leaders were making a huge mistake by writing off Stassen "as an ambitious kid who wouldn't cause trouble" in the nomination process. "In the late spring," Wilson continued, "the leaders awoke from this dream to discover that Stassen, once only the nation's most youthful governor, had become a grown man, with a fine war record. More important, he enjoyed the closest association with grass-roots politicians ever developed by a Presidential candidate." Wilson's assessment was undoubtedly true, particularly when it came to pinpointing the party establishment's intense distrust of Stassen, which dated back to the Republican Convention of 1940. Party leaders never forgave Stassen for his act of betrayal that led to Willkie's nomination. That the people had wanted Willkie was beside the point. As a party outsider, Willkie was unconventional and untested and therefore beyond the sway of Republican leaders. That Stassen had played such a critical role in bringing Willkie to the fore eight years earlier only added to their hostility. And now that Stassen's primary victories appeared to be coming from voters to whom Willkie had previously appealed, the gloves were about to come off. As Wilson put it, "They resolved in 1940, after Wendell L. Willkie was beaten by Roosevelt, that never again would an outsider capture the fruits for which the leaders had worked." Stassen's relentless and forthright campaigning might have made him a frontrunner, but to the party elite he would always remain an unwelcome outlier.[19]

In May of 1948, with the nominating convention just weeks away, Harold Stassen made a series of mistakes that played right into his opponents' hands. His first blunder came in Ohio, where Stassen chose to challenge Robert Taft on the senator's home turf. The move was audacious, "for there had long been an unwritten rule in Presidential politics that a candidate's status as 'favorite son' should not be threatened by outsiders." Stassen would need a big win to offset the damage caused by such a blatant breach of tradition. To make matters worse, Taft repeatedly called on Stassen to explain where he stood on a number of important issues. Stassen's 1947 treatise, *Where I Stand*, seemed uninspired and pedestrian when viewed through the lens of a bare-knuckled political campaign. One reviewer had described Stassen's position on most matters discussed in his book as "more than nothing but less than something." Now he was being called to account by Bob Taft— Mr. Republican himself—who had been in the U.S. Senate for nearly ten years and had an extensive voting record to show for it. Suddenly Stassen was on the defensive. On May 4 Ohioans went to the polls and, as expected, more than half of them voted for Taft. Stassen won nine of the twenty-three delegate seats that he had contested (Ohio had fifty-three delegates in all), but he also managed to further alienate conservatives in the Republican

Party who found his self-described liberalism repugnant. Attention shifted to Oregon, where Stassen's express train to the nomination ran off the rails once and for all.[20]

~

The turning point in the 1948 Republican presidential primaries came on Monday, May 17. The forty to sixty million listeners who tuned in to a nationwide broadcast that evening had no way of knowing that they were about to make radio history. But then again neither did the two men they anxiously waited to hear. History unfolded in dramatic fashion on this particular night and then, as if to assure its rightful place in the ranks of radio legend, it was folded up again quickly and neatly and all but forgotten by the American public. Until now, that is.

That night's program would by most estimates attract the single largest national radio audience to date—a fact that might have thrilled Tom Swafford if only he could spare a few seconds to think about it. At the moment, however, he was producing the most important broadcast of his career, and there was no time to congratulate himself. Swafford, program director at KEX in Portland, Oregon, had helped think up this whole thing, and now, as he sat in the radio station's control room, he no doubt shared in the listening public's anticipation. At exactly 6 PM Pacific time, Swafford pointed his left forefinger to veteran announcer Sherman Washburn, whose smooth voice projected the professional tone and quiet confidence that characterized American radio in the 1940s. Washburn began, "You are about to hear a debate between Governor Thomas E. Dewey and Harold E. Stassen—candidates for the Republican nomination to the Presidency of the United States. They will be introduced by the chairman of the Multnomah County Republican Central Committee, Mr. Donald R. Van Boskirk of Portland, who is acting as moderator for tonight's broadcast. Now, Mr. Van Boskirk . . ."[21]

If Tom Dewey had stuck to his first instincts, this night never would have come to pass. He told his assistant Paul Lockwood that he wasn't interested in debating Stassen in Oregon, or anywhere for that matter. But Thomas Dewey was not comfortable playing the role of underdog in a political fight, especially among fellow Republicans, and that's exactly where he found himself in the spring of 1948. Despite being the GOP's standard-bearer during the last presidential election, Dewey—along with several other prominent Republican hopefuls—was still reeling from Harold Stassen's early and decisive primary victories in Wisconsin, Nebraska, and Pennsylvania. When Governor Dewey arrived in Oregon just three weeks before the primary, he quickly announced that he "was tired of losing elections by default" and that he would "stop Stassen" then and there.[22]

Tom Swafford also sensed the growing importance of Oregon's primary, scheduled for Friday, May 21. Years later he recalled what it felt like to be inundated with "politics around the clock" in May of 1948. "I spent much of that month bucketing around Oregon in DC-3s," Swafford wrote. "I can't say I got to know either of the candidates, but I did spend a lot of time with them both, usually in some place like a locker room at a high school gym, waiting for broadcast time. And I would hear the speech, from either Dewey or Stassen, night after night."[23]

Swafford was therefore well acquainted with each man's political philosophies and rhetorical skills. He knew their positions on the issues that had come to define the campaign thus far, and he had even spoken in person with both Dewey and Stassen when negotiations over the debate's format reached an impasse. There was a lot riding on this evening's debate, nobody denied that, and it was not just voters on the West Coast who could feel the pressure mounting as Friday's election drew near. Page one of the morning's *New York Times* announced PRESIDENCY RIVALS FACE DECISIVE TEST IN OREGON PRIMARY. Political correspondent James A. Hagerty (father of James C. Hagerty, Governor Dewey's press secretary) reminded readers that the contest came "just one month before the convention opens in Philadelphia. Unlike preferential primaries in other states, the vote in Oregon is binding and defeat could be a serious setback for either [Stassen or Dewey] in his candidacy for the Presidential nomination." But as Chairman Van Boskirk introduced the candidates, simply knowing how high the stakes were could not have fully prepared Tom Swafford—not to mention the millions of Americans who were listening in—for the dramatic scene that was about to take place. Van Boskirk began: "Good evening, Ladies and Gentlemen. For the past few weeks Oregonians have been participating in a red-hot political campaign between Governor Thomas E. Dewey of New York and former Governor Harold E. Stassen of Minnesota. As the campaign has progressed it appears that the primary issue on which these candidates are diametrically opposed is: Should the Communist Party in the United States be outlawed?"[24]

Dewey agreed to the debate on three conditions. First, he nixed the original plan of broadcasting the exchange with Stassen from the Portland Civic Auditorium in front of nearly five thousand people. Acknowledging Stassen's popular appeal, Dewey's staff "derided the proposal as a circus stunt, which would subject their candidate to unseemly heckling and perhaps booing." According to Swafford, "Dewey insisted that there be no audience, that it be done in a radio station." The fifty-plus reporters and photographers who packed themselves into station KEX's studio could safely cover the debate without tipping the scales in favor of one candidate over the other.[25]

Thomas Dewey had another compelling reason to avoid sharing a stage with Harold Stassen. At five feet eight inches, the larger-than-life governor of New York looked downright puny next to the six-foot-three, two-hundred-and-twenty-pound Stassen. Tom Dewey must have felt a bit like Stephen Douglas sizing up the prospects of a debate with Abraham Lincoln in 1858. Dewey's supporters thought his physical appearance projected the professionalism and shrewdness of a tough, battle-hardened district attorney, which of course he was. But some observers criticized his trademark mustache and stern demeanor. He aspired, after all, to become president of the United States, and charisma was not his strong suit. Alice Roosevelt Longworth, Teddy's eldest and frequently caustic daughter, quipped that when she saw Dewey she couldn't help thinking of "the little man on top of the wedding cake." (That's the same Alice Longworth, incidentally, who opposed nominating Dewey for a second run at the White House on the principle that "you can't make a *soufflé* rise twice.")[26]

A radio broadcast clearly favored Dewey under these circumstances, but the medium had not always worked to his advantage. Four years and one presidential campaign earlier, Franklin Roosevelt had outwitted Dewey, thus demonstrating the president's mastery of the airwaves. One evening in 1944, Roosevelt reserved time for a quarter-hour radio address on the National Broadcasting Company network. Dewey purchased the following fifteen minutes on NBC to tap into President Roosevelt's large listening audience for his reply. Roosevelt spoke for exactly fourteen minutes and then left sixty seconds of paid air time in dead silence after his remarks. It must have felt like an eternity to folks tuned in across the country who anxiously fiddled with their radio dials, searching for sounds on other wavelengths. Unfortunately for Dewey, millions of listeners found other stations as they twiddled and were simply not there when the Republican candidate came on the air to speak.[27]

Thomas Dewey could rest assured that nothing like what happened in 1944 would occur this evening. In addition to dictating the format of the debate, Dewey demanded that the entire discussion be limited to the question of whether or not the Communist Party should be outlawed in America. Looking back on that era, it is difficult to imagine a more controversial topic in 1948, but Harold Stassen, still flush from his earlier primary victories and recent polling data, exuded confidence. (A May 14 Gallup Poll tracking favored candidates among Republican voters nationwide put Stassen at 37 percent and Dewey at 24 percent. Reacting to Stassen's stunning victory in Nebraska a month earlier, syndicated columnist Joseph Alsop wrote, "If Stassen's onward march continues through the next primaries, a very great number of Republican professionals, herding delegates with the peevish ferocity of aging collie dogs, are going to be needed to stop the Minnesota former Governor at Philadelphia.")[28]

Few pleasantries were exchanged when the candidates arrived and posed for some quick photographs before assuming their assigned places for the broadcast. The brief, cordial conversation went something like this:

STASSEN: *Good evening, Tom. We've certainly stirred up a lot of interest.*
DEWEY (laughing): *We sure did.*
STASSEN: *We've both seen a lot of Oregon.*
DEWEY: *We sure have.*[29]

Stassen grinned wide for the cameras, but according to Swafford "it was obvious that Dewey wasn't eager to have their meeting preserved on film." Judging from the uncomfortable encounter, both men were saving their smartest rhetoric for the debate itself.[30]

Harold Stassen spoke first and for the affirmative. (As a final condition, Dewey demanded that he be afforded the last word in the debate. It proved a wily maneuver on Dewey's part and one that many firsthand observers looking back on the event considered fatal for Harold Stassen's position and line of reasoning.) While Tom Swafford listened to Stassen's opening remarks, he watched Governor Dewey from the control room. Dewey "sat there, hands folded in his lap, staring off across the studio, totally composed, almost detached," Swafford reported. Dewey had done his homework and was absolutely prepared to make his case. And so he waited patiently as Harold Stassen began speaking with characteristic eloquence and conviction:

Chairman Van Boskirk—Your Excellency Governor Dewey—My Fellow Citizens—During the recent war, I saw many young Americans killed. I watched ships explode and burn, planes crash in flames, men, our men, my friends, fall. I met thousands of prisoners of war as they were liberated from indescribable conditions of imprisonment and suffering. I viewed the devastation of cities and of farms. In the midst of these experiences, I thought more deeply than ever before of the way in which men should live, of the preciousness of freedom, of the future of America. I made a quiet resolve to do everything within my power after V-J Day to keep America free and to prevent a third world war.[31]

Two minutes into his opening remarks, Stassen had yet to address the central question of the debate: "should the Communist Party in the United States be outlawed?" He was taking a most unorthodox—though hardly uncharacteristic—approach to the issue at hand. But the great multitude of his fellow citizens who had already seen and heard Harold Stassen on the campaign trail knew that his run for the White House had been anything but conventional thus far.

Since announcing his candidacy on December 17, 1946, Stassen had taken his case directly to the American people and in the process virtually redefined the rules for presidential campaigns. Just a month before the debate in Oregon, *Newsweek* announced that "Stassen had covered no less than 16,000 miles visiting 42 states" in his bid for the presidency. "By pure hard work," the story continues, "Stassen stumped the experts. He became the most indefatigable campaigner in history—making no fewer than 325 major addresses and hundreds of lesser speeches in 476 days, taking unequivocal, courageous stands on just about everything from the Communist Party (for outlawing it), to oleomargarine (for taxing it), shaking literally hundreds of thousands of hands, and mounting the stump thrice daily in crucial pre-primary states."[32]

Stassen had to admit that although Dewey arrived in Oregon late in the game, he and his staff had improvised a masterful campaign. He must have read the recent *New York Times* story suggesting "Governor Dewey has taken over lock, stock, and barrel the methods of his opponent . . . campaigning harder than Oregonians do when they run for statewide office." But even as he spoke, Stassen sensed that the momentum was still on his side, and his confidence began to get the best of him. Convinced that both history and public opinion justified his hard line regarding political subversives, he took the offensive by chiding Dewey for advocating a "soft policy toward Communists." Stassen's accusation likely referred to comments Dewey had made at a number of campaign stops just two days earlier. "In no moment of hysteria, in no moment of campaigning for votes should we ever consider outlawing the communist party," Dewey told listeners in language as prophetic as it was reasonable. "You can't shoot ideas with a gun."[33]

The die was cast. With no room to maneuver on this divisive issue—an issue that he had deliberately made central to his presidential campaign—Stassen tried to back Dewey into a corner. Based upon his recent travels around the world, which included a personal conference with Joseph Stalin in Moscow, Stassen confidently asserted that he had "reached the conclusion that the Communist organizations in the world are absolutely directed by the rulers of Russia in the Kremlin." Furthermore, he was convinced that the objectives of Communists in America and other democratic nations were "to overthrow free governments and to destroy the liberties of man." Citing the very recent communist coup in Czechoslovakia, Stassen warned, "The free countries do not now have adequate laws to safeguard themselves in the face of this menace."

Stassen's argument finally began to take form. He acknowledged the inherent dangers involved with trying to combat the subversion of democratic institutions while not trampling upon the very rights one intends to preserve. But he took aim at those for whom outlawing the Communist Party smacked of unconstitutionality. There is "no such thing as a freedom to destroy freedom," Stassen declared. There exists no "constitutional right to overthrow our government." Then he boldly defended his position by identifying the specific portion of the Constitution that made outlawing the Communist Party both necessary and proper, namely Article 4, Section 4 (frequently referred to as the Guarantee Clause), which states, "The United States shall guarantee to every State in this Union a Republican Form of Government, and shall protect each of them against Invasion; and on Application of the Legislature, or of the Executive (when the Legislature cannot be convened) against domestic Violence." Stassen was in effect arguing that Congress not only had the right but indeed the obligation to make legislation that would prevent Communists from destroying democracy in any of the forty-eight states that made up the United States of America in 1948.

It just so happened that there was at that very moment a bill addressing communist activities in America up for debate in the U.S. House of Representatives. Cosponsored by Congressmen Karl Mundt of South Dakota and Richard Nixon of California, both Republicans, the bill received considerable press coverage in the days preceding and following that night's debate. On May 11, only six days earlier, the House Committee on Un-American

Activities (HUAC) released a report containing "what it called documentary proof that the Communist party of the United States and its leaders advocated the Government's overthrow by force and violence." Committee chairman J. Parnell Thomas (R-New Jersey) added that the report "provided the most effective argument possible for passage of the Mundt-Nixon bill to curb communistic activities."[34]

Stassen decided to issue a direct challenge to Dewey by invoking the substance and intent of the Mundt-Nixon bill, a move that entirely changed Governor Dewey's strategy in the debate and eventually came back to haunt the former governor of Minnesota. Claiming, incorrectly as it turns out, that the bill definitely outlawed the Communist Party in America, Stassen asked Dewey to reconsider his opposition to the idea by remarking, in perhaps his most memorable phrase of the evening, "We must not coddle Communism with legality." And then he digressed. With a tone that most likely struck his listening audience as pedantic oration, Harold Stassen gave a hurried lecture on the origins of communism in Russia, suggesting that the Bolsheviks succeeded in 1917 precisely because the czar had not outlawed them. To further bolster his argument, Stassen added for good measure, no doubt to the delight of Thomas Dewey, that the chairman of the American Communist Party—Mr. William Foster—publicly stated that he was opposed to the Mundt-Nixon bill because in his opinion it outlawed the Communist Party in the United States. Linking Dewey's position to Foster's on an issue that seemed so black and white was apparently too big a temptation for Stassen to pass up. Unfortunately for him and in particular his prospects for victory in the Oregon primary, it provided Dewey with a magnificent opportunity.

Tom Swafford watched from the KEX control room as Governor Dewey approached the microphone. "When it was time for him to speak, he did so without a note," Swafford remembered. "As he began, his voice, a deep baritone, was pitched at its lowest register. His pace was deliberate; his tone thoughtful." The young program director was immediately impressed by Dewey's poise as the former federal prosecutor proceeded to methodically dismantle Stassen's argument for outlawing the Communist Party. "From time to time, as he'd begin to make a point," Swafford recalled, "he'd reach out with his left hand, looking for all the world like a surgeon in the midst of an operation, reaching for an instrument, knowing that the nurse would slap the correct one into his palm." Three of Dewey's aides sat at a nearby table fingering through boxes of three-by-five note cards. Elliott

Bell, superintendent of banks for the state of New York, would periodically thrust his hand forward with one of the cards, and "Dewey would glance at it without interrupting or varying the rhythm or flow of his remarks, see what he wanted, hand it back without looking at Bell, and continue to build his case."[35]

Dewey ad-libbed beautifully. He began by quickly conceding three seemingly obvious points to Stassen. As to the question of whether or not the American Communist Party was directed by Moscow, *certainly* it was, said Dewey. As to whether or not its objective was to overthrow the U.S. government, *certainly*. As to whether or not such an objective represented a threat to world peace, *certainly* it did, said Dewey. But when it came to the central question of the debate, Dewey declared, "I am unalterably, wholeheartedly, unswervingly against any scheme to write laws outlawing people because of their religious, political, social, or economic ideas."

Then Dewey proceeded to take Stassen to task for not sticking to the topic they had agreed to debate and for completely misrepresenting the Mundt-Nixon bill. Stassen had most definitely gone astray with his remarks, more or less using the free radio time to place an exclamation point on his Oregon campaign and to reach millions of other voters across the nation. It may have been a shrewd use of the airwaves (Dewey, it should be remembered, had been known to dabble in similar tactics in 1944), but given what Stassen claimed about the Mundt-Nixon bill and Dewey's subsequent effort to set the record straight, listeners must have wondered if the former governor of Minnesota had been caught cramming for a test for which he was ill prepared.

Exploiting his opponent's lack of knowledge regarding the bill in question, Dewey maintained that it did *not* outlaw the Communist Party. To prove his point, he went right to the source by quoting Congressman Karl Mundt, who said on May 14, "This bill does not outlaw the Communist party." Then Dewey scored a direct hit when he suggested that Mr. Mundt, the bill's coauthor, represented a more reliable authority on the meaning of the proposed legislation than did Mr. Foster, head of the American Communist Party. One can't help but wonder if Stassen blushed upon hearing Dewey frame the issue in such straightforward terms. If it did give him pause, Stassen didn't have much time to recover, because the governor of New York, catching his stride, began to pour it on. Long since abandoning his prepared remarks, Dewey grabbed a copy of the HUAC report on communism Karl Mundt had read to his House colleagues on April 30 and quoted it extensively: "The committee gave serious consideration to the many well-intentioned proposals which were before it which attempted to meet the problem by outlawing the Communist Party . . . The committee believes there are several compelling arguments against the outlawing approach. There are grave constitutional questions involved in attempting to interfere with the rights of the states to declare what parties and individuals may qualify for appearance on the ballot."[36]

Finally, after shedding considerable light on Stassen's mishandling of the Mundt-Nixon issue, Governor Dewey attacked the entire premise behind banning subversive political parties. He rejected the use of totalitarian methods in what was essentially a war of ideas. "I believe in keeping the Communist party everlastingly out in the open so we can defeat it and all it stands for," he said. "The free world looks to us for hope, for leadership, and most of all for a demonstration of our invincible faith that the free way of life will triumph so long as we keep it free." Dewey once again invoked the April 30 HUAC report to drive his point home: "Illegalization of the party might drive the Communist movement further underground, whereas exposure of its activities is the primary need . . . Illegalization has not proved effective in Canada and other countries which have tried it . . . We are willing to permit the theories of communism and democracy to clash in the open market place of political ideas."[37]

Dewey's twenty minutes were up. It had been a remarkable turn of events. Stassen had rarely sounded so conservative, and Dewey would have been hard-pressed to chart a more suitable course for liberal opponents of the measure. President Truman himself had entered the fray days earlier, saying "he thought the outlawing of a political party was entirely contrary to our principles" and making it clear "that if a conspiracy to overthrow the government developed, laws already in the statute books were adequate to deal with it."[38]

Stassen stood and walked toward the microphone to deliver his rebuttal. Tom Swafford looked on in amazement at what appeared to be "a different man." As he spoke, Swafford noted, Stassen "was wearing the kind of half smile a boxer puts on after taking a damaging blow when he wants the judges to think it didn't hurt. The radio audience couldn't see that, of course, but it could hear the uncertain, diffident delivery that had replaced the earlier booming confidence." Stassen had already lost the debate, but he either didn't know it yet or was unwilling to let on that he even suspected it. Instead, he held firm to his original position, ignored virtually every aspect of his opponent's argument, and tried to bring back from the dead an issue that Dewey had buried under six feet of facts. The thrust of his rebuttal came in the form of another direct challenge, this one sounding even more desperate than the first: "I submit to the governor that he earnestly reconsider his position. And specifically, if he will say that he will now agree to support the Mundt-Nixon bill, unequivocally, then I will agree that we have reached a point of union on this important issue, and we will go forward with a constructive campaign in Oregon on those other very important questions that are before the people of this great state and before our America in the wake of war."[39]

Thomas Dewey came out swinging even harder in the second round of the debate. He had eight and a half minutes to deliver his closing arguments, and he began by hammering away at Stassen's weak rebuttal: "I gather from Mr. Stassen's statement that he has completely surrendered . . . And he is willing to settle now, when confronted with facts, for a law which the author and the Committee say does not outlaw the [Communist] party, which of course it doesn't." He even echoed President Truman's denunciation of the bill by pointing out that there were currently twenty-seven federal laws on the books (several of which he named and described in detail) that dealt with the threat of political subversion.

Finally, Governor Dewey gave a little history lesson of his own. Drawing from the young republic's experiences during the French Revolution almost exactly one hundred and fifty years earlier, he reminded his listeners that trying to outlaw political ideas was hardly new. In fact, the Adams administration and its allies in Congress had attempted to silence their political opponents when they passed the Alien and Sedition Acts in 1798. What resulted was the violation of constitutionally protected rights, false imprisonment, and the subsequent destruction of the Federalist Party. "In these United States," Dewey said, "we should prosecute men for the crimes they commit but never for the ideas that they have." Sounding more like an attorney for the American Civil Liberties Union than a candidate for the presidency of the United States, Dewey closed by defending his record against the Communists in New York. "We licked 'em," he said, "because we kept them out in the open. Because we everlastingly believe in the Bill of Rights. Because we know that if in this country we will always keep every idea that's bad out in the open we will lick it. It will never get any place in the United States."

And with that the debate was over. The entire program had lasted just under an hour. The candidates quickly offered one another an obligatory

handshake and departed the KEX studios to take advantage of the four
remaining days until the Oregon primary. No one yet knew the outcome
of the upcoming vote, not to mention how the debate would affect it, but
the implications for Harold Stassen would turn out to be monumental.
That evening's debate marked the beginning of his political demise.

Dewey won the Oregon primary by only four percentage points, but the
swiftness with which he put an end to his opponent's aura of invincibility
helped convince Republican voters that Stassen's popularity could not possibly last through November. In Philadelphia that summer Dewey clinched
the nomination on the second ballot (Taft and Stassen came in second and
third, respectively) and then embarked upon a lackluster campaign to unseat
Harry Truman. The president crisscrossed the nation from one whistle-stop
to the next (acting more like Stassen every day), while Dewey and his advisors acted as if they should have their mail forwarded to 1600 Pennsylvania
Avenue to avoid the holiday rush. Hindsight being what it is, one is left to
wonder why more people didn't perceive a Greek tragedy in the offing.

It would be unfair to suggest that Truman's victory on November 2 was
written in the stars. The pollsters certainly didn't see it that way; nor did the
vast majority of journalists who covered the campaign. The reasons for
Dewey's unexpected loss are varied and complicated and involve issues
beyond the scope of this study. But Stassen's role in the entire episode bears
remembrance because he started a movement that in due time transformed
presidential elections. As Roscoe Drummond put it long before anyone knew
how things would shake out in 1948, "[Stassen] firmly believes in the direct-
primary system. He thinks that people should have a chance to nominate
their Presidents as well as to elect them. And he believes that the American
people should have a direct opportunity to pass on his candidacy . . . For
Harold Stassen does not want to master and manage the people of his country but to serve them." Writing several years after the fact, James Reston of
the *New York Times* offered an even more penetrating analysis of Stassen's
assets and liabilities as a candidate. "He had come into the political arena,"
Reston wrote, "as the young man who really would rather be right than
be President; he had arrived on the scene crying for a new political moral-
ity, and in the clutch had seemed to embrace the same old tactic of political
expediency." Calling for the Communist Party to be outlawed at a time
when most Americans were decidedly anti-communist no doubt qualifies
as one such moment. "As a result," continued Reston, "he lost caste with
the liberals, who branded him as a turncoat, although he never convinced

the conservative Republicans that he was anything but a Republican New Dealer." Harold Stassen—the "boy wonder" of Minnesota, the progressive Republican from the Middle West, the man whose political fortunes had risen so far and so fast—had finally lost his luster, never to find it shining quite so brightly again. The man who had made a career out of sticking to the middle way was finding out just how hard it is to remain unscathed at the center of the political spectrum. It would fall to Dwight Eisenhower to make that position seem tenable.[40]

~

Stassen licked his wounds and pursued an entirely new opportunity that doubtless appealed to the everlasting scholar inside of him. On September 17, 1948, he formally began his brief but influential tenure as president of the University of Pennsylvania. Stassen's time at Penn coincided with Dwight Eisenhower's presidency at Columbia University, which provided the backdrop for a working relationship that would in time have dramatic effects upon both of their futures. Eisenhower took a leave from Columbia in early 1951 to assume command of North Atlantic Treaty Organization (NATO) forces in Europe at President Truman's request. Duty had always been Ike's watchword, and in characteristic fashion he headed promptly to Paris and began organizing efforts to achieve collective security among America's allies in Western Europe. The task proved more political than military, as it required maintaining a delicate balance between former enemies—France and England on one hand and a democratic West Germany on the other. The real threat to peace, however, remained the incalculable consequences of Soviet aggression now that both superpowers possessed atomic weapons. Eisenhower, like Truman, bore the burdens of such knowledge day in and day out while serving as supreme commander of NATO.

A series of meetings were taking place back in the United States during the spring and summer of 1951 that would radically alter Eisenhower's plans. According to Bernard Shanley, who became one of Eisenhower's most trusted advisors in the White House, a number of prominent Republicans had begun seriously discussing the possibility of an Eisenhower-for-president movement. Because Eisenhower had not yet expressed interest in such a plan—indeed, no one knew if he was even available—Shanley contends that he "was asked by numerous Governors, Senators, and congressmen to head up a delaying action for Eisenhower" as a means of buying time for others to convince Eisenhower to run. "It was their consensus," Shanley continues, "that unless this were done, Senator Taft would be the nominee;

so that I spent almost the whole of 1951 visiting key people all over the country and arranging to battle Senator Taft in the main primaries with a stalking horse."[41]

Shanley makes no bones about the fact that Harold Stassen was that stalking horse. At a meeting held in mid-June at the Clarksboro, New Jersey, home of Amos Peaslee—a lawyer and well-known Stassen supporter—forty-one Republican leaders from across the nation agreed in principle to back Stassen's candidacy as a means of countering Taft's pathway to the nomination. The list of conditions settled upon by the attendees—including Minnesota's Ed Thye, Walter Judd, and Warren Burger—contained a proviso stating, "This may be modified by obtaining information whether General Eisenhower: a. is a Republican; b. would not run on Democratic ticket; c. intends to run on the Republican ticket in '52."[42]

In the meantime, several people traveled to Paris in the hopes of convincing Ike to bear the Republican Party's standard in 1952. According to Eisenhower, the most influential visitor was Henry Cabot Lodge, Jr., who arrived at NATO supreme headquarters on September 4, 1951. In the course of their lengthy and cordial conversation, Lodge reviewed the challenges facing the United States and then declared point-blank, "You are the only one who can be elected by the Republicans to the Presidency. You *must* permit the use of your name in the upcoming primaries." By Eisenhower's own admission, that was the turning point. "For the first time," he wrote in his memoirs, "I had allowed the smallest break in a regular practice of returning a flat refusal to any kind of proposal that I become an active participant. From that time onward, both alone and through correspondence, I began to look anew—perhaps subconsciously—at myself and politics."[43]

Next it was Stassen's turn to make a direct appeal for Eisenhower's candidacy. In December of 1951, he traveled to Paris and frankly presented his views to the general. His goal, Stassen stated, was to do everything in his power to stop Taft from securing the nomination because it would lead to yet another defeat for Republicans in November. He intended to engage in a vigorous campaign during the primary season, and he had the support of other moderate members of the party who feared a Taft nomination. As Bernard Shanley puts it, "Consequently with the uncertainty as to the Eisenhower situation, it seemed not only expedient but absolutely necessary that Harold Stassen drive ahead in order to prevent commitments being made to the Taft people which could not be broken and also because in the event that General Eisenhower was not a candidate, Harold Stassen would be left as the only one to oppose Senator Taft." Stassen left Paris without any definitive assurances from Eisenhower regarding the general's own plans. For the time being Ike was keeping his cards close to his chest, but sooner or later he would have to decide whether or not he wanted to make a run at the presidency.[44]

In March of 1952 events moved swiftly and forced Eisenhower from the fence. He reluctantly agreed to let his name appear on the ballot in New Hampshire's primary, which was scheduled for March 11. He lifted not a finger to help his cause in the run-up to the election (he was still stationed in Paris) and then seemed genuinely surprised when one in two voters chose him over Taft and Stassen. Any doubts he had harbored regarding his political appeal were beginning to wear off. One week later, voters went to the polls in Minnesota, where Eisenhower was not officially entered as a candidate. Stassen won, as expected, but more than a hundred thousand people voted for Ike thanks to a last-minute write-in campaign organized by "Minnesotans for Eisenhower." It was a remarkable and completely unprecedented demonstration of support for a man who had still not officially declared himself a candidate for the Republican nomination. Ironically, it also confirmed what Stassen had been saying about the primary system since 1948: let the voters decide. Suddenly it appeared as though even Stassen's favorite-son status could not completely diminish the rising tide of support for Ike.

After receiving news of the election returns from Minnesota, General Eisenhower wrote to President Truman requesting relief from his command effective June 1, 1952. By that time he hoped that NATO would be sufficiently bolstered and organized to allow him the liberty of returning stateside and testing the political waters firsthand. Meanwhile, "Ike for President" clubs kept popping up all over the country, and his supporters made sure that his name appeared on the ballot in several upcoming primary contests. That process revealed a geographic trend with which Eisenhower would have to contend if he was serious about wanting the nomination. While Ike fared well among Republican voters on the East and West Coasts, Taft still enjoyed a considerable advantage in midwestern states like Wisconsin, Nebraska, Illinois, Ohio, and South Dakota. And that's where Harold Stassen came in. By challenging Taft in the states where the senator seemed unbeatable, Stassen was essentially reversing the role he had played in 1948. Now his primary objective was to undermine the air of invincibility that accompanied Taft while Eisenhower fulfilled his duty to the nation and its European allies.

By the time Republicans arrived in Chicago on July 7 to choose their party's candidate, it was essentially a two-man race. The inevitable back-room deal making and jockeying for delegates seemed rather perfunctory as everyone at the convention knew that Taft was the old guard establish-ment's choice and Eisenhower appealed to the masses. Yet still the party leaders found a way to haggle over procedural matters and the seating of contested delegates. An up-and-coming attorney from St. Paul named Warren Burger helped settle the dispute, and balloting finally commenced on July 11. The roll call of states proceeded in predictable fashion, with most delegations backing their favorite-son candidates for the sake of loyalty and tradition. At the end of the first ballot, Eisenhower had 595 delegates to Taft's 500, which left Ike just nine votes shy of the minimum number needed to secure the nomination. Suddenly Senator Edward Thye, head of the Minnesota delegation, asked to be recognized by convention chairman Joseph Martin. According to Stassen, this had all been arranged by Bernard Shanley and Warren Burger prior to the balloting process. Martin recog-nized Thye before officially announcing the result of the first ballot, and the senator shouted, "Mr. Chairman, Minnesota wishes to change its vote to Eisenhower." Spontaneous applause interrupted the exchange, so Martin called the convention to order and spoke forcefully into the microphone, "What is the vote from Minnesota?" Thye replied, "Minnesota casts its 28 votes for Eisenhower." That was all it took. Other delegations quickly fol-lowed suit, but Minnesota had put Eisenhower over the top. The party faith-ful had finally chosen a candidate—and an outsider at that—who possessed both the reputation and the political philosophy necessary to return a Repub-lican administration to the White House for the first time in twenty years.[45]

In his acceptance speech, Eisenhower likened the coming campaign to a great crusade. "I take up this task, therefore, in a spirit of deep obliga-tion," he declared. "Mindful of its burdens and of its decisive importance, I accept your summons. I will lead this crusade." And then in a gesture designed to encourage party unity, Ike said, "Since this morning I have had helpful and heartwarming talks with Senator Taft, Governor Warren, and Governor Stassen. I wanted them to know, as I want you to know, that in the hard fight ahead we will work intimately together to promote the principles and aims of our party. I was strengthened and heartened by their instant agreement to support this cause to the utmost. Their cooperation means that the Republican Party will unitedly move forward in a sweep-ing victory."[46]

In choosing Senator Richard Nixon of California as his running mate, Eisenhower had managed to balance the ticket in terms of age, geography, and political philosophy. At sixty-two years of age, Ike would be the oldest president since James Buchanan, assuming he could defeat Democratic nominee Adlai Stevenson in November. Nixon was only thirty-nine, and as a native Californian he would undoubtedly help deliver electoral votes from a part of the nation that had been solidly in the Democrats' column since 1932. Nixon also appealed to conservatives in the Republican Party because of his well-publicized pursuit of Communists in America, which led to the conviction of Alger Hiss on perjury charges and helped pave the way for a very different kind of crusade spearheaded by Senator Joseph McCarthy. Eisenhower for his part would get a lot of play out of the phrase "middle way" on the campaign trail because it best represented his developing political creed. Like Harold Stassen, Eisenhower was a loyal Republican who gravitated toward the center because that's where things get done in our system. His interactions with voters across the country convinced him that most Americans felt the same way. Ike's landslide victory in November only reinforced his belief that cooperation and compromise held the greatest hope for prosperity at home and peace abroad. Once in office, he would have countless opportunities to put that philosophy to work. For Harold Stassen, however, Eisenhower's victory would lead to the most exhilarating and disappointing phase of his career as he sought permanent peace with America's enemy while finding little professional harmony with his colleagues in Washington.

8 Try to Figure Him Out

Harold Stassen surprised very few people when he left the University of Pennsylvania for good in January of 1953. He had become a trusted member of Eisenhower's inner circle. He proved an able and articulate advisor on the campaign trail by remaining faithful to his and the candidate's core principles. That Eisenhower shared so many fundamental beliefs with Stassen—on "the middle way," on the possibilities and limitations of federal power, on the importance of maintaining peace while ensuring national security—made Minnesota's former governor a natural source of counsel across a wide spectrum of issues.

Despite their repeated attempts to figure him out, fellow cabinet officials failed to comprehend the nature of the Eisenhower-Stassen relationship. Where administration insiders saw Stassen as the "undeterrable candidate" seeking any opportunity to advance his career, Eisenhower saw "a professional politician" with refreshingly moderate views who could supplement his own working knowledge of political exigencies. Where many within the councils of government perceived blinding ambition on Stassen's part, Eisenhower sensed "sincerity of purpose" and "tireless energy." And what department heads like John Foster Dulles (state) and George Humphrey (treasury) considered Stassen's unremitting habit of sticking his nose where it didn't belong, President Eisenhower would one day characterize as "loyal friendship" and "readiness to express to me frankly your views on the many subjects that have been of common interest to us both." In truth, the relationship was not nearly as complicated as Stassen's contemporaries would have had us believe. But that did not make it any less controversial.[1]

John Foster Dulles, President Dwight D. Eisenhower, and Harold Stassen, seated at the president's desk in the Oval Office, 1953

On the day after Eisenhower's victory, Harold Hinton of the *New York Times* reported that Stassen was widely viewed as a possible choice for secretary of labor. His work in securing passage of Minnesota's Labor Peace Act in 1939, which helped bring to a close the state's worst era of labor unrest, suggested that his nomination might be palatable to both management and labor interests at a time when Eisenhower was pledging to "support and strengthen, not weaken, the laws that protect the American worker." Stassen's progressive, middle-of-the-road brand of Republicanism resonated with Eisenhower's campaign promise that organized labor would "always get both justice and fairness from him." Both men agreed the time had come to break the Democratic Party's twenty-year stranglehold on big labor and vice versa. Voters demanded a change in leadership, and for the first time in two decades a Republican, though hardly a typical one at that, would occupy the White House. Only fresh, new approaches to such complex problems as labor-management relations, the war in Korea, inflation, the arms race, and civil rights could produce movement on issues that had become frozen in rhetoric and recrimination. This had been the overarching theme of Eisenhower's drive to the presidency, and this was the type of change for which Americans resoundingly demonstrated their approval on November 4, 1952.[2]

But once the campaign ceased and the administration prepared to assume power, the president-elect enlisted Stassen's experience and skill for a much more daunting challenge than the one facing America's workers. Eisenhower knew of Stassen's efforts to get the United Nations up and running and respected his enlightened views on foreign policy matters. Stassen, it should be remembered, was among the first midwestern politicians to acknowledge the death of isolationism. And he showed his willingness to set partisanship aside when he accepted Franklin Roosevelt's invitation to help negotiate the UN Charter in San Francisco. That was exactly the type of cooperative spirit Eisenhower hoped to make the hallmark of his presidency. The question in any case appears not to have been whether Harold Stassen could be of considerable assistance to the new president but rather where he could be most effective.

It may well have been Stassen's legendary initiative and penchant for making snap decisions that helped determine his role in the new administration. In an intriguing episode laced with the sort of cloak-and-dagger maneuvers one expects from cold warriors, Stassen chose to fire off an urgent warning to Eisenhower just four days after the election, the reverberations of which would be far reaching for Stassen both politically and personally. As he sat in his University of Pennsylvania office on November 7, 1952, Stassen received a mysterious phone call from a man who claimed to be an American Foreign Service officer with important information for President-elect Eisenhower. The caller refused to give his name and volunteered no other proof of his reliability. Stassen was immediately suspicious. He quickly asked the man to identify the current American ambassador to Brazil, who had spent his entire career in the U.S. Foreign Service and with whom Stassen had become familiar through the United Nations. The caller knew the ambassador's name and accurately described how long he had held his current post. Stassen tested the man three more times and then, convinced of his authenticity, urged the caller to proceed with his information. At the end of the conversation, Stassen thanked the man and glanced at his watch. It was 10:43 AM. Using an old navy method for identifying dispatches, he told the informant: "If you want to talk to me again identify yourself to my secretary with the code 10:43–11–7–52. I'll leave word for her to put you right through to me." According to Stassen, the man never called back and his identity remains a mystery.[3]

What the anonymous caller revealed to Stassen served to confirm a fear that Eisenhower and his advisors already held. Though the late campaign had been focused on defeating Adlai Stevenson, to a great extent the Republicans' most penetrating messages had come at Harry Truman's expense, particularly when it came to foreign policy. Ever since the "police action" in Korea had turned into a bloody stalemate with limited objectives and no end in sight, Truman's approval ratings seemed to be inversely proportional to the mounting number of American causalities. When Eisenhower boldly proclaimed, "I shall go to Korea," he unwittingly set the stage for a thorny transition from candidate to commander in chief. As historian Stephen Ambrose observed, Truman's objection to such a statement was "its implication that in Korea Eisenhower would find some magic formula to end the war, one that escaped the [Truman] Administration and the Joint Chiefs of Staff," including Eisenhower's old friend and confidant Omar Bradley, current chairman of the JCS. Now that the election was over, the Eisenhower camp worried that the outgoing administration—namely Truman and Secretary of State Dean Acheson—would try to get the president-elect to publically endorse all commitments made to Korea before the inauguration and thus tie his own hands in the process. That is precisely what Stassen's mysterious caller suggested was in the works.[4]

Harold Stassen moved swiftly. The next morning he sent a confidential letter to Eisenhower, who was taking a long-overdue vacation at Augusta National Golf Club in Georgia. It is an extraordinarily candid missive, suggesting this was not the first time (and it certainly would not be the last) that Stassen offered unsolicited advice to Eisenhower. The difference now of course was that Eisenhower was just a few weeks removed from becoming the leader of the free world, and Stassen held neither elective office nor an official standing within the president-elect's administration. That did not seem to deter either man from expressing himself freely given the seriousness of what was at stake.

Stassen began the letter by referring directly to "confidential information received from a reliable source." He proceeded to outline Truman's alleged plan to force Eisenhower's hand on negotiations regarding Korea and then made a convincing case for taking no immediate action by suggesting, "It would reduce the possible range on your future policy decisions and do so at a time when you do not yet have complete information in the hands of your own people, nor the authority to implement your own policies." But Stassen did not stop there. He recommended a series of measures aimed at sidestepping Truman's perceived overtures while laying the groundwork for future discussions on issues ranging from communist aggression in Formosa to Indian neutrality to Mideast peace to European unification. Taken as a whole, Stassen's letter represented a broad and bold attempt to influence Eisenhower's view of the world in 1953. It culminated in the following assessment that continued to hew the party line: "In summary your first foreign policy decision can be a great asset in establishing the foundation for a peaceful world, and, on the contrary, these foundations would be injured if your first foreign policy move was an agreement with a discredited retiring President who has seriously blundered in his conduct of foreign policy."[5]

Eisenhower responded two days later. He thanked Stassen for the information and addressed several specific points directly. He characterized his response as "the hastiest kind of reply," promising that he would give the entire letter careful consideration and discuss it with two or three others, among them, no doubt, John Foster Dulles. The president-elect closed by mentioning he would be returning to his home in New York the following week and extending a warm invitation that Stassen could hardly refuse: "I hope you will find it possible to come and see me during that time—I should like to have a long talk with you." The former "boy wonder" from Minnesota who had doggedly pursued the highest office in the land and dreamed of world peace since his college days was about to find out what wonders the future held in store for him.[6]

In the meantime, Eisenhower began assembling his cabinet. When he wrote his memoirs a decade later, the president referred to his choice for secretary of state as "an obvious one," noting that John Foster Dulles "had carried on a lifelong study of American diplomacy." Indeed, if ever a man had the right pedigree for taking charge of America's foreign policy matters, it was Dulles. His grandfather, John Watson Foster, had been Benjamin Harrison's secretary of state, and his uncle served in the same capacity under Woodrow Wilson. Nineteen-year-old John Foster Dulles quickly put his Princeton education to good use when he attended the Second Hague Conference in 1907 and then helped represent the United States in Paris during negotiations over the Treaty of Versailles. As the Second World War came to a close, he advised American delegates, including Stassen, at the founding of the United Nations. By the early 1950s, Dulles was a seasoned

international lawyer, a former U.S. senator, and arguably the most experienced foreign policy scholar in the nation. Eisenhower later described Dulles
as "a vigorous Republican who had represented bipartisanship in earlier
years, a man of strong opinions and unimpeachable character." The president privately quipped to friends, "Foster has been studying to be Secretary
of State since he was five years old."[7]

In late November Harold Stassen made his way to New York City to visit
the Eisenhower home at Morningside Heights on the Columbia University
campus. The meeting was informal—two Ivy League presidents (one of
whom had recently been elected president of the United States) chewing
the fat, so to speak—and no official record of the meeting exists. But according to Stassen's recollection, the discussion focused immediately on the type
of role Eisenhower envisioned Stassen playing in the new administration.
Namely, the president-elect wanted him to succeed Averell Harriman as
director of mutual security. If Stassen accepted the appointment, he would
become a member of the National Security Council and rank among the
president's highest-level executive officers, which required a willingness to
advise him on issues beyond one's primary area of accountability. As Eisenhower later explained to all of his cabinet nominees, he expected them to
be mindful of "virtually any question that concerned the government. No
one was relieved of his responsibility or the opportunity to think broadly
and to make suggestions." Such an understanding was indicative of Eisenhower's leadership style. He wanted to have all relevant facts, information,
and perspectives at his disposal before making a decision for which he and
only he would be held responsible. Stassen took the president-elect at his
word and would in time make the most of his opportunities to be candid and
direct, qualities not equally valued by several of his future colleagues. Without realizing it, Eisenhower had just planted the seeds of a bitter rivalry that
would dominate the next six years of Stassen's career in government.[8]

Though Harold and Esther originally intended to stay in Philadelphia
no matter the outcome of his meeting with Eisenhower, the lure of public service and the prospect of contributing to the new president's foreign
policy initiatives proved more than Stassen could resist. He resigned from
the University of Pennsylvania and moved Esther and their two children—
Glen, seventeen, and Kathleen, eleven—to Washington, DC. With characteristic zeal, Stassen plunged headlong into the duties of coordinating a relatively young and, as fate would have it, short-lived executive department
known as the Mutual Security Agency. At long last he could devote all of his

professional responsibilities to building upon the foundations of world peace he had helped establish at San Francisco in 1945. Unfortunately for Harold Stassen, bureaucratic squabbles combined with clashing wills and administrative missteps ultimately rendered much of his work toward lasting security unfulfilled. And though he certainly bore responsibility for occasional errors in judgment during his tenure, Stassen was charged with the unenviable task of rising to the service of Dwight D. Eisenhower from under the immense shadow of John Foster Dulles. It's a wonder he lasted as long as he did.

∼

The federal agency Stassen took over after Eisenhower's inauguration was created late in Truman's presidency and played a vital role in U.S. efforts to check the growth of communism. When Congress passed the Mutual Security Act in October of 1951, it authorized the president to vastly increase the type of foreign aid administered under the Marshall Plan, the massive economic relief program aimed at helping rebuild war-torn Europe. Predicated on the notion that America's long-term security and economic well-being was intertwined with the fate of other free nations, the Mutual Security Agency dispersed billions of dollars annually in overseas military, technical, and humanitarian assistance. The program was not without its critics, and Stassen had to contend with competing interests regularly, both at home and abroad. His operations had obvious implications for the Departments of State, Treasury, and Defense, and the flow of money depended upon congressional appropriations. Still, Eisenhower and Stassen were firmly committed to the principles of foreign aid and collective security. Together these offered the best hope for unity in Western Europe and provided a strong bulwark against communist aggression.

Ten days after assuming his new post, Stassen accompanied Secretary of State Dulles on a tour of European capitals at the president's behest. Writing to a close associate at NATO, Eisenhower said he "wanted the European governments to be assured on an official basis that I had neither changed my personal views nor did I have any intention of denying the basic truth that only in collective security was there any real future in the free world." Eisenhower would devote a great deal of his time as president alternately placating and prodding his European allies in order to maintain a united front against Soviet aggrandizement. It was no easy task given the myriad issues at play—economic recovery and unification, a divided Germany, nuclear proliferation, decolonization, nation building, containing the spread of communism in both Europe and Asia, and so on—but one Eisenhower deemed absolutely essential to the cause of peace in the world.[9]

By 1953 the United States was publicly supporting a French plan to form the European Defense Community—a supranational European army incorporating soldiers from several NATO countries including West Germany. The controversial treaty was designed to facilitate German rearmament for deterring Soviet aggression without allowing ultranationalists in Germany to have a large and fiercely loyal military establishment at their disposal. (Memories of the post–Great War era understandably dominated the minds of policy makers on both sides of the Atlantic in the wake of World War II. Parallels abound. For instance, the French National Assembly's vote to reject the EDC Treaty in 1954, despite the fact that the plan originated with its own premier, sounds remarkably like the U.S. Senate's failure to ratify President Woodrow Wilson's hard-fought Treaty of Versailles in 1919. Likewise, French premier Georges Clemenceau's vision for a so-called "cordon sanitaire" to forestall the spread of Bolshevism after World War I provided in part the philosophical foundations for America's policy of containment in the late 1940s.)

Dulles and Stassen clearly had their work cut out for them in Europe. No matter how indispensable collective security appeared from America's perspective, Europeans were the ones who would have to live with its consequences. The past still loomed large on the continent, and making partners of such recent and bitter enemies required a great deal more than wishful thinking. Dulles cabled Eisenhower every evening to keep the administration updated on their discussions with various European leaders. On February 3 he reported, "Yesterday devoted wholly to talks with top French officials largely in relation to EDC. While political difficulties are great, Stassen and I feel that there is real determination on part of present government . . . to push this to a successful conclusion. There is still a hard road ahead, but we feel that ultimate success is possible and even probable."[10]

With the benefit of hindsight and to the extent that the EDC was still-born, the optimism Dulles transmitted in early February of 1953 appears misplaced. But then again collective security was and always is a work in progress, so the discussions he had with Europeans paved the way for mutual understanding and coordinated efforts to maintain vital diplomatic, military, and economic ties as the Cold War intensified. Harold Stassen's role in the meetings remains less clear and may in fact have strained his relationship with the secretary of state. As director of the Mutual Security

Agency, Stassen was looking for specific needs his organization could fulfill through economic aid. That process would soon put him at odds with several prominent members of the administration. Dulles, on the other hand, in addition to conveying Eisenhower's pledge of support, was gauging European attitudes about collective security. A pragmatist at heart, he was assessing the willingness of European leaders to make and then follow through on international commitments. There, of course, was the rub. A unified Western Europe, or hemisphere for that matter, would only exist if individual leaders could garner the political will to supplant their national interests for the collective good. Ironically, but perhaps not surprisingly, Eisenhower had the toughest sales job of all. Contentious battles within his own political party hindered the new president's efforts to increase international cooperation. Once again, the middle way that he and Stassen and others in the administration so desperately wanted to pursue with respect to foreign affairs was being threatened by the same Republicans who never wanted to see an Eisenhower presidency in the first place.

~

Eisenhower fancied himself a middle-of-the-roader, but policy decisions that dominated the first year of his administration betrayed a tendency to favor the right side of the road. This was most evident in his dealings with the increasingly extremist elements of the Republican Party. Senator Joseph McCarthy, the anti-communist crusader from Wisconsin, still captivated the nation's attention and was becoming as big a thorn in Eisenhower's side as he had been in Harry Truman's. That McCarthy belonged to the same political party as the president in 1953 served only to widen his appeal and sharpen his attacks. The senator had managed to become perhaps the most powerful and feared man in America, and even the president of the United States avoided a direct frontal assault on McCarthy and his methods, no matter how repugnant they appeared to be.

The passage of time—not to mention McCarthy's subsequent self-destruction—has helped validate Eisenhower's efforts to steer clear of Senator McCarthy. Ike's famous comment to campaign aides—"I'm not going to get into the gutter with that guy"—now sounds like the proclamation of a seasoned statesman who refused to tarnish the dignity of his office by slinging mud at a professional mudslinger. Unfortunately, that's not how everyone interpreted it at the time, particularly after McCarthy's blistering attack on General George C. Marshall and Eisenhower's failure to defend his old friend's honor. By the spring of 1953, when he was at the pinnacle

of his influence, Joe McCarthy seemed to have cast a spell on nearly everyone in the administration except Harold Stassen, whose attempt to cut
McCarthy down to size in March marked the first significant conflict between
a senior member of the president's staff and Wisconsin's junior senator.
The manner by which Eisenhower defused the situation lent considerable
credence to the notion that no one, not even the president of the United
States, could stand up to McCarthy and get away with it. Looks can be
deceiving as the facts and hindsight demonstrate in this particular case, but
observers near and far generally agreed that Stassen was the one who took
it on the chin.

The episode went public in late March 1953, with McCarthy dropping
another bombshell at one of his now-famous televised press conferences.
Standing at his side was a young aid named Robert Kennedy, assistant counsel to the Senate's Permanent Subcommittee on Investigations. McCarthy
had hired Bobby, then fresh from the University of Virginia Law School,
as a means of mollifying his father, former ambassador Joseph P. Kennedy,
who generously supported McCarthy's reelection campaign in 1952. For
several weeks prior to the press conference, Bobby Kennedy had been roll-
ing up his sleeves and chasing down leads to verify McCarthy's hunch that
U.S. allies were in fact trading with China, whose very forces American soldiers were battling on the Korean Peninsula. As it turns out, an extensive
paper trail proved McCarthy's contention, and in typical fashion he headed
straight for the cameras. The senator announced that he "had effected an
agreement with Greek owners of 242 merchant ships to break off all trade
with Communist China, North Korea, and Far Eastern ports of the Soviet
Union." When pressed by reporters as to why he, a member of Congress,
had been dealing directly with foreign interests—a process clearly within
the State Department's purview—McCarthy responded that his "negotiations had been carried out secretly and without advising the State Department because of their 'extremely delicate' nature. He expressed confidence,
however, that the results would be welcomed by the department."[11]

The next day John Foster Dulles managed keep his cool and hold his
tongue. Harold Stassen did not. In his capacity as Mutual Security director,
Stassen worked closely with America's allies and resented McCarthy's inter-
ference. He accused the senator of meddling with the functions of the executive branch, saying, "You are in effect undermining and are harmful to
our objective" of trying to halt trade with the Communists. While Stassen
was technically in the right, his timing could not have been worse. Just two

days earlier, Charles "Chip" Bohlen, the president's choice for ambassador to the Soviet Union, won Senate confirmation despite McCarthy's vigorous opposition. Eisenhower was doubtless gratified to receive the support of Senator Robert Taft—"Mr. Republican" himself—in what threatened to be a very messy and public breaking of the GOP ranks over Bohlen's nomination. Crisis averted, Eisenhower was more determined than ever not to fall into McCarthy's trap and split the party asunder. Stassen's remarks had the potential to do just that.[12]

The president, along with Dulles and Vice President Nixon, acted quickly to smooth things over. Nixon arranged for Dulles and McCarthy to meet privately over lunch. The two spoke for nearly an hour and a half, during which time the secretary of state apparently gave Senator McCarthy a short civics lesson. Dulles pulled out a copy of George Washington's farewell address and proceeded to familiarize his guest with the first president's view on separation of powers. No one kept a record of the exchange, but it is not difficult to imagine which portions of Washington's 1796 speech Dulles chose to underscore for the junior senator: "The necessity of reciprocal checks in the exercise of political power, by dividing and distributing it into different depositories, and constituting each the guardian of the public weal against invasions by the others, has been evinced by experiments ancient and modern . . . Let there be no change by usurpation; for, though this, in one instance, may be the instrument of good, it is the customary weapon by which free governments are destroyed."

If McCarthy happened to spy a calendar during the meeting—the date was April 1—he must have grinned uncomfortably and felt the fool. His only solace could have been that it was a private rebuke rather than a public one. And that had been the administration's intent all along, even though McCarthy rarely if ever extended such a courtesy to his foes, real or imagined. Dulles and Eisenhower decided to soften the blow by providing McCarthy an out. Unfortunately for Harold Stassen, his old protégé Joe McCarthy was allowed to save face at *his* expense. After the luncheon Dulles praised the senator from Wisconsin for acting in "the national interest" while McCarthy acknowledged "that it was the prerogative of the President to conduct American foreign policy." But the damage to Stassen's credibility did not end there. At his weekly press conference the next day, Eisenhower took several questions about "the little incident" and tried to downplay its significance. When pressed to identify with whom he was more disappointed, McCarthy or Stassen, Eisenhower equivocated. While maintaining that McCarthy had no real authority to "negotiate" with foreign interests on behalf of the United States, the president suggested that Stassen "probably meant an infringement rather than undermining" when he mistakenly criticized McCarthy's discussions with Greek ship owners. Publicly, Harold Stassen had to endure the mild but unmistakable displeasure of his president. According to Arthur Krock of the *New York Times*, however, Eisenhower was privately furious with McCarthy. "Once again," writes McCarthy biographer Thomas Reeves, "out of a sense of personal dignity, out of respect for the separation of powers, and from a deep appreciation of the value of the right-wing to this administration, he [Eisenhower] elected to avoid a direct confrontation."[13]

If Eisenhower had hoped that showing considerable restraint in this episode would have a reciprocal effect upon Joe McCarthy, he was sadly mistaken. The senator from Wisconsin ratcheted up his attacks on the president, on U.S. allies, on the Chinese, and on virtually anyone who did not conform to his brand of anti-communist zeal. By late spring 1953 his criticism had started to alienate the British government, something Eisenhower desperately wanted to avoid as he tried to maintain the delicate though heretofore united coalition of Western European states against communism. Former Prime Minister Clement Attlee took to the floor of Britain's Parliament in mid-May to offer a poorly veiled attack on McCarthy and his ultra-conservative cronies. He said in part, "I hope that no one will suggest that I am in any way anti-American . . . I am very conscious of all that the Americans have done for the world, besides in the war . . . The American Constitution was framed for an isolationist state . . . one sometimes wonders who is more powerful, the President or Senator McCarthy."[14]

Attlee's remarks no doubt stung Americans on both ends of Pennsylvania Avenue. But again Eisenhower proved that discretion is the better part of valor while McCarthy let loose another barrage of insults. His immediate target was the British, whom he accused of continuing to do business with Communists, but his ire was more generally directed at American cooperation with Europe. One such denunciation on the Senate floor culminated in the following: "Let us sink every accursed ship carrying materials to the enemy and resulting in the death of American boys, regardless of what flag those ships may fly . . . We can go it alone." Going it alone was exactly the type of antiquated foreign policy position Eisenhower, Dulles, and Stassen were trying to move America away from. After meeting with the president to discuss the growing controversy, Stassen took another swipe at McCarthy, telling reporters, "We need less headline hunters and more Eisenhower backers for the good of America."[15]

With respect to foreign policy, the administration's loudest critics came from within the GOP, and now Senator Robert Taft entered the fray to rekindle conservative memories of the good old days when American charity began at home. Taft seized the moment—his last, as he was dying of cancer—and added his voice to the rising chorus of "go-it-aloners" in Congress. On May 26 Taft suggested the United States should pursue a unilateral policy in Korea, adding, "we might as well abandon any idea of working with the United Nations in the East and reserve to ourselves a completely free hand." Taft obviously hit a nerve. At a weekly press conference two days later, Eisenhower responded at length to a question about Taft's comments. It is perhaps the most candid and succinct explanation Eisenhower ever offered for his pursuit of international cooperation. That it was delivered "off the cuff," so to speak, makes it all the more remarkable. He said,

> If you are going to go it alone one place, you of course have to go it alone everywhere. If you are going to try to develop a coalition of understanding based upon decency, on ideas of justice, common concepts of governments, established by the will of free men, then you have got to make compromises. You have got to find the way in between the conflicting partisan considerations that will serve the best good of all.
>
> Now, that is what we are up against today, because our whole policy is based on this theory: No single free nation can live alone in the world. We have to have friends. Those friends have got to be tied to you, in some form or another. We have to have that unity in basic purposes that comes from a recognition of common interests. That is what we are up against.[16]

It was a brilliant statement of principle, one that captured the essential spirit of "the middle way." It marked the beginning of Eisenhower's break with the right wing of his party, and he immediately drew praise from the *New York Times* editorial staff:

> As a newcomer in politics General Eisenhower may have placed more emphasis on party unity than it deserves. He may too little have realized that great decisions these days usually cross party lines, and that in issues of high principle he must expect to lose some support in his own party and gain some support in the opposite party. But when it came to a parting of

the ways he abandoned Mr. Taft in favor of the greater unity of the free nations . . .

Isolationism is a sort of chills and fever, from which Senator Taft suffers, not all the time but at intervals. Fortunately, only a small minority of the Senate Committee on Foreign Relations has been bitten by the same mosquito.[17]

By December of 1954 Eisenhower's conversion was complete. In an extraordinary moment of confidence, he confided to press secretary James C. Hagerty that he could no longer work with the radical right wing of the Republican Party and that he was ready to fight them every step of the way. The president added, "This party of ours has to realize that they won't exist unless they become a party of progressive moderates—unless they can prove to the American people that they are a middle-of-the-road party and turn their backs on the extremes of the left and particularly the extremes of the right." Then, as if campaigning for reelection before a one-man constituency, he promised Hagerty, "These next two years I have just one purpose, outside of the job of keeping this world at peace, and that is to build up a strong progressive Republican Party in this country."[18]

Never had Eisenhower and Stassen's political philosophies been so similar. Peace and progressivism were the building blocks of Harold Stassen's career back in the 1930s, and now his vision for America finally had a dedicated champion in the Oval Office. The "middle way" was at long last gaining momentum as Eisenhower attempted to navigate the political mainstream in both domestic and foreign affairs. He sought greater efficiency and accountability in the making of national policy for the common good and looked to state and local governments to pick up their share of the burden. However, he refused to rewrite American history by dispensing of federal agencies that had proven successful simply because conservatives decried big government. As the president once told his brother Edgar, "Should any political party attempt to abolish Social Security, unemployment insurance, and eliminate labor laws and farm programs, you would not hear of that party again in our political history." Like Stassen, Eisenhower's political instincts told him to stick with the wishes of Middle America, naturally familiar territory for someone reared on the virtues and values of central Kansas but well versed on how the rest of the world worked.[19]

Eisenhower continued to solicit Stassen's advice on matters beyond the scope of mutual security, much to the chagrin of his fellow cabinet members.

In the summer of 1953 the president abolished the Mutual Security Agency and reorganized its activities under the Foreign Operations Administration. He appointed Stassen director of the new organization, and within a year's time FOA was overseeing the distribution of $2.8 billion in foreign aid, grants, and loans. Stassen continued on as a member of the National Security Agency and reported directly to the president, even though his duties clearly had major implications for the Departments of State, Treasury, and Defense.

Though an effective communicator and manager, Stassen collided with many personalities—both large and small—within the administration. His penchant for making quick decisions and operating independently frustrated more than a few of Eisenhower's closest advisors, chief among them Clarence Randall, the successful steel executive to whom Eisenhower turned for advice on foreign trade. As chairman of the Commission on Foreign Economic Policy, Randall became the president's point man on global trade initiatives. The former president of Inland Steel was at heart a fiscal conservative who sought relationships that stimulated American production while keeping tariff levels high enough to protect U.S. companies from rising foreign competition. The commission's much-heralded "Randall Report," which was released to the public in the spring of 1954, quickly drew jeers from over a dozen of the nation's leading economists. They condemned the report for its "want of basic philosophy and for its failure to assert American leadership or to enlighten the American people as to their international responsibilities and opportunities."[20]

Clarence Randall, who helped develop national policy on foreign trade, and Harold Stassen, who oversaw the distribution of foreign aid to developing nations, occupied executive offices approximately two hundred feet from one another. But in terms of professional experiences, political philosophies, and leadership styles, they were worlds apart. Years earlier, when Stassen was campaigning for the presidency, he made note of a celebrated verse from the book of Job: "Would that mine adversary had written a book." In Randall's case, that book came in the form of a personal journal documenting his eight years of public service in the Eisenhower administration. Randall discretely vented many frustrations in his journal but none more frequently than his unfavorable impressions of Harold Stassen. Entry after entry suggests, at least from Randall's perspective, that the director of FOA had far more ambitions than allies in the government. And though the observations are clearly not impartial, they do nevertheless reflect a persistent and unflattering image Stassen projected and never managed to shake during his time in the White House. To Clarence Randall and other officials with a working knowledge of corporate and government bureau-cracies, Harold Stassen's legendary initiative smacked of insubordination. Time and again Randall hammered away at that fundamental issue, as evi-denced by the following journal entries:

March 1, 1954
There can be no doubt that Harold possesses some perfectly magnificent qualities, but that he is one of the most difficult men in America to fathom. When I look into those eyes of his I am not at all sure what is going on behind them. I sense that he is measuring me and weighing how best he may use me to further his own thinking.[21]

May 2, 1954
I think by now it is clear to all thoughtful people in the Administration that Harold is a very dangerous man. I have no way of knowing what the Presi-dent thinks about him although I suspect he thinks well of him. But below the Presidential level he hasn't one single friend. He seems to thrive on enmity, however, and no one seems to know how to stop him. He hasn't the slightest instinct for team play. He takes breath-taking decisions on his own oftentimes those which are not his to take, and tells no one . . .
    . . . I have become convinced that Stassen lacks basically the quality of sound judgment, even in those rare instances where his actions are not motivated by personal ambition. His success rests upon lightning-fast men-tal agility and great facility in the use of words.

October 23, 1954
To be fair, I do not credit this altogether to selfishness. I just think Harold doesn't understand what government really is, but it is without parallel in recent history, in my judgment, for one man below the rank of President to move boldly into new plans and schemes in which he makes announce-ments and commitments without any consideration for the viewpoints of those upon whose apparent responsibility he is impinging.[22]

One day in the middle of March 1955, Clarence Randall opened up his morning newspaper to discover that Harold Stassen had been offered and had accepted a new position within the administration. Referring to it as "the very best secret in Washington where only a few secrets are kept," Randall must have been overjoyed by the news. For several months he had been alluding to his desire for Stassen to be transferred to another area of responsibility. A year earlier he had even noted in his journal that some in the administration were tossing around the idea of an ambassadorship for Stassen as a means of getting him out of Washington. When someone suggested elevating him to the State Department's official representative in Great Britain, Randall dismissed the notion wryly: "Harold in England would be a very dangerous man indeed. He might even try to run for King over there."[23]

The president had other plans for Stassen. On March 19, 1955, Eisenhower formally announced the creation of an entirely new administrative post—special assistant to the president for disarmament. The official statement began with Eisenhower's personal feelings regarding nuclear weaponry:

> The massive resources required for modern armaments, the huge diversion of materials and of energy, the heavy burden of taxation, the demands for years of service of vast numbers of men, the unprecedented destructive power of new weapons and the international tensions which powerful armaments aggravate have been of deep concern to me for many years.
>
> At the same time the tragic consequences of unilateral disarmament, the reckless moves of Hitler when the United States was weak, the Korean aggression when our armed strength had been rapidly diminished and the vast extent of the armament now centered around the opposing ideology of communism have been equally apparent to me.[24]

Eisenhower appointed Stassen to the new position and charged him with the task of "developing, on behalf of the President and the State Department, the broad studies, investigations, and conclusions which, when concurred in by the National Security Council and approved by the President, will become basic policy toward the question of disarmament." News of Stassen's reassignment may have caught official Washington off guard, but it was almost universally hailed as a step in the right direction, if for extremely different reasons. From the perspective of people like Clarence Randall, Secretary of the Treasury George Humphrey, Budget Director Joseph Dodge, and Commerce Secretary Sinclair Weeks, Harold Stassen would now be someone else's problem. For Stassen, however, the opportunity of a lifetime—to make substantial progress toward lasting world peace—had finally come his way. His political capital may have been at an all-time low, particularly among fellow Republicans, but helping to steer America away from the perilous brink of nuclear annihilation offered Stassen the prospect of fulfilling his earliest professional ambition.[25]

For Eisenhower's part, this attempt to ease tensions between the United States and the Soviet Union demonstrated his growing frustration with the status quo. Since the end of hostilities in 1945, the two superpowers had engaged in a dangerous game of one-upmanship dominated by aggressive rhetoric and the sort of provocative gesture politicking that had historically resulted in war. But now of course, in an atomic age, the implications of war had changed dramatically. The logic of force, containment, the Truman Doctrine, collective security, and the domino theory may have prevented a third world war in the short run, but the hostile ideologies and misunderstandings driving such policies offered few guarantees upon which to pin the hopes of humankind. Eisenhower clearly understood this, and he continually sought opportunities to break through the acrimony in order to further the cause of peace.

His first efforts came just a few weeks after the inauguration, when news of Joseph Stalin's imminent death reached Washington. At a meeting of the National Security Council on March 4, 1953, just hours before the Kremlin officially announced that the Russian leader had indeed died, discussions focused on how the administration should respond to the impending changes in Soviet leadership. While Secretary of State John Foster Dulles counseled caution for fear of alienating the Soviets at such a sensitive time, Eisenhower sensed a unique opportunity. "I want to reach out to the Russians—the people and the Politburo—to see if we can't somehow crack the Iron Curtain and thaw out the Cold War," he said.[26]

The president decided to make the most of the situation. He was determined to deliver a message to the Soviets and the world at large underscoring his desire for peace. He solicited ideas from a number of key advisors and speech writers, Stassen prominent among them, and carefully tailored an impassioned speech that ranks among the greatest of his entire career. Dubbed "The Chance for Peace," the address signified a major psychological and diplomatic coup for the new president. Speaking before the American Society of Newspaper Editors on April 16, 1953, Eisenhower—the soldier turned statesman—boldly proclaimed,

> Every gun that is made, every warship launched, every rocket fired signifies, in the final sense, a theft from those who hunger and are not fed, those who are cold and are not clothed . . .

... This, I repeat, is the best way of life to be found on the road the world has been taking.

This is not a way of life at all, in any true sense. Under the cloud of threatening war, it is humanity hanging from a cross of iron.

The economic and moral implications of such dramatic trade-offs was unmistakable. Eisenhower hoped that the Russian people and their leaders could embrace his "firm faith that God created men to enjoy, not destroy, the fruits of the earth and of their own toil." He became even more candid, speaking at once to the American people (the president's address was broadcast over television and radio from the Statler Hotel in Washington) but undoubtedly aiming his remarks directly at Moscow:

So the new Soviet leadership now has a precious opportunity to awaken, with the rest of the world, to the point of peril reached and to help turn the tide of history . . . This we do know: a world that begins to witness the rebirth of trust among nations can find its way to a peace that is neither partial nor punitive. With all who will work in good faith toward such a peace, we are ready, with renewed resolve, to strive to redeem the near-lost hopes of our day.[27]

Over the course of the next several months, Eisenhower concluded that while the Soviet leaders, including Molotov, Malenkov, Bulganin, and Khrushchev (no one in the United States knew for sure who the true heir to Stalin was), had not dismissed his overtures out of hand, they needed further evidence of America's willingness to match words with deeds. Making Stassen the point man for disarmament policy would be an important step in that process. In early May of 1955, the Soviets offered a preliminary disarmament proposal, "in which Moscow expressed its willingness to accept inspectors on Soviet soil." But the move also highlighted a growing rift in Eisenhower's administration between hardliners of the Dulles type and more outspoken proponents of negotiation and conciliation like Stassen. In reflecting upon this appointment to be what columnist Richard Rovere called the "Secretary of Peace," Stassen would later write, "The challenge of this new assignment hovered over all my waking thoughts: How I could help the President break the tensions of the Cold War by promoting disarmament, but do it in a way that would work in tandem with Secretary Dulles, instead of clashing with him!"[28]

That dynamic would prove the source of Stassen's greatest frustration during the next two and half years and, ultimately, marked the beginning of his demise as a member of Eisenhower's inner circle. On May 17, 1955, less than two months after the appointment, Dulles met with the president to express his concerns that Stassen, "consciously or unconsciously, was extending his jurisdiction, at least in the popular mind, so as to include the whole area of 'peace.'" Pointing out "that Stassen was appointed to work out in cooperation with the interested Departments a national program for the limitation and control of armaments," Dulles was concerned that referring to Stassen as the "Secretary for Peace" would undermine the efforts of the State Department and the entire foreign service.[29]

Eisenhower made clear that he did not object if writers dubbed Stassen "Secretary for Peace." In doing so, they were essentially furthering Eisenhower's original intent of advertising America's desire to avoid war. He went so far as to suggest to Dulles that "if we could do something to dramatize our interest in 'peace' to counteract the Soviet peace offensives that might be good." Dulles responded by saying that the relationship would likely not work unless Stassen "accepted foreign policy guidance" from the secretary of state as he had done as head of the Foreign Operations Administration. Dulles suggested that he and Stassen sit down "to work out the proper relationship," and Eisenhower fully agreed.[30]

Three days later Dulles and Stassen met to clarify their responsibilities with respect to disarmament. The memorandum Dulles prepared following that meeting shines considerable light upon the two men's differing approaches and foreshadows their inevitable parting of ways. Stassen began by outlining his general thesis on arms control, which Dulles characterized as a "freeze" of armaments at present levels. The secretary of state shared his skepticism "as to whether the Soviet Union would accept a freeze at a point where we had substantial atomic superiority." On this point Dulles was dead on, as would be demonstrated later that summer when the Soviets rejected Eisenhower's "Open Skies" proposal. So long as they were behind in the arms race and war with the Americans was a possibility, the Russians had little incentive to abandon their production of nuclear weapons.[31]

Dulles moved on to other matters. He bluntly informed Stassen that he "did not like his use of the title 'Secretary for Peace.'" The ensuing conversation essentially amounted to a reminder of who was in charge of the peace process. Dulles shared his concern "that it was not good for the State

Department and Foreign Service to feel that some outside agency had primary responsibility for peace." Stassen pointed out that the issue "had come about more or less naturally without his instigation" and that "he would drop any use himself of this title, although he could not prevent it being used by others." Dulles used the exchange to underscore his primary message, the reason for which he wanted to discuss matters with Stassen in the first place: "I said once there was an agreed United States position [on disarmament], I thought then the carrying out of it ought to be under the direction and guidance of the Secretary of State, and that he should cooperate with us and take policy guidance from us. He said this would be highly agreeable to him." Now that the jurisdictional issues had been settled, Stassen could move forward with his new responsibilities so long as he remembered who was in charge of foreign affairs.[32]

Despite their philosophical differences, Dulles and Stassen managed to carry on a cordial working relationship for the time being. Pursuant to Stassen's new role in the administration, the Foreign Operations Administration was slated to be phased out on July 1, 1955, and its primary functions taken over by the Department of State. On June 30, Dulles wrote Stassen a formal letter commending him for his oversight of the FOA and praising the former governor's administrative abilities. He wrote, "I find myself recalling with deep gratification the pleasant relationship we have enjoyed over the past two and a half years during your stewardship of our mutual security program. It was a period of great accomplishment in our aid operations, and this was due in large measure to your wholehearted devotion to the task and your inspiring leadership. I have never ceased to admire your ready grasp of the many facets of the complex problems which you were called upon to handle." Successful as he had been in the past, Stassen was just now entering perhaps the most challenging and controversial phase of his service to the Eisenhower administration and the nation.[33]

～

In July 1955 leaders of the four major powers—the United Sates, Great Britain, France, and the Soviet Union—gathered in Geneva, Switzerland, for highly anticipated summit talks. Though subsequent references to the "spirit of Geneva" may be overblown considering how little was actually accomplished at the summit, it did mark the first time an American and Soviet chief of state had conferred directly since Truman and Stalin met at Potsdam precisely ten years earlier. Considering how contentious and potentially deadly the Cold War had become, just getting the two sides to sit down and have a civil conversation seemed to represent a major step forward on the path to peace.

Once again, President Eisenhower seized the opportunity to make substantial progress in his negotiations with the Soviets. Working in close consultation with a coterie of advisors including Harold Stassen, General Alfred Gruenther (supreme allied commander in Europe), Admiral Arthur Radford (chairman of the Joint Chiefs of Staff), and Nelson Rockefeller (special assistant to the president), Eisenhower explored an innovative approach to mutual security that came to be known as the "Open Skies" proposal. Stassen wrote in 1990 that the original idea for aerial inspection, upon which "Open Skies" was based, developed out of his conversations with air force General James Doolittle. Perhaps best known for organizing and leading the famed B-25 raid over Tokyo in April of 1942, by the 1950s Doolittle had become a respected advisor on issues ranging from atomic energy and defense spending to foreign intelligence and national aeronautics. In 1955 Stassen tapped Doolittle to serve on a committee working to develop specific plans for disarmament. Although Sherman Adams, Eisenhower's chief of staff, gave Nelson Rockefeller credit for suggesting aerial inspection, Stassen maintained to the end of his life that James Doolittle first brought the idea to his attention. With characteristic self-effacement, Doolittle briefly addressed the subject in his 1991 autobiography, writing, "Typically of jobs like that, whatever input I had is buried in the minutes of the many meetings I attended, and many of our deliberations were and still may be classified."[34]

Regardless of where, when, or with whom the concept originated, it was Eisenhower, at Stassen's persistent urging, who put the proposal before his fellow conferees at Geneva. On Thursday, July 21, the fourth day of meetings, the president began to deliver his prepared remarks on the subject of disarmament. Without warning Eisenhower paused briefly, removed his glasses, and looked directly at the Soviet delegation, which included Bulganin, Molotov, Khrushchev, and the president's old friend Marshall Zhukov—Russia's greatest living military hero. Then, according to his recollections, Eisenhower spoke "quickly and partially extemporaneously," saying,

> Gentlemen, since I have been working on this memorandum to present to this conference, I have been searching my heart and mind for something that I could say here that could convince everyone of the great sincerity of the United States in approaching this problem of disarmament.

I should address myself for a moment principally to the delegates from the Soviet Union, because our two great countries admittedly possess new and terrible weapons in quantities which do give rise in other parts of the world, or reciprocally, to the fears and dangers of surprise attack.

I propose, therefore, that we take a practical step, that we begin an arrangement, very quickly, as between ourselves, immediately.[35]

Now that he had their attention, the president proceeded to outline his plan. He proposed a mutual exchange of blueprints for military facilities to be followed up by prearranged aerial reconnaissance for the purpose of verifying and photographing each nation's military capabilities. These measures, taken as whole, offered the best possible assurances against a surprise attack, "thus lessening danger and relaxing tension" between the two superpowers. Eisenhower's seemingly impromptu suggestion was received warmly at the conference table by the other leaders (he had previously tipped his hand to British prime minister Anthony Eden, who enthusiastically supported the plan). At a reception following the day's meetings, however, Nikita Khrushchev made a point of informing the president that he had no intention of permitting such inspections in Soviet territory. Eisenhower was naturally disappointed and hoped that he could persuade the enigmatic Soviet leader to reconsider. Unfortunately, he never did.[36]

Years later, Khrushchev's son Sergei provided the simplest but most compelling explanation for why his father was so quick to dismiss Eisenhower's "Open Skies" proposal. Nearly forty-five years after the fact and well beyond the reach of Soviet authorities, the younger Khrushchev wrote, "Father rejected the plan outright. Not that he was against the idea itself. But if the American President feared a Soviet attack, Father was afraid of something quite different: that in the process of flying over our country, the Americans would discover our most important secret—how much weaker we were than they—and that discovery might prompt the United States to carry out a preventive strike. In subsequent years Father continued to oppose inspections for the same reason."[37]

John Foster Dulles was a pragmatist. He believed that while the "Open Skies" initiative never had any real chance of gaining Soviet support, just floating the idea for the entire world to see constituted a diplomatic victory for the United States. The Soviet leaders could either accept it or reject it, but either way the United States could claim the moral high ground. Most importantly, Dulles believed that a clear line of distinction had been drawn on the entire issue of aerial inspection and that the Americans should stick to their original proposal rather than negotiate it to death, risking the appearance of weakness or lack of decisiveness.

On that point, Harold Stassen completely disagreed. He believed the Geneva summit marked a turning point in Cold War relations and that the time had come for "a new direction to US disarmament policy." He rejected the all-or-nothing approach advocated by Dulles, preferring instead to work out partial arrangements, "conducted by means of negotiations and concessions on both sides. Stassen meant to offer America and the world the security that nuclear disarmament could provide, but without insisting on that unattainable target." He proceeded to explore and prepare a sort of incremental plan for bilateral disarmament with the Soviets. He and Dulles were now clearly on a collision course with one another, and the stakes kept getting higher.[38]

On July 20, 1956, presidential aide Arthur Larson was headed toward the Oval Office when he encountered Harold Stassen on his way out of a meeting with the president. When Larson entered the room he found Eisenhower fuming. This was a particularly challenging time for the president, who was recovering from intestinal surgery, and Larson knew that relations with Egyptian president Gamal Nasser were deteriorating rapidly. Just the day before, Dulles had withdrawn America's offer to help finance construction of the Aswan High Dam, thus helping drive Egypt into the Soviet camp. As if that weren't bad enough, six days later Nasser would nationalize the Suez Canal, which ultimately led to a combined British, French, and Israeli invasion of Egypt. That ill-advised operation (about which Eisenhower knew nothing in advance) would receive universal condemnation, drive a wedge between the United States and its allies, and radically change the dynamics of Middle East relations. Though all of this lay on the horizon, Eisenhower was losing patience with Egypt's leader, and it showed. "Art," he demanded, "have you ever been Nasserized and Stassenized on the same day?"[39]

Apparently Stassen had chosen this day of all days to inform Eisenhower that Vice President Richard Nixon should not be on the Republican ticket in November. Stassen offered some polling evidence and argued that Nixon would potentially cost Eisenhower the election. With the Republican National Convention set to begin in just four weeks, Stassen's timing could not have been worse. Unless of course his "Dump-Nixon" campaign gained traction, in which case the party would need to find a viable alternative and quickly. Eisenhower was shocked but did little to discourage Stassen's meddling on that or any subsequent day. By his own admission, Eisenhower had more pressing matters on his mind and quickly advised, "You are an American citizen, Harold, and free to follow your own judgment in such matters."[40]

Stassen took the hurried comment as tacit approval and ran with it. At a press conference the following Monday he proposed that Massachusetts governor Christian Herter be the Republican candidate for vice president. That announcement precipitated a flurry of activity in Washington news circles. Fellow Republicans waited for a sign, any sign, as to how the president wanted to proceed, but, according to writer Chris Matthews, "the silence emanating from 1600 Pennsylvania Avenue lent the stop-Nixon campaign a certain stature." Within a few days it became obvious that Stassen had gone out too far on the limb. No prominent Republicans were rallying to the cause, and Democrats could hardly contain their glee. Herter, who gained an appointment as assistant secretary of state out of the entire affair, described Stassen's one-man stop-Nixon campaign as a "comic opera." Perhaps the only man who wasn't laughing was Nixon himself, who later described the period as one of "agonizing uncertainty." Richard Nixon would never forget Stassen's blatant attempt to derail his political career, nor would the powers that be in the Republican Party. Adding insult to injury, Stassen was compelled to second Nixon's nomination at the convention as a symbol of party unity and political fence mending. Unfortunately for Stassen, the fence was well beyond repair.[41]

This became increasingly evident as his relations with John Foster Dulles continued to deteriorate. Stassen pursued his own plans on disarmament, considering himself the president's lead advisor on this issue, and doggedly prepared for the 1957 London Arms Control Conference. To complicate matters further, Eisenhower appointed Stassen deputy representative of the United States on the United Nations Disarmament Commission, which meant he was technically under the authority of UN ambassador Henry Cabot Lodge. Stassen now had three bosses—Eisenhower, Dulles, and Lodge—but his critics complained that he continued to act independently, a charge consistently supported by Stassen's actions. In May of 1957, Dulles spoke with Nixon about the London conference and related disarmament proposals. Dulles reported, "The Vice President expressed the view that Stassen would be willing to sign any agreement, however improvident, merely for the sake of getting any agreement and the consequent renown."[42]

Dulles feared that Stassen would make commitments at the London conference that the administration was not willing or prepared to meet. In April Stassen returned to the states to bring his colleagues up to speed on the proceedings, and Dulles cautioned him to tread lightly in negotiations with the Russian delegates. The secretary of state was most concerned about Stassen's use of informal or "personal" proposals as a means of finding out what the Soviets might be willing to accept in the way of partial disarmament. Dulles said that "unless these reflected positions had in fact been approved, it was highly dangerous." The Soviets had accused the Americans of backing out of agreements in the past, and according to Dulles, "we could not afford to be put in that position by withdrawing from 'personal' positions put forward by Stassen."[43]

That is precisely what happened but with an added twist of irony that came back to haunt Stassen. On May 31 he offered his Soviet counterparts an "informal memorandum" outlining a detailed disarmament proposal. It contained among other things a scaled-back plan for mutual aerial and ground inspections, provisions for reduced military expenditures, and a ten-month suspension of nuclear testing. Stassen believed he was on the verge of brokering a historic arms control agreement with the Soviet Union. It would be the crowning achievement of his tireless work on behalf of world peace and disarmament. Unfortunately, according to his assistant Robert Matteson, Stassen "was skating on thin ice." When Prime Minister Harold Macmillan found out that Stassen had offered a bilateral proposal to the Soviets without consulting the British, he was furious. Now the Americans were guilty of acting alone, the very charge Eisenhower had levied at the British and French during the Suez crisis. Dulles and Eisenhower scrambled to pick up the pieces. The president fired off a cable to Macmillan trying to assure the British leader that Stassen's actions "took place without the knowledge or authorization of any of us here in Washington." He added, "I realize that once the Soviets have a piece of paper in their hands from the Head of the United States Delegation, it puts you and our other allies in an awkward position, one that is not easy to redress, but we shall do the best that we can."[44]

It was, in effect, the final straw. Dulles ordered Stassen to return home, and the secretary of state headed to London to take over negotiations personally. But the damage was already done. Harold Stassen had come closer than anyone else to solidifying a substantial arms control deal with the Soviets, and now he had essentially had his wings clipped. He was discredited and disgraced. But the final blow came later that fall when Dulles met with

Stassen to discuss his future in the administration. Both men agreed that "a situation might be developing which would make it undesirable for him to continue on in this disarmament work." Then Dulles lowered the boom. He informed Stassen that "there was a considerable measure of personal distrust of him in this matter" and that members of Congress and prominent European allies—Konrad Adenauer of Germany and Harold Macmillan included—preferred to distance themselves from any proposal that was attached to his name. "They did not," according to Dulles, "want to preside over the political rehabilitation of Harold Stassen." So there it was. No matter how much he had achieved during his nearly half decade of service in the Eisenhower administration, Stassen had been unable to shed the sullied image of a political opportunist and a bad one at that. Eisenhower had believed in him all along, but even that was little consolation given the circumstances. The time had come for Harold Stassen to bow out gracefully and chart a new course. Time and again, however, that had proven easier said than done.[45]

Thus, nearly one year to the day after Eisenhower's dramatic appeal in Geneva, two unrelated miscalculations combined to make Stassen's premature departure from the White House virtually unavoidable. One was self-inflicted and the other involved an unexpected war halfway around the world. The first would earn Stassen the perpetual disdain of a future U.S. president (not to mention the subsequent admiration of at least a few of his fellow citizens) and the second would in a roundabout way serve to exacerbate the damage from Stassen's own diplomatic blunder.

There is a fascinating postscript to Stassen's political activities in 1956 that up until now has gone either unnoticed or unexplored. It reveals a great deal about Richard Nixon and the people with whom he surrounded himself. Many years before the worst of the Watergate revelations rendered Nixon helpless before the bar of history, he had acquired a reputation for practicing a rough brand of politics. He was not one to forgive and forget, and it is hardly surprising that Nixon held a special grudge against Stassen after the events leading up to both the 1952 and 1956 elections. Although Stassen was certainly not the only prominent Republican to urge Nixon off the presidential ticket, the former "boy wonder" from Minnesota seemed to relish the task. In truth, Stassen was unequivocally opposed to a Nixon-led GOP, and he let his objections be known to Eisenhower and other Republican leaders. He once confided to his son Glen that he respected virtually everyone with whom he had come into contact during his many years of public service—

except Richard Nixon. After years of close observation, Stassen had come to the conclusion that Nixon lacked the moral fiber and sound judgment necessary to fulfill the role of America's chief executive.[46]

None of this came as much of a surprise to Richard Nixon, who had to fend off not one but two attempts by Harold Stassen to derail his political aspirations. In the spring of 1962, *Life* magazine ran a series of excerpts from Nixon's soon-to-be-released political memoir titled *Six Crises*. The first crisis Nixon recounted involved the now infamous "secret fund" that nearly ended his vice presidential career before it even began. When news broke in September of 1952 that Senator Richard Nixon and his family allegedly received financial gifts from wealthy campaign donors to the tune of twenty thousand dollars, all hell broke loose in the Republican ranks. Nixon wrote, "In a 300-word telegram Harold Stassen advised me to offer my withdrawal from the race. He even spelled out a suggested text for my withdrawal message and stated that Earl Warren should be named to step in if my offer was accepted." Nixon went on the offensive by taking to the nation's airwaves and vindicated himself virtually overnight in the eyes of most Americans and, more importantly, in the opinion of Dwight Eisenhower, the Republican Party's presidential nominee.[47]

Under the circumstances, Stassen's attempt to replace Nixon on the ticket again in 1956 must have struck a deep, bitter, and lasting chord in the vice president. Nixon ultimately survived that crisis as well, but he and his close political advisor—James Bassett—may have had the last laugh after all, even if it involved an inside joke. Bassett worked as Nixon's press secretary in 1952 and then shifted to campaign manager in 1956. Ten years earlier he served on Fleet Admiral William "Bull" Halsey's staff, where he no doubt crossed paths with Commander Harold Stassen. Bassett left politics after Nixon's 1960 presidential campaign and concentrated on his writing career full time. In 1962, the same year Richard Nixon's *Six Crises* appeared in print, James Bassett published an action-packed war novel entitled *Harm's Way*. The story was set in the Pacific during World War II and centered around a rugged, no-nonsense American admiral named Rockwell Torrey, later portrayed by John Wayne on the silver screen. Bassett included a perfunctory disclaimer at the beginning of the book that reads, "Except for the historical persons whom I have not endeavored to disguise, none of the characters in this fiction are based on any actual person, living or dead. Only the heroes may have subconscious counterparts in the author's mind. Such villains as might appear have been cut from whole khaki cloth."[48]

Here's where the story within the story takes a bizarre twist. Bassett's tale of naval warfare and clashing personalities includes an antagonist who bears a striking resemblance to Harold Stassen. The character in question, Commander Neal Owynn, is a former lawyer and senator who gave up his seat in Congress to join the U.S. Naval Reserve. Bassett describes him as "the aging boy wonder of the ageless Middle Atlantic hill country" who "had gone to an undistinguished land grant university." Another character in the story warns a colleague to tread lightly around the commander, explaining that a "chap like Neal Owynn might even wind up as President." And at one point Owynn reminds his superior that "after the war, politicians with combat records will be sitting pretty. Hell. Being entitled to sport the right ribbon in your buttonhole should be worth a half a million votes in my state alone." Bassett next mentions the navy's Legion of Merit decoration, which Commander Stassen was awarded in April of 1945.[49]

The similarities between Neal Owynn and Harold Stassen are too numerous to dismiss as mere coincidence. It seems much more plausible that James Bassett knew full well what he was writing or, more precisely, about whom he was writing. And his motive might have been as simple and as straightforward as his most piercing characterization of Neal Owynn: "As he spoke, the Senator's spurious Harvard accent wore away, along with his elegant rhetoric, for now he was at his enthusiastic best, scheming to confound an adversary, or destroy him, all in the name of good clean political fun."[50]

Richard Nixon played the role of Harold Stassen's adversary during most of the 1950s, and he'd nearly been destroyed in the process. But now, thanks to Bassett's mighty pen, Stassen had received his just rewards. Perhaps Nixon and Bassett joked privately about the not-so-hidden inspiration for Commander Neal Owynn. Maybe they told close friends and associates. Maybe they didn't have to. By then Stassen's political career was past the point of no return.

~

Stassen officially left the Eisenhower administration on February 15, 1958. In response to Stassen's letter of resignation, the president wrote, "I have valued highly your loyal friendship, as well as your readiness to express to me frankly your views on the many subjects that have been of common interest to us both." Stassen was heading back to Philadelphia, ostensibly to practice law and campaign for a spot on the Republican ticket in Pennsylvania's upcoming gubernatorial race. But that was only part of the story, and both men knew it. Stassen had locked horns with many influential Republicans over the years, as demonstrated by his complicated relationships with Thomas Dewey, Robert Taft, Arthur Vandenberg, Joseph McCarthy, and Richard Nixon. To a certain extent that was to be expected in national politics, particularly come election time. But Stassen's unrelenting policy disputes with John Foster Dulles and others in the administration were a different matter because they ultimately reflected poorly on the president. Stassen had simply gone out on a limb one too many times, only to find that he was alone and lacking the political capital needed to warrant rescue. Eisenhower clearly recognized the errors in judgment that had culminated in Stassen's demise, but he also appreciated the sheer brilliance and determination that preceded them. And he hoped that there were still more victories to be had for Harold Stassen—personally and professionally—because the nation owed him a debt of gratitude. "I am free to express my deep conviction," Eisenhower wrote, "that because of your long and varied experience in state government and in military and civil posts in the Federal government, you have much to contribute to the future of our country. Certainly your sincerity and integrity will command the respect of all citizens, no matter in what activity you may engage."[51]

If only others had been so gracious. Harold Stassen became a punch line for political satirists rather quickly, and his past accomplishments faded from most memories in proportion to his future defeats. And there would be many. Within only a few weeks of Stassen's departure from Washington, journalist Arthur Krock published a pithy little doggerel (think Humpty Dumpty) that proved remarkably prophetic:

> Harold sat on the White House wall.
> Foster caused Harold to have a great fall.
> And only the State of William Penn
> Can put poor Harold together again.[52]

Stassen's political fortunes did not rebound in Pennsylvania or anywhere for that matter, but it wasn't for lack of trying. He pursued several more elective offices over the years—governor of Pennsylvania, mayor of Philadelphia, and at various times governor, congressman, and senator from Minnesota. Then there was the always-elusive Republican nomination for president, which he sought six more times between 1964 and 1992. Johnny Carson once told his *Tonight Show* audience that Harold Stassen was still campaigning, this time for citizenship in Minnesota. Others joked about a major gathering of Stassen supporters taking place in a telephone booth. And upon hearing that the former governor was running for president again in 1964, "a politically precocious youngster in Queens dubbed his soapbox derby car 'Harold Stassen's Ticker Tape Parade.'" On and on the ribbing went, and year after year Stassen announced his candidacy for some office or another. He never won an election again. Nor did he ever lose the will to run.[53]

Stassen took it all in stride and continued to speak candidly on the important issues of the day. He resumed his legal practice upon returning to Philadelphia, specializing in international law and leveraging his vast knowledge of geopolitics on behalf of clients with overseas interests. He had formed many important relationships with leaders from around the world during his years of service under Eisenhower, and his concern with global affairs lasted long after he left office. But the winds of change eventually brought much of the world's attention back to the United States in the 1960s, and Stassen supported the struggle for human rights at home. A devout Baptist his entire life, Stassen served as president of the American Baptist Convention in 1963. That summer he joined Martin Luther King, Jr.—

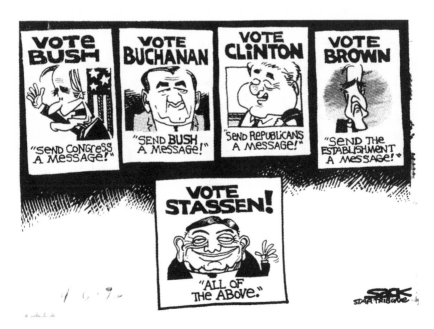

Cartoon by Steve Sack, *Minneapolis Star Tribune*, April 6, 1992

fellow Baptist and peace advocate—for the March on Washington because equality of opportunity had always been central to Stassen's notion of justice. As governor of Minnesota, he attempted to integrate the Minnesota National Guard by commissioning its first black officer in 1942. He also made it possible for black football players to compete at the University of Pennsylvania beginning in 1948, less than a year after Jackie Robinson broke the color barrier in Major League Baseball. Stassen also shared King's growing opposition to the Vietnam War. When Dr. King received word that he had won the Nobel Peace Prize for his work in promoting nonviolence and civil rights, Harold Stassen lauded him via telegram the very next day, writing,

ENTHUSIASTIC CONGRATULATIONS TO YOU UPON YOUR THOROUGHLY WELL DESERVED AWARD OF THE NOBEL PEACE PRIZE FOR 1964 . . . IT IS ESPECIALLY SIGNIFICANT THAT THIS AWARD TO YOU RIGHTLY RECOGNIZES THE INTERRELATIONSHIP TO WORLD PEACE OF THE SUCCESSFUL ESTABLISHMENT OF THE RIGHTS OF ALL WITHIN THE UNITED STATES WHICH YOU HAVE SO COURAGEOUSLY ELOQUENTLY AND EFFECTIVELY ADVANCED THROUGH NON-VIOLENT MEANS.[54]

The year 1964 was also one for a presidential election. Stassen and several other moderate Republicans tried to stop the extremist wing of their party from taking over the nomination process. Despite their efforts, Senator Barry Goldwater of Arizona reigned supreme at the convention, prompting political chronicler Teddy White to observe, "History would have to record that the Republican Party had not submitted docilely to this new leadership, but had resisted to the end—so that from this resistance and defeat, others, later, might take heart and resume the battle." Stassen later referred to Goldwater's nomination as the "tragic shift of our party," but he never lost hope in the GOP and its capacity for change. After all, he'd been witnessing it all his life.[55]

By 1978 Harold Stassen was back in Minnesota for good. He resumed practicing law in West St. Paul, just a stone's throw from the site of his childhood home, and he surveyed the political landscape with the same keenness he had displayed a half century earlier. He quickly set his sights on a U.S. Senate seat and campaigned vigorously for the primary election. He lost again, this time to a retail business owner and political newcomer by the name of Rudy Boschwitz. Stassen accepted the defeat with grace (his critics would claim practice makes perfect), and he issued a short statement reaffirming his loyalty to the Republican Party and promising his unconditional support for Boschwitz in November. Then he concluded,

"I will continue, as I resolved to do as a young student at the University of Minnesota, to endeavor, with humility, to contribute to the future peace and well-being of all humanity on this earth, under God." Rudy Boschwitz ended up going to the Senate, and in 1980 Harold Stassen was campaigning for president again.[56]

Stassen appeared on C-SPAN's *Booknotes* in the fall of 1990 to promote *Eisenhower: Turning the World Toward Peace,* a book he coauthored with his friend Marshall Houts. It offers unabashed praise for Eisenhower's foreign policy, which, according to Stassen, "moved the world from the icy brinks of World War III to the hopes of enduring peace, with devotion to freedom, justice, and human rights." The book presents a unique, insider's account of the 1952 presidential campaign and election as well as the inner workings of Eisenhower's national security team. It is also the closest thing to an autobiography that Stassen ever produced. In a 1990 *Booknotes* interview, host Brian Lamb couldn't help bringing up his distinguished guest's numerous bids to become president. Then he asked the obvious question: "Are you going to run again?" Stassen smiled broadly, shook his head, and replied, "No. I'm not gonna run any more. I'm just walking for peace now." Two years later he was trudging through wet New Hampshire snow for the umpteenth time, meeting voters and seeking their support on primary day. At eighty-four years of age, Harold Stassen had become the political equivalent of the Energizer Bunny.[57]

More of Him
Than We Have Now

Like the indefatigable Don Quixote, Stassen has been reduced to a cari-
cature of himself—hapless and helpless—tilting at voting booths in an
unending quest to capture the presidency or newspaper headlines. Ambition, so the story goes, was his fatal flaw. That is how most Americans, if
they remember him at all, still picture Harold Stassen, who passed away
peacefully on March 4, 2001. But those who dismiss Stassen out of hand as
a wannabe or a might-have-been betray either ignorance of history or contempt of principle. Neither is worthy of the man or his abiding purpose in
life, which reminds us that the race is not always to the swift nor the battle
necessarily to the strong. Stassen's long and winding and frequently bumpy
road in politics demonstrates the timeless truth of Abraham Lincoln's observation: "The probability that we may fail in the struggle ought not to deter
us from the support of a cause we believe to be great." Stassen knew this all
along. When the *New York Times* printed his obituary, the editors included
Stassen's own appraisal of his nearly seventy years of public service. "I
know I've had an impact," he said, "that some things I've done have really
counted for world peace, for the passion of the individual. I sometimes wish
people would ask not how many times I've run a political campaign, but
how many times I've been right on the issues." That's all that really mattered to the man who sought the presidency so many times, not for power's
sake but to advance the cause of peace whenever and wherever he could.[1]

To the very end of his life, Harold Stassen tried to make substantive
contributions toward ensuring justice, security, and peace throughout the
world. In 1995, when the United Nations approached the fiftieth anniversary

of its founding, Stassen was still hard at work trying to keep the organization abreast with the times and its principle mission, "to save succeeding generations from the scourge of war." He wrote and published what he called *United Nations: A Working Paper for Restructuring* to commemorate the important milestone and stimulate a broad-based discussion regarding the future of the organization. "With the ending of the cold war," Stassen suggested in the book's preface, "the peoples of the world need the United Nations Organization today more than ever. The United Nations must become more effective in peacemaking, more efficient in peacekeeping, and more dynamic in securing the well-being of the children, women, and men of the world."[2]

Stassen then laid out his plans for revision in a very straightforward manner. He printed the original UN Charter on the left-hand side of the book and presented his proposed reforms on the adjacent pages for the sake of easy comparison. Most of his recommendations reflected the myriad changes in circumstances and attitudes that had taken place in the half century since the end of World War II. He acknowledged "varied religions, divergent ethnic origins" and "violent terrorism" in his new preamble, phrases that never appeared in the UN Charter he helped draft in 1945. And he explicitly recognized that "the United Nations Organization of the future must become a world-changing, creative center, functioning within the extremes of economic, political, social, religious, and philosophical thought." Indeed, much had changed in the world since Stassen had been at the peak of his professional career and influence. But his basic political philosophy and purpose in life had in truth changed very little over the years.[3]

~

On Friday, March 9, 2001, Harold Stassen lay in state in the Minnesota State Capitol rotunda. Family and friends and a few hundred supporters turned out to mourn his passing and honor his memory. Governor Jesse Ventura referred to his predecessor as "a man of the people" and praised the former-governor-turned-naval-officer for his "bravery and selfless dedication to his country." Then Ventura, a colorful politician in his own right, paused for a moment to reflect upon Stassen's accomplishments and said, "I am humbled." But Ventura wasn't the only one. Ordinary people with extraordinary memories came out of the woodwork to pay their respects. Eighty-five-year-old Dan Jones perhaps put it best when asked by a reporter why he felt compelled to attend the ceremony. "Harold Stassen was the first vote I ever cast. He was a very gentle man, a highly ethical man, a highly moral man.

He never brought disrespect to the state of Minnesota. I just admired him as a man, as a human being. I thought of him as Minnesota's No. 1 Citizen."[4]

Even the target of Stassen's "Dump-Nixon" campaign understood what very few of his fellow countrymen have been willing or able to admit. In 1993 Stassen's longtime friend and associate Robert Matteson wrote to Richard Nixon soliciting his opinion of Stassen. Almost exactly a year before his own death, Nixon replied graciously to Matteson's request. The only man to ever resign the presidency had apparently let bygones be bygones. "Despite his activities in 1956," Nixon wrote, "I still have a high opinion of Stassen as a political leader. I supported him in 1948 and believe he would have made a good President primarily because of his enlightened vision on foreign policy. He served with distinction in the Eisenhower administration. He failed to go to the top because he gave the appearance of wanting it too much . . . History should treat him with respect because of his rare abilities."[5]

I am standing near the top of what folks in these parts call Pilot Knob, a distinctive knoll high above the Minnesota and Mississippi Rivers. The Dakota people call this spot *Oheyawahi*, "the hill much visited," because they consider it sacred. They used to meet here to bury their dead and bid them safe travels to the spirit world. A different kind of traveler coming up the Mississippi River in a steamboat long ago could see Pilot Knob in the distance and know that he had reached the end of his journey. Civilization began or ended here at one time, depending upon one's perspective. Maybe it still does.

It is fall. The leaves have turned and the air is crisp and the bright sunshine provides me with more hope than warmth. So too does my youngest son, who is standing next to me. He points down to the ground and asks who is buried there. It is the final resting place for Harold Stassen and his beloved wife of seventy-one years, Esther, who died just five months before him. A tribute printed below Stassen's name on the grave marker reads HE LAID THE FOUNDATION FOR LASTING PEACE. To the right of us, an American flag unfurls in the brisk breeze, all fifty stars clearly visible at once. I seem to recall that there were only forty-five states in the union when Harold Stassen was born. Old Glory changed often in those days, even if what it symbolized did not. Then I glance at my boy and realize that he is the same age Harold's mother was when she made the long trip across the Atlantic Ocean to begin a new life in America. Hope accompanied all the passengers on that remarkable journey just as surely as it attends us on ours. I am suddenly reminded of Mark Twain's supposed observation that "History does not repeat itself, but it does rhyme." I think about the poet Carl Sandburg and the free man and the United States of the Earth and moderation, tolerance, compromise, and the middle way. Then I thank God for Harold Stassen and wish that we had more of him than we have now.

Acknowledgments

The only thing lonelier than reading a book that no one has heard of is writing one. And if you do it like I did over the span of eight years and begin telling folks what you're up to, quizzical looks and skeptical head nods become commonplace. Fortunately, many people have encouraged me along the way, and without their kindhearted assistance and advice, this book would not have been possible.

I am most indebted to the Werle and Rourke families for their continuous love and support. Writing is a solitary task, and I greatly regret that it often occupies far more of my time and attention than my family deserves. Several years ago I was talking on the phone with Harold Stassen's son Glen, who lived in California, when my two worlds—personal and professional—collided in a most revealing way. One of my own sons wanted me to help him with something or other around the house, and I explained that I couldn't possibly do it right then because I was in the middle of a very important conversation related to the Stassen book. A few minutes later, Glen shared with me a poignant story about a conversation he had with his father when the elder Stassen was about eighty-five years old. For the first time, Glen admitted how much he had missed his father during the war years, when Commander Stassen was serving as a naval officer in the Pacific. Harold suddenly turned to his son, now an adult, and asked, "Did you resent me for going to war?" Glen recalled being startled and a bit ashamed by the question at first, but he eventually came to appreciate it as a wonderful illustration of his father's emotional presence and his sensitivity to other people's feelings. It has taken me many years, not to mention the example of Harold and Glen Stassen, to realize that my greatest duty rests where my heart resides—at home. Thank you, Colleen, Jacob, Joshua, and Simon Abraham, for your endless patience, love, and encouragement.

My research was aided by generous and courteous professionals at the Minnesota Historical Society Library in St. Paul, the Dwight D. Eisenhower Presidential Library in Abilene, Kansas, and the United Nations Archives in New York City. Special thanks go to research librarian extraordinaire Rebecca Snyder at the Dakota County Historical Society in South St. Paul and Chad Roberts, president of the Ramsey County Historical Society. Thanks, Chad and Rebecca, for believing in me long before I believed in myself.

I am grateful also for the many people who read portions of the story and provided me with valuable feedback: Chad Roberts, Dave Dempsey, Doug Hoverson, Chuck Nixon, May Ginder, Pam Boston, Karlyn and Craig Coleman, Al and Betty Werle, Chuck Knapp, Dan Caffrey, Paul Laux, Kevin McMahon, John Halter, John Rosengren, Kate Roberts, Elise Rethlake, and hundreds of APUSHers from the Academy of Holy Angels, who remind me day after day and year after year why I love history so darn much. There is nothing quite like a captive audience.

Thank you as well to Harold Stassen's relatives, many of whom met, spoke, or corresponded with me over the years. They include Glen Harold Stassen, Bob Stassen, Rachel Stassen-Berger, Lois Glewwe, and Rollie Crawford. I appreciate the time and perspective that each of you was willing to share with me as well as the implicit trust that goes along with discussing a loved one's life and legacy.

I am especially grateful to two pros in the publishing business: author Rhoda Gilman, for encouraging me to take a shot at telling this story, and Ann Regan, editor in chief at MNHS Press, for helping see it through to completion. I hope to have done both of you proud.

Notes

NOTES TO PROLOGUE

1. *Ocala Star Banner,* February 16, 1988, 8B; interview with Arlen Erdahl conducted by the author, November 9, 2008, Lakeville, MN.

2. Interview with Charles Reid conducted by the author, October 12, 2013, Richfield, MN.

3. Reid interview.

4. *Washington Post,* March 8, 2001.

5. Carl Sandburg, *The People, Yes* (New York: Harcourt Brace & Co., 1936).

6. *New York Times,* August 26, 1917.

NOTES TO CHAPTER 1

1. Details on state history, Theodore C. Blegen, *Grassroots History* (Minneapolis: University of Minnesota Press, 1947), 32.

2. William G. LeDuc and Family Papers, 1760–1967, box 4, folder 7, Minnesota Historical Society, St. Paul, MN; *Minnesota Pioneer,* October 27, 1853; Mark Twain, *Life on the Mississippi* (New York: Harper & Brothers, 1883), 489.

3. *New York Times,* July 16, 1898, 4.

4. Sherwood Anderson, *Winesburg, Ohio* (New York: Signet Classics, 2005), 56.

5. Theodore C. Blegen and Philip D. Jordan, *With Various Voices: Recordings of North Star Life* (St. Paul, MN: Itasca Press, 1949), 343.

6. Theodore Roosevelt, *An Autobiography* (New York: Macmillan Co., 1913), 568.

7. Mario R. DiNunzio, ed., *Theodore Roosevelt: An American Mind: Selected Writings* (New York: Penguin Books, 1995), 129–30; Robert F. Bruner and Sean D. Carr, *The Panic of 1907: Lessons Learned from the Market's Perfect Storm* (Hoboken, NJ: John Wiley & Sons, Inc., 2007), 26–32.

8. *USA Today*, December 31, 1999, 31A; *New York Times*, January, 19, 1901, BR9.

9. *USA Today*, December 31, 1999, 31A.

10. Allan Nevins and Henry Steele Commager, *America: The Story of a Free People* (Boston: Little, Brown and Co., 1943), 374.

11. Theodore C. Blegen, *Minnesota: A History of the State,* 2nd ed. (St. Paul: University of Minnesota Press, 1975), 292.

12. Richard C. Cortner, *The Iron Horse and the Constitution: The Railroads and the Transformation of the Fourteenth Amendment* (Westport, CT: Greenwood Press, 1993), 3.

13. Cortner, *The Iron Horse and the Constitution,* 9.

14. *Minneapolis Tribune*, March 4, 1885, 4.

15. *Minneapolis Tribune*, April 6, 1907, 8.

16. *Minneapolis Tribune*, February 8, 1907, 3.

17. *Ex Parte Young*, 209 U.S. 123, 142 (1908).

18. Cortner, *The Iron Horse and the Constitution,* 196.

19. Richard Hofstadter, *The Age of Reform* (New York: Vintage Books, 1955), 264–65.

20. Woodrow Wilson, *The New Freedom* (Englewood Cliffs, NJ: Prentice-Hall, Inc., 1961), 35.

21. Cortner, *The Iron Horse and the Constitution,* 206.

22. Joseph Frazier Wall, *Andrew Carnegie* (Pittsburgh, PA: University of Pittsburgh Press, 1989), 917; *New York Times,* April 24, 1907, 8.

23. Barbara Tuchman, *The Proud Tower: A Portrait of the World Before the War, 1890–1914* (New York: MacMillan Co., 1966), 278.

24. Tuchman, *The Proud Tower,* 278.

25. *New York Times,* June 16, 1907, C1.

26. *New York Times,* June 16, 1907, C1.

27. *New York Times,* June 16, 1907, C1.

28. Tuchman, *The Proud Tower,* 281.

29. John A. Garraty and Peter Gay, eds., *The Columbia History of the World* (New York: Harper & Row, 1972), 968.

30. Neil Betten, "Strike on the Mesabi, 1907," *Minnesota History* 40.7 (Fall 1967): 341.

31. Philip S. Foner, *History of the Labor Movement in the United States. Volume IV: The Industrial Workers of the World, 1905–1917* (New York: International Publishers Co., 1965), 490.

32. Betten, "Strike on the Mesabi," 342.

33. Foner, *History of the Labor Movement,* 491.

34. Andrew Carroll, ed., *Letters of a Nation* (New York: Kodansha America, Inc., 1997), 187.

35. Nell Irvin Painter, *Standing at Armageddon: The United States, 1877–1919* (New York: W. W. Norton & Co., 1987), 213.

36. Painter, *Standing at Armageddon*, 213.

37. Harold E. Stassen, *Where I Stand* (New York: Doubleday & Co., Inc., 1947), 2.

38. *St. Paul Dispatch*, November 9, 1938, 2.

39. *St. Paul Dispatch*, November 9, 1938, 2.

40. Stassen, *Where I Stand*, 2.

41. Stassen, *Where I Stand*, 3.

42. Stassen, *Where I Stand*, 3.

43. John Gunther, *Inside U.S.A.* (New York: Harper & Brothers, 1947), 297; Harrison E. Salisbury, *A Journey for Our Times: A Memoir* (New York: Harper & Row, 1983), 83.

44. President Theodore Roosevelt's Fourth Annual Message to Congress, *A Compilation of the Messages and Papers of the Presidents*, vol. 16 (New York: Bureau of National Literature, Inc., 1916), 6923.

45. L. Ethan Ellis, *Frank B. Kellogg and American Foreign Relations, 1925–1929* (New Brunswick, NJ: Rutgers University Press, 1961), 70.

46. Harold E. Stassen, "National Will or International Goodwill," speech, Harold E. Stassen Papers, box 1, folder 14, page 1, Minnesota History Society, St. Paul, MN (hereafter, Stassen Papers). All quoted portions are taken from this draft.

47. Stassen, "National Will or International Goodwill," 1.

48. Stassen, "National Will or International Goodwill," 4–5.

49. Stassen, "National Will or International Goodwill," 5–6.

50. Stassen, "National Will or International Goodwill," 6.

51. Wilfred P. Deac, "Fire from the Hills," *Military History* (August 1990): 38; Ellis, *Frank B. Kellogg*, 74, 75.

52. Deac, "Fire from the Hills," 45.

53. Richard Freund, *Zero Hour: Policies of the Powers* (New York: Oxford University Press, 1937), 198.

54. Alan Brinkley, *American History: A Survey*, 13th ed. (New York: McGraw-Hill, 2009), 709.

55. E. David Cronon, "The End of a Dream," in *Portrait of America*, 3rd ed., ed. Stephen B. Oates (Boston: Houghton Mifflin Co., 1983), 2:142, 143; Freund, *Zero Hour*, 200, 202.

NOTES TO CHAPTER 2

1. John D. Hicks, *The American Nation: A History of the United States from 1865 to the Present* (Cambridge, MA: Riverside Press, 1955), 465, 466.

2. George H. Mayer, *The Political Career of Floyd B. Olson* (St. Paul: Minnesota Historical Society Press, 1987), 16.

3. Mayer, *The Political Career of Floyd B. Olson*, xiv.

4. Ivan Hinderaker, "Harold Stassen and Developments in the Republican Party in Minnesota, 1937–1943" (PhD diss., University of Minnesota Political Science Department, June 1949), 44.

5. Interview with Lois Glewwe conducted by the author, September 28, 2008, South St. Paul, MN; Ivan Hinderaker, "Harold Stassen," 44.

6. Hinderaker, "Harold Stassen," 45–46.

7. *South St. Paul Daily Reporter*, August 5, 1932, 1.

8. *South St. Paul Daily Reporter*, August 5, 1932, 1.

9. *South St. Paul Daily Reporter*, August 5, 1932, 5.

10. *West St. Paul Booster*, August 12, 1932, 1; *South St. Paul Daily Reporter*, August 11, 1932, 1.

11. Neal Karlen, *Augie's Secrets: The Minneapolis Mob and the King of the Hennepin Strip* (St. Paul: Minnesota Historical Society Press, 2013), 14; Paul Maccabee, *John Dillinger Slept Here: A Crooks' Tour of Crime and Corruption in St. Paul, 1920–1936* (St. Paul: Minnesota Historical Society Press, 1995), 9; *South St. Paul Daily Reporter*, July 9, 1932, 1, 4; *West St. Paul Booster*, September 1, 1933, 1.

12. *Dakota County Tribune*, December 22, 1933, 1.

13. *Berkeley Daily Gazette*, December 21, 1933, 1; *South St. Paul Daily Reporter*, May 4, 1936, 1.

14. Frederick Lewis Allen, *Since Yesterday: The 1930s in America*, Bantam Matrix ed. (New York: Harper & Row, 1965), 68.

15. Gunther, *Inside U.S.A.*, 298.

16. Allen, *Since Yesterday*, 69.

17. Interview with Walter Klaus conducted by author, February 10, 2009, Hastings, MN.

18. *Home Building and Loan Association v. Blaisdell*, 290 U.S. 398 (1934).

19. *State of Minnesota v. Blasius*, 290 U.S. 1 (1933); *St. Paul Pioneer Press*, July 10, 1998, 5B.

20. *St. Paul Pioneer Press*, July 10, 1998, 1B.

21. *St. Paul Pioneer Press*, July 10, 1998, 1B, 5B; *State of Minnesota v. Blasius*, 290 U.S. 1 (1933).

22. Quoted by Russell W. Fridley in Mayer, *The Political Career of Floyd B. Olson*, xix.

23. Steven J. Keillor, *Shaping Minnesota's Identity: 150 Years of State History* (Lakeville, MN: Pogo Press, 2008), 176; Albert Eisele, *Almost to the Presidency* (Blue Earth, MN: Piper Co., 1972), 46; Gunther, *Inside U.S.A.*, 296.

24. Quoted in the Young Republican League of Minnesota's 25th Anniversary Program pamphlet, "From '37 to '62, the Story of the Winning Crew" (1962).

NOTES TO CHAPTER 3

1. Mayer, *The Political Career of Floyd B. Olson*, 297.

2. Mayer, *The Political Career of Floyd B. Olson*, 278, 279–80.

3. Mayer, *The Political Career of Floyd B. Olson,* 287.

4. Blegen, *Minnesota,* 529.

5. *Niagara Falls Gazette,* October 15, 1936, 16; *Snohomish County Forum,* October 22, 1936, 6.

6. *New York Times,* October 12, 1936, 21.

7. FDR to Mr. Delaney, Western Union telegram, October 6, 1936, in author's possession.

8. Arthur S. Link and William B. Catton, *American Epoch: A History of the United States Since the 1890s,* 3rd ed. (New York: Alfred A. Knopf, 1967), 418.

9. William E. Lass, *Minnesota: A History* (New York: W. W. Norton & Co., 1998), 226.

10. Keillor, *Shaping Minnesota's Identity,* 179–80; *Brainerd Daily Dispatch,* April 7, 1937, 1; Blegen, *Minnesota,* 536.

11. *Hastings Herald,* April 30, 1937, 1.

12. *South St. Paul Daily Reporter,* November 19, 1937, 1.

13. *South St. Paul Daily Reporter,* December 17, 1937, 1.

14. "Memorandum of State Political Situation" (1938), box 4, Stassen Papers. All quoted portions are taken from this document.

15. Gunther, *Inside U.S.A.,* 300.

16. *West St. Paul Booster,* March 11, 1938, 1; *West St. Paul Booster,* April 15, 1938, 1.

17. Gunther, *Inside U.S.A.,* 300.

18. Newspaper editorials from the 1938 gubernatorial campaign, box 4, Stassen Papers.

19. *South St. Paul Daily Reporter,* August 16, 1938, 1; *South St. Paul Daily Reporter,* August 9, 1938, 1; Box 4, Stassen Papers.

20. Campaign brochure prepared for Harold E. Stassen, South St. Paul, by Stassen All-Party Volunteers, Dr. George O. Orr, chairman, 649 Lowry Building, St. Paul, MN (1938); *Minneapolis Journal,* October 28, 1938, 7.

21. *West St. Paul Booster,* November 4, 1938, 1; *Dakota County Tribune,* November 4, 1938, 1.

22. William Manchester, *The Glory and the Dream: A Narrative History of America, 1932–1972* (New York: Bantam Books, 1974), 170; Keillor, *Shaping Minnesota's Identity,* 182.

NOTES TO CHAPTER 4

1. *Life,* February 17, 1941, 61.

2. Hinderaker, "Harold Stassen," 389.

3. *South St. Paul Daily Reporter,* January 3, 1939, 1–2.

4. *St. Paul Dispatch,* January 3, 1939, 1; *South St. Paul Daily Reporter,* January 3, 1939, 2; Hinderaker, "Harold Stassen," 392.

5. Stassen, *Where I Stand,* 153.

6. *Life*, October 19, 1942, 125, 126.

7. Stassen, *Where I Stand,* 140.

8. Stassen, *Where I Stand,* 140–41.

9. *Life*, October 19, 1942, 126.

10. Stassen, *Where I Stand,* 152.

11. Hinderaker, "Harold Stassen," 495, 541.

12. Hinderaker, "Harold Stassen," 538.

13. *Booknotes* interview with Harold Stassen conducted by Brian Lamb on C-SPAN. Program originally aired on Sunday, October 14, 1990. Produced and transcribed by National Cable Satellite Corporation, 1990.

14. *New York Times,* December 10, 1939, 62.

15. Nevins and Commager, *America,* 482–83.

16. Winston S. Churchill, *Their Finest Hour* (New York: Houghton Mifflin Co., 1949), 21.

17. Charles Peters, *Five Days in Philadelphia* (New York: PublicAffairs, 2005), 49.

18. *New York Times,* April 30, 1940, 1.

19. *New York Times,* April 30, 1940, 12; Gunther, *Inside U.S.A.,* 302.

20. Gunther, *Inside U.S.A.,* 302.

21. Peters, *Five Days in Philadelphia,* 75; *New York Times,* June 25, 1940.

22. *New York Times,* June 25, 1940.

23. Churchill, *Their Finest Hour,* 102.

24. Peters, *Five Days in Philadelphia,* 76.

25. Winston S. Churchill, *The Grand Alliance* (New York: Houghton Mifflin Co., 1950), 24.

26. Hinderaker, "Harold Stassen," 640.

27. Dave Kenney, *Minnesota Goes to War: The Home Front during World War II* (St. Paul: Minnesota Historical Society Press, 2005), 38.

28. Interview with Arlene Shramek conducted by author on January 25, 1996.

29. Alec Kirby, "Harold Stassen: A Biographical Memoir," *Proceedings of the American Philosophical Society* 147.3 (September 2003): 319.

30. *Time*, Monday, May 3, 1943.

NOTES TO CHAPTER 5

1. *New York Times,* October 29, 1944, E2.

2. Eric Sevareid, *Not So Wild a Dream* (New York: Alfred A. Knopf, 1947), 198.

3. Carl Sandburg, *Home Front Memo* (New York: Harcourt, Brace and Co., 1943), 192, 250.

4. Sinclair Lewis, *It Can't Happen Here* (New York: Triangle Books, 1935), 433; Mark Schorer, *Sinclair Lewis: An American Life* (New York: McGraw-Hill Book Co., Inc., 1961), 693.

5. *South St. Paul Daily Reporter,* April 27, 1943, 2.

6. *Booknotes* Stassen interview.

7. William F. Halsey and J. Bryan III, *Admiral Halsey's Story* (New York: Whittlesey House/McGraw-Hill Book Co., Inc., 1947), 184–85.

8. Walter Karig, *Battle Report: Victory in the Pacific* (New York: Rinehart and Co., Inc., 1949), 526; Halsey and Bryan, *Admiral Halsey's Story*, 141, 143.

9. *New York Times*, February 21, 1945.

10. Halsey and Bryan, *Admiral Halsey's Story*, 144; *Booknotes* Stassen interview.

11. Karig, *Battle Report*, 514.

12. Karig, *Battle Report*, 514–15.

13. Karig, *Battle Report*, 515, 526.

14. William Craig, *The Fall of Japan: The Chronicle of the End of an Empire* (New York: Galahad Books, 1967), 274; Malcolm Kennedy, *A Short History of Japan* (New York: Mentor Books, 1964), 291.

15. Paul Fussell, *Wartime: Understanding and Behavior in the Second World War* (New York: Oxford University Press, 1989), 119.

16. Gavan Daws, *Prisoners of the Japanese: POWs of World War II in the Pacific* (New York: William Morrow and Co., Inc., 1994), 257.

17. Daws, *Prisoners of the Japanese*, 257.

18. Daws, *Prisoners of the Japanese*, 257.

19. Hampton Sides, *Ghost Soldiers: The Forgotten Epic Story of World War II's Most Dramatic Mission* (New York: Doubleday, 2001), 10, 11.

20. Craig, *The Fall of Japan*, 141–43, 214, 215.

21. Gregory Boyington, *Baa Baa Black Sheep* (New York: Dell Publishing Co., Inc., 1958), 337.

22. Fussell, *Wartime*, 232–33.

23. Karig, *Battle Report*, 517.

24. Alex Kershaw, *Escape from the Deep: A True Story of Courage and Survival during World War II* (Philadelphia: Da Capo Press, 2008), 183; Boyington, *Baa Baa Black Sheep*, 341.

25. Kershaw, *Escape from the Deep*, 184.

26. Karig, *Battle Report*, 518.

27. Karig, *Battle Report*, 518.

28. Boyington, *Baa Baa Black Sheep*, 342, 343; Sharon Boswell, interviewer, "Robert F. Goldsworthy: An Oral History," Washington State Oral History Program, 35.

29. Karig, *Battle Report*, 518–19.

30. *New York Times*, September 1, 1945, 1; Karig, *Battle Report*, 521.

31. *New York Times*, August 31, 1945, 1, 3.

32. Karig, *Battle Report*, 520–21.

33. Theodore White, *In Search of History: A Personal Adventure* (New York: Warner Books, 1978), 298, 301.

34. Interview with Robert Mackey, June 6, 2003, trans. and ed. by Robert Mathes, Veterans' History Project, Library of Congress; William Manchester, *American Caesar: Douglas MacArthur, 1880–1964* (New York: Dell Publishing Co., Inc., 1978), 529.

35. Manchester, *American Caesar*, 526; White, *In Search of History*, 301–2.

36. White, *In Search of History*, 302; John Toland, *The Rising Sun: The Decline and Fall of the Japanese Empire* (New York, Bantam Books, Inc., 1971), 981.

37. Toland, *The Rising Sun*, 981.

38. Manchester, *American Caesar*, 529, 530.

39. White, *In Search of History*, 303–4.

NOTES TO CHAPTER 6

1. Arthur H. Vandenberg, Jr., ed., *The Private Papers of Senator Vandenberg* (Boston: Houghton Mifflin, 1952), 215.

2. Vandenberg, ed., *Private Papers*, 215–16.

3. Ernie Pyle, *Brave Men* (New York: Henry Holt and Co., 1944), 466.

4. Jim Bishop, *FDR's Last Year: April 1944–April 1945* (New York: Pocket Books, 1975), 229.

5. Robert E. Sherwood, *Roosevelt and Hopkins: An Intimate History* (New York: Harper & Brothers, 1948), 825–26.

6. C. David Tompkins, *Senator Arthur H. Vandenberg: The Evolution of a Modern Republican, 1884–1945* (East Lansing: Michigan State University Press, 1970).

7. Louis L. Snyder, *The War* (New York: Dell Publishing, Co., Inc., 1960), 241.

8. Vandenberg, ed., *Private Papers*, 10.

9. Vandenberg, ed., *Private Papers*, 1, 11.

10. Harold Stassen, "A Proposal of a Definite United Nations Government," address given at joint session of the Minneapolis and St. Paul branches of the Foreign Policy Association, Coffman Memorial Union, University of Minnesota, January 7, 1943.

11. William B. Ziff, *The Gentlemen Talk of Peace* (New York: MacMillan Co., 1944), 351.

12. Wendell Willkie, *One World* (New York: Simon and Schuster, 1943), 202.

13. Ziff, *The Gentlemen Talk of Peace*, 350.

14. Vandenberg, ed., *Private Papers*, 55.

15. Vandenberg, ed., *Private Papers*, 132.

16. Vandenberg, ed., *Private Papers*, 135.

17. Vandenberg, ed., *Private Papers*, 138.

18. Gunther, *Inside U.S.A.*, 307; *Time*, February 26, 1945.

19. Gunther, *Inside U.S.A.*, 307.

20. *New York Times*, March 14, 1945, 8.

21. Sherwood, *Roosevelt and Hopkins,* 879–80.

22. Bishop, *FDR's Last Year,* 778.

23. Stephen C. Schlesinger, *Act of Creation: The Founding of the United Nations* (Boulder, CO: Westview Press, 2003), 5–6.

24. Richard D. McKinzie, oral history interview with Harold Stassen, Philadelphia, Pennsylvania, June 26, 1973; Cord Meyer, *Facing Reality: From World Federalism to the CIA* (New York: Harper & Row Publishers, 1980), 38, 40.

25. Brian Urquhart, *Ralph Bunche: An American Life* (New York: W. W. Norton & Co., Inc., 1993), 117, 118, 119.

26. *The Rotarian,* May 1945, 51.

27. Willkie, *One World,* 174; United Nations Conference on International Organization, Verbatim Minutes of Technical Committees (11/4), Committee on Trusteeship System, Second Meeting (May 10, 1945), United Nations Archives and Record Management Section, New York (hereafter, UNARM).

28. Verbatim Minutes from Trusteeship Committee's Third Meeting (May 11, 1945), UNARM; Verbatim Minutes from Trusteeship Committee's Fourth Meeting (May 14, 1945), UNARM.

29. Verbatim Minutes from Trusteeship Committee's Sixth Meeting (May 17, 1945), UNARM.

30. Verbatim Minutes from Trusteeship Committee's Sixth Meeting (May 17, 1945), UNARM.

31. Verbatim Minutes from Trusteeship Committee's Eleventh Meeting (May 31, 1945), UNARM; Carlos P. Romulo, *Crusade in Asia: Philippine Victory* (New York: John Day Co., 1955), 270.

32. Romulo, *Crusade in Asia,* 270.

33. United Nations Charter, chapter XI, article 76, section B.

34. Verbatim Minutes from Trusteeship Committee's Twelfth Meeting (June 1, 1945), UNARM.

35. Verbatim Minutes from Trusteeship Committee's Twelfth Meeting (June 1, 1945), UNARM.

36. Schlesinger, *Act of Creation,* 256, 260.

37. *Winthrop News,* July 5, 1945, 4.

NOTES TO CHAPTER 7

1. *St. Petersburg Times,* Friday, June 18, 1948, 6; *Life,* March 1, 1948, 44–52.

2. *Newsweek,* April 19, 1948, 45; Frank Capra, *The Name Above the Title: An Autobiography* (New York: Da Capo Press, Inc., 1997), 390.

3. *United States News,* October 17, 1947, 21.

4. Stassen, *Where I Stand,* viii.

5. Barbara Stuhler, *Ten Men of Minnesota and American Foreign Policy, 1898–1968* (St. Paul: Minnesota Historical Society Press, 1973), 94.

6. Jules Abels, *Out of the Jaws of Victory* (New York: Henry Holt and Co., 1959), 54; Stuhler, *Ten Men of Minnesota*, 153.

7. Stassen, *Where I Stand*, 12.

8. *United States News*, October 17, 1947, 31; Stassen, *Where I Stand*, 23.

9. Walter LeFeber, *The American Age: United States Foreign Policy at Home and Abroad since 1750* (New York: W. W. Norton & Co., 1989), 451.

10. David McCullough, *Truman* (New York: Simon & Schuster, 1992), 608.

11. Dean Acheson, *Present at the Creation: My Years in the State Department* (New York: W. W. Norton & Co., Inc., 1969), 219; Eric F. Goldman, *The Crucial Decade— And After: America, 1945–1960* (New York: Vintage Books, 1960), 59.

12. Acheson, *Present at the Creation*, 222; McCullough, *Truman*, 549.

13. McCullough, *Truman*, 551, 553.

14. *Time*, August 25, 1947, 21; Walter Millis, ed., *The Forrestal Diaries* (New York: Viking Press, 1951), 310.

15. *Time*, August 25, 1947, 19; Irwin Ross, *The Loneliest Campaign: The Truman Victory of 1948* (New York: New American Library, Inc., 1968), 37, 40; Abels, *Out of the Jaws of Victory*, 50.

16. *Life*, March 1, 1948, 50.

17. Ross, *The Loneliest Campaign*, 42–43; *New York Herald-Tribune*, April 8, 1948.

18. Abels, *Out of the Jaws of Victory*, 52.

19. *Look*, June 22, 1948, 56.

20. Ross, *The Loneliest Campaign*, 46; Abels, *Out of the Jaws of Victory*, 56.

21. A digital recording of the entire Stassen-Dewey radio debate is stored on the UR Research Center website at the University of Rochester. The *New York Times* also reprinted a transcript of the debate in its May 18, 1948, edition. Quoted portions of the debate come from both sources. Tom Swafford, "The Last Real Presidential Debate," *American Heritage* 37.2 (February/March 1986): 66–71.

22. Swafford, "The Last Real Presidential Debate," 66–71.

23. Swafford, "The Last Real Presidential Debate," 66–71.

24. *New York Times*, May 17, 1948, 1.

25. Ross, *The Loneliest Campaign*, 51; Swafford, "The Last Real Presidential Debate," 66–71.

26. David Halberstam, *The Coldest Winter: America and the Korean War* (New York: Hyperion, 2007), 210; Abels, *Out of the Jaws of Victory*, 62.

27. Theodore H. White, *The Making of the President 1972* (New York: Bantam Books, 1973), 334.

28. Ross, *The Loneliest Campaign*, 45.

29. Ross, *The Loneliest Campaign*, 51.

30. Swafford, "The Last Real Presidential Debate," 66–71.

31. Swafford, "The Last Real Presidential Debate," 66–71.

32. *Newsweek*, April 19, 1948, 28.

33. *New York Times*, May 15, 1948, E10, 59.

34. *New York Times*, May 12, 1948, 1.

35. Swafford, "The Last Real Presidential Debate," 66–71.

36. *New York Times*, May 18, 1948, 16; *The Annals of America*, vol. 16, 1940–1949 (Encyclopaedia Britannica, Inc., 1976), 523–27.

37. *The Annals of America*, 523–27.

38. *New York Times*, May 14, 1948, 15.

39. Swafford, "The Last Real Presidential Debate," 66–71.

40. *Life*, March 1, 1948, 52; *New York Times*, October 11, 1955.

41. Bernard Shanley, "Preface to Eisenhower Memoirs," Diaries, 1951–57, box 1, folder 1, p. 1, Dwight D. Eisenhower Library, Abilene, KS (hereafter, Eisenhower Library).

42. Shanley, "The Delaying Action," Diaries, 1951–57, box 1, folder 1, p. 1, Eisenhower Library.

43. Dwight D. Eisenhower, *Mandate for Change: 1953–1956* (New York: Doubleday & Co., Inc., 1963), 18.

44. Shanley, "The Delaying Action," 7.

45. Harold Stassen and Marshall Houts, *Eisenhower: Turning the World Toward Peace* (St. Paul, MN: Merrill/Magnus Publishing Co., 1990), 35, 36.

46. Dwight D. Eisenhower, "Address Accepting the Presidential Nomination at the Republican National Convention in Chicago," July 11, 1952, available at John T. Woolley and Gerhard Peters, *The American Presidency Project*, www.presidency.ucsb.edu.

NOTES TO CHAPTER 8

1. Emmet John Hughes, *The Ordeal of Power: A Political Memoir of the Eisenhower Years* (New York: Atheneum, 1963), 21; Arthur Larson, *The President Nobody Knew* (New York: Charles Scribner's Sons, 1968), 9; DDE to HES, February 15, 1958, Woolley and Peters, *The American Presidency Project*.

2. *New York Times*, November 2, 1952, 1; *New York Times*, September 18, 1952, 18.

3. Stassen and Houts, *Eisenhower*, 89–90.

4. Stephen Ambrose, *Eisenhower: The President, 1952–1969* (Norwalk, CT: Easton Press, 1984), 2:15.

5. Stassen and Houts, *Eisenhower*, 91–92, 95.

6. Stassen and Houts, *Eisenhower*, 98.

7. Eisenhower, *Mandate for Change*, 86; Robert J. Donovan, *Eisenhower: The Inside Story* (New York: Harper & Brothers, 1956), 162.

8. Eisenhower, *Mandate for Change*, 99.

9. Eisenhower, *Mandate for Change*, 140.

10. Eisenhower, *Mandate for Change*, 141.

11. *New York Times*, March 29, 1953, 34.

12. Goldman, *The Crucial Decade*, 252.

13. Thomas C. Reeves, *The Life and Times of Joe McCarthy* (New York: Stein and Day Publishers, 1982), 487; *New York Times*, April 3, 1953, 12.

14. *New York Times*, May 17, 1953, E1.

15. Reeves, *Life and Times of Joe McCarthy*, 619.

16. Donovan, *Eisenhower*, 136–37; *New York Times*, May 29, 1953, 4.

17. *New York Times*, May 29, 1953, 24.

18. Robert H. Ferrell, ed., *The Diary of James C. Hagerty: Eisenhower in Mid-Course, 1954–1955* (Bloomington: Indiana University Press, 1983), 129.

19. Louis Galambos and Daun van Ee, "A President's First Term: Eisenhower's Pursuit of 'The Middle Way,'" *Humanities* 22.1 (January/February 2001).

20. *Time*, April 5, 1954.

21. Clarence B. Randall, Journals, 1953–56, Washington after the Commission, 1954, Volume I (February 16—March 1, 1954), Eisenhower Library.

22. Randall, Journals, Volume V (September 8–November 2, 1954).

23. Randall, Journals, Volume III (May 3, 1954).

24. *New York Times*, March 20, 1955, 3.

25. *New York Times*, March 20, 1955, 3.

26. Stassen and Houts, *Eisenhower*, 161.

27. Eisenhower, *Mandate for Change*, 145.

28. David Tal, "The Secretary of State versus the Secretary of Peace: The Dulles-Stassen Controversy and US Disarmament Policy, 1955–58," *Journal of Contemporary History* 41.4 (2006): 724; Stassen and Houts, *Eisenhower*, 283.

29. Memorandum of conversation between JFD and DDE, May 17, 1955 at 2:00 PM, John Foster Dulles Papers, 1951–59 (Secretary of State), Eisenhower Library.

30. Memorandum of conversation between JFD and DDE, May 17, 1955.

31. Memorandum of conversation between JFD and HES, May 20, 1955, John Foster Dulles Papers, Eisenhower Library.

32. Memorandum of conversation between JFD and HES, May 20, 1955.

33. Letter from JFD to HES, June 30, 1955, John Foster Dulles Papers, Eisenhower Library.

34. Stassen and Houts, *Eisenhower*, 351; James H. "Jimmy" Doolittle and Carroll V. Glines, *I Could Never Be So Lucky Again* (New York: Bantam Books, 1991), 467.

35. Eisenhower, *Mandate for Change*, 520.

36. Stassen and Houts, *Eisenhower*, 339.

37. Sergei Khrushchev, "The Cold War Through the Looking Glass," *American Heritage* 50.6 (October 1999): 37.

38. Tal, "The Secretary of State versus the Secretary of Peace," 726.

39. Larson, *The President Nobody Knew*, 8–9.

40. Dwight D. Eisenhower, *Waging Peace: 1956–1961* (New York: Doubleday & Co., Inc., 1965), 10.

41. Chris Matthews, *Kennedy and Nixon: The Rivalry that Shaped Postwar America* (New York: Touchstone, 1996), 112.

42. Memorandum of Conversation with Vice President Nixon, May 15, 1957, John Foster Dulles Papers, Eisenhower Library.

43. Memorandum of Conversation with Governor Stassen, April 20, 1957, John Foster Dulles Papers, Eisenhower Library.

44. Robert E. Matteson, *Harold Stassen: His Career, the Man, and the 1957 London Arms Control Negotiations* (Inver Grove Heights, MN: desk top ink, 1993), 52; telegram from DDE to Macmillan, June 4, 1957, John Foster Dulles Papers, Eisenhower Library.

45. Memorandum of Conversation with Mr. Stassen, September 17, 1957, John Foster Dulles Papers, Eisenhower Library.

46. Telephone interview with Glen Harold Stassen by the author, May 14, 2011.

47. *Life*, March 16, 1962, 112.

48. James Bassett, *Harm's Way* (New York: Signet Books, 1962), precede.

49. Bassett, *Harm's Way*, 169, 208, 209.

50. Bassett, *Harm's Way*, 208.

51. DDE to HES, February 15, 1958, Woolley and Peters, *The American Presidency Project*.

52. Arthur Krock, *In The Nation: 1932–1966* (New York: Paperback Library, 1969), 252.

53. Rick Perlstein, *Before the Storm: Barry Goldwater and the Unmaking of the American Consensus* (New York: Nation Books, 2009), 325.

54. Western Union telegram from HES to MLK, October 15, 1964, available at www.thekingcenter.org.

55. Theodore H. White, *The Making of the President 1964* (New York: New American Library, 1966), 240; *Booknotes* Stassen interview.

56. "Statement of Harold Stassen," September 13, 1978, H.E.S Correspondence, Dakota County Historical Society, South St. Paul, MN.

57. Stassen and Houts, *Eisenhower*, i; *Booknotes* Stassen interview.

NOTES TO EPILOGUE

1. James C. Humes, *The Wit and Wisdom of Abraham Lincoln: A Treasury of Quotations, Anecdotes, and Observations* (New York: Gramercy Books, 1996), 35; *New York Times*, March 5, 2001.

2. Preamble to the United Nations Charter; Harold Stassen, *United Nations: A Working Paper for Restructuring* (Minneapolis, MN: Lerner Publications Co., 1995), 11.

3. Stassen, *United Nations*, 11.

4. *St. Paul Pioneer Press*, March 10, 2001, 7A.

5. Matteson, *Harold Stassen*, 24.

Index

Abbreviation "HS" stands for Harold Stassen. Page numbers in *italics* indicate photographs.

Olson, Floyd B., 46–47, 48, 61–63, 65–68, 70, 78
Omori Prison Camp, 107–8, 111–16
One World (Willkie), 129
"Open Skies" proposal, 196–98
Operation Swift Mercy, 103
Oregon, 1948 presidential primary, 158–67
organized crime, 54–56

Palawan Island, 110
Panama, 37–38
Panic of 1907, 31–32
Pavlak, Leo, 55, 56
Pearl Harbor, Japanese attack on, 97–98, 127
Pearson, Drew, 143
Peaslee, Amos, 170
Peckham, Rufus, 23–24
Pennsylvania, 1948 presidential primary, 156
The People, Yes (Sandburg, 1936), 8
Petersen, Hjalmar, 74, 77
Petriella, Teofilo, 30
Philadelphia, PA, HS's law practice, 205
Philippines, UN Charter participation, 137, 139, 140
Pilot Knob, 211–12
Pokegama Sanitarium, 49–50
political patronage, 66
Popular Front protest, 70–71
populism, 45–46
presidential elections: 1936, 69–70; 1940, 97; 1948, 168; 1952, 173
presidential primaries: 1940, 92–97; 1948, 5, 143–47, 152–67; 1952, 169–72; 1968, 4–5; 1980, 207; 1984, 7; 1988, 3–4; 1992, 207; direct primary system, 168
prisoners of war (POWs), in Japan, 107–18

progressivism, 14, 16–18, 44, 188
Pyle, Ernie, 124, 131

Quie, Albert, 87

Radford, Arthur, 196
railroads, state regulation of, 20–26
Randall, Clarence, 189–91
Reeves, Thomas, 186
Reid, Charles, 4–5
Reno, Milo, 57
Republican National Convention: 1940, 92–97; 1948, 168; 1964, 206
Republican Party, Minnesota: gubernatorial campaign (1938), 72–73, 77–78; HS's impact on, 87–88; William Stassen's Dakota County leadership, 33; Young Republican League, 63, 65, 71–72
Republican Party, U.S.: HS's identification with, 45; HS's relationship with, 156–57, 168–69, 204; midterm election gains (1938), 80; presidential campaign (1940), 92–97; presidential campaign (1948), 153–67; progressivism in, 14, 16–18, 24–25, 188
Reston, James, 168–69
Riverview Baptist Church, 12, 50
Rockefeller, John D., 29, 31
Rockefeller, Nelson, 196
Rolvaag, Karl F., 68
Romulo, Carlos, 139, 140
Roosevelt, Franklin Delano: Boyington's Medal of Honor, 113; Churchill correspondence during WWII, 91, 97; death of, 133; election of 1940, 97; fireside chats, 95; "Good Neighbor Policy," 42; inscription on GI Bibles, 111–12; Lend-Lease Act of 1941, 126–27; "middle way" approach, 129; New Deal, 59–60; radio debate with Dewey (1944), 160; reelection of 1936,